Archaeological Thinking

Archaeological Thinking

How to Make Sense of the Past

Second Edition

Charles E. Orser, Jr.

ROWMAN & LITTLEFIELD
Lanham • Boulder • New York • London

Published by Rowman & Littlefield
An imprint of The Rowman & Littlefield Publishing Group, Inc.
4501 Forbes Boulevard, Suite 200, Lanham, Maryland 20706
www.rowman.com

86-90 Paul Street, London EC2A 4NE

British Library Cataloguing in Publication Information Available

Library of Congress Cataloging-in-Publication Data

Names: Orser, Charles E., Jr., 1950- author.
Title: Archaeological thinking : how to make sense of the past / Charles E. Orser, Jr.
Other titles: How to make sense of the past
Description: Second edition. | Lanham : Rowman & Littlefield, [2023] | Includes bibliographical references and index.
Identifiers: LCCN 2023018315 (print) | LCCN 2023018316 (ebook) | ISBN 9781538177228 (cloth) | ISBN 9781538177235 (paperback) | ISBN 9781538177242 (epub)
Subjects: LCSH: Archaeology—Study and teaching. | Archaeology—Methodology. | Critical thinking—Study and teaching.
Classification: LCC CC83 .O77 2023 (print) | LCC CC83 (ebook) | DDC 930.1—dc23/eng/20230420
LC record available at https://lccn.loc.gov/2023018315
LC ebook record available at https://lccn.loc.gov/2023018316

Contents

Preface

The idea for the first edition of this book developed after years of teaching an undergraduate course on archaeological thinking. The goal of the course was to examine how archaeologists create plausible interpretations of the past using scattered and incomplete evidence. While teaching the course, I knew that most students interested in archaeology would probably never have the opportunity or maybe even the desire to become professional archaeologists. Archaeology is a demanding field and fierce competition exists for the limited jobs that are annually available. The scarcity of professional posts at museums and universities has always been smaller than the number of people available to fill them, and today most archaeologists find employment in government or the private sector.

The examples I used in the course came mostly from the fringe side of archaeology, what is best called pseudo-archaeology. I used such examples, as I do in this book, because the outlandish tales of space aliens, sunken cities, and mysterious creatures are easy to analyze. Comparing them with actual archaeological findings usually demonstrates pseudo-archaeology's silliest claims. My goal was never to debunk the examples per se, but to help students learn to think critically about more realistic alternatives.

That most students will never become professional archaeologists is not a deterrent. In fact, that most students enter other fields proved to me the importance of the course. Teaching the basics of archaeological thinking provides students with critical thinking skills they can use for the rest of their lives. Regardless of their eventual professions, they will all confront outrageous interpretations of history whenever they search the web, watch television, or read blogs. The development of the internet and the expansion of cable TV has been a boon to pretend archaeologists, those individuals who have created a cottage industry by promoting outrageous claims, or what they deceptively term "alternative history." As a result of the seemingly tireless efforts of these pseudo-archaeologists, a large number of people now think that humanity's accomplishments result from interactions with ancient space aliens, that medieval monks once lived in North America, and that a race of giants once plodded across the American landscape.

After having taught the course for a few years I realized that even the well-educated can be susceptible to the yarns of untrained pseudo-archaeologists. Individuals can be easily fooled if they have not developed the thinking skills needed to make their own, independent evaluations. The proponents of the most outlandish accounts are often well-spoken, thoroughly convincing individuals who appear to present reasonable interpretations. That their views cannot be sustained with archaeological evidence does not deter them. Archaeologists know that ancient Britons built Stonehenge and that the Mayas constructed complex pyramids without any help from outer space. Human history is fascinating on its own terms and no need exists to insert outrageous storylines into it.

I also discovered that a person does not necessarily need to have a great deal of archaeological knowledge to refute the pseudo-archaeologist's most outlandish interpretations. Having such knowledge is certainly helpful, but all a person must do is to evaluate the claim, judge its assumptions, and consider alternative interpretations based on what is tangibly known.

As I mention in this book—and as every professional archaeologist knows—most of the most ridiculous interpretations of the human past are harmless and easily refuted with archaeological evidence. But some of the most flawed, politically motivated interpretations can be extremely dangerous, and professional archaeologists have a duty to refute them.

Some professional archaeologists think it is beneath them to acknowledge the world of pseudo-archaeology, believing that it does not merit serious attention. Some of the ideas currently floating around on the internet are so silly they do not deserve refutation. But the problem is that the general public may not feel the same way. A good story is always compelling and the idea that our human ancestors once interbred with spacemen intrigues people across the world.

Education is the most effective means for combating the use of archaeology to create preposterous or dangerous histories of humanity. But knowing precisely how archaeologists reach their conclusions—their thought processes and intellectual methods—is not widely known outside the profession. This book seeks to make some of the most basic thinking in archaeology available to a wide audience, including everyone who has never taken an archaeology course but who are nevertheless fascinated by our collective human story.

I attempt to present my arguments using straightforward language. I do not cover everything possible, and some professional archaeologists may find much of the content too simplistic for their liking. Simplicity and a lack of archaeological jargon was my goal. My view is that an explanation that cannot be understood is no explanation at all. Complex terminology may drive people to the often more clearly spoken pseudo-archaeologists.

I have completely rewritten the text for this second edition, removing one chapter and adding four more. Some reviewers were correct that the first edition leaned too heavily on examples from the historic past. In this edition, I have attempted to broaden the time depth of the examples because all archaeologists, regardless of their period of interest, engage in the same process of thinking.

Numerous people have helped me as I prepared this second edition. I would like to acknowledge my editor Erinn Slanina, whose enthusiasm and guidance was extremely gratifying. Equally important are the original readers of the prospectus. Their insightful ideas considerably improved my presentation. Merilee Salmon, noted philosopher of science and well known to professional archaeologists, kindly read and commented on my logic chapter. Her guidance was crucial in helping me avoid a couple of serious mistakes.

A large number of individuals helped me obtain the images for this book. Many of them assisted me simply in the spirit of collegial kindness, and I deeply appreciate their help. They are Stephen Kay, British School at Rome; Briggs Buchanan, University of Tulsa; Andy Chopping, Museum of London Archaeology; Lisa Buchanan, Parks Canada; Nora White, Ogham in 3D Project; Ross Smith, Queen Victoria Museum and Art Gallery, Tasmania; Innocent Pikiyari, University of Pretoria, South Africa; Don Hitchcock, Armidale, Australia; and Karin Zimmermann of the University of Heidelburg Library, Germany. Tina Ross drew figure 5.2.

Lastly, but certainly not least, I must acknowledge, as I always do, the encouragement, support, editorial abilities, and thoughtful ideas of Janice. Everyone who knows me understands the contribution she makes to my research and writing, and once again, her assistance has made this book considerably better than it would have been without her input.

1

Thinking in Archaeology

In his satirical book, *Bluff Your Way in Archaeology*, archaeologist Paul Bahn writes that "If history is bunk, then Archaeology is junk." He continues by noting that archaeology involves "seeking, retrieving, and studying the abandoned, lost, broken, and discarded traces left by human beings in the past." Bahn concludes that archaeologists are the opposite of waste collectors (although he admits that archaeologists sometime dress like them!). A less colorful textbook definition of archaeology is that it involves the investigation of "the social and cultural past through material remains" with the goal of learning more about the lives of people who lived in the past. Regardless of how one chooses to define the field, the discoveries made by archaeologists have rewritten huge portions of the human story. Much of what they have found would have been lost to history without archaeology. The new finds range from the bones of *Ardipithecus ramidus*, an early hominid dating to around 4.4 million years ago, to the design of Cold War missile silos. Such studies have allowed archaeologists to fill the blank spots left by written history.

Most people know that archaeologists have long trod the stones of Egypt and cut through the jungles of Mesoamerica, but less well known is that some archaeologists study our contemporary world, investigating the curious history of the tin can or questioning why the design of computer mice have changed over time. In every case, recent or ancient, what archaeologists have learned about the past and its artifacts has informed, confounded, and sometimes even challenged, what we think we know about ourselves.

Despite the many advances in archaeological knowledge, an important question remains. How do archaeologists know that what they have determined about the past is correct? After all, as L.P. Hartley famously wrote in his novel, *The Go-Between*, "The past is a foreign country; they do things differently there." The distance in time (as thus also of behavior) between a past era and our own time can present immense difficulties of interpretation, and the problems increase the further back in time we travel.

It should come as no surprise that archaeologists in this high-tech age have several tools to help them unravel the mysteries of the past. The shovel and trowel are still mainstays, but the archaeological tool kit now ranges from highly sophisticated dating methods to handheld computers and drones. Mapping, photography, and notetaking are all done digitally today in ways that were not even contemplated only a few years ago.

Despite all the tools at the archaeologists' disposal, the greatest tool is the mind. Without the ability to think creatively, archaeologists would be completely lost in the foreign country of the past. But, because all individuals are different—with unique personal histories, cultural backgrounds, and educational experiences—how do archaeologists distill the vast intricacies of the past into the telling of history, especially since the largest segment of the human past occurred before the invention of writing?

Much of the answer to this question involves education and experience. Archaeologists have spent years reading excavation reports, scholarly papers, and books about aspects of the past that interest them. As renowned British archaeologist Stuart Piggott wrote in *Approach to Archaeology*, archaeologists "spend a surprising large part" of their time "reading the results of other peoples' work." In addition, archaeologists gain firsthand experience by taking part in excavations, literally getting their hands dirty with what interests them. But reading reports and digging in the dirt are only part of the process. Archaeologists must also hone their minds to think critically, to challenge themselves to accept ideas that they may not have previously considered or that they once thought were entirely out of the question.

In short, archaeologists must also train their minds. But how do they do this? An example will help.

Imagine this. You've had a long day at your job, in classes, or running errands, and you've decided to let things go for a while and just surf the internet looking for interesting videos. You remember reading something in a blog about the pyramids of Egypt, those massive stone monuments that have fascinated the world for centuries. They have entered the human imagination and caused infinite wonder. Generations have marveled at how a pharaoh could have marshaled the power and authority to command his people to spend years constructing the stone mountains in the middle of the Egyptian desert.

So, you decide to find videos that might help you understand why the Egyptians built the pyramids. The first video you find is about the Great Pyramid of Giza. The smooth-talking narrator, accompanied by several professional archaeologists, is explaining that the pyramid was built during the Fourth Dynasty as a tomb for Pharaoh Khufu. The pyramid is thus about 4,500 years old. The experts in the video make it clear that the Great Pyramid is one of the world's most impressive historical monuments. A cut-away of the inside of the pyramid shows a series of shafts and chambers, two of which archaeologists have named the King's Chamber and the Queen's Chamber (figure 1.1). The

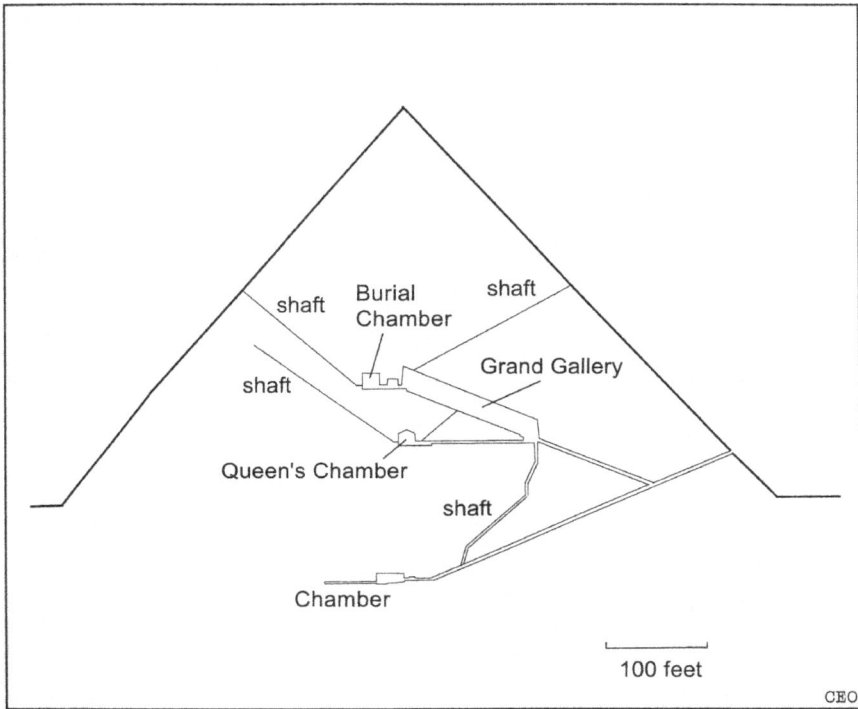

Figure 1.1. Inside the Great Pyramid, showing the chambers and shafts
Source: *Adapted from John Romer,* The Great Pyramid: Ancient Egypt Revisited. *Cambridge: Cambridge University Press, 2007. Drawing by author.*

archaeologists carefully explain what they know about Egyptian pyramids but admit that much remains to be learned.

The video ends and you've learned some interesting things about ancient Egypt and its Great Pyramid. But you notice that other videos have also been made about the pyramid. Wondering what else there is to know about it, you click on another video. In this one, however, all that stuff about the pyramid being a burial vault for the pharaoh has disappeared. Now there's no mention of archaeological research or the results of any recent excavations. Instead, the narrator is saying that the pyramid was really used to create nuclear energy! It wasn't a tomb at all; it was really a plutonium mill built by some mysterious, long-forgotten civilization. He says that archaeologists—like the ones in the first video—think Egyptians built it, but they're wrong. Ancient Egyptians had nothing to do with it. Just think about it, he says. Why would anyone build such a gigantic structure, using such heavy stones, as a resting place for just one or two people, even if the people were supposed to be semidivine? Why would so many people work so hard to build a pyramid when they could build much smaller tombs or simply bury their dead under the sand? The immense size of the pyramid implies that it must have had a more important function, doesn't it? He claims that archaeologists are just ignoring the obvious or hiding the real evidence.

Wow! This wasn't mentioned at all in the other video. This narrator really seems to know what he's talking about. He's mentioned isotopes, Cesium-137, and Strontium-90, and he's convinced that building a huge pyramid for a few mummies is just silly. He also seems more enthusiastic than the professional archaeologists in the other video. Maybe he really has discovered a secret history, a story that no one knows.

So, having watched both videos, you're faced with an interesting situation. You've been given two competing interpretations about the purpose and meaning of the Great Pyramid. Both seem believable and the presenters of each appear to have been knowledgeable. The nuclear guy seemed more scientific than the archaeologists because he mentioned isotopes and such, but the archaeologists conducted excavations and historical research. The nuclear pyramid guy didn't mention anything about excavation or even Egyptian history. And he was so enthusiastic and seemed so sure of his interpretation.

As the viewer, you are presented with ideas that are mutually exclusive: either ancient Egyptians built the pyramid as a tomb for their pharaoh, or some mysterious people built it as a nuclear facility. Both interpretations cannot be true, but how are you supposed to know which to accept? You cannot accept both because they are incompatible.

Puzzled but intrigued by the Great Pyramid, you begin to weigh the pros and cons of each video. In the first one, the professional archaeologists had spent years, sometimes their entire adult lives, trying to unravel the mysteries of the ancient Egyptians. You know that ancient Egyptian civilization is one of the most fascinating cultures that has ever existed, and you know from visiting museums that archaeologists have attributed some pretty incredible works of art to them. At the same time, though, you also know that archaeologists still don't know everything about ancient Egyptian life. You know because the archaeologists in the first video openly admitted it.

True, the archaeologists were extremely knowledgeable and dedicated, and they seemed to know what they were talking about. But why didn't they try to discount the man's atomic interpretation? Why did they just ignore it? Does this mean that the nuclear guy is correct that professional archaeologists sometimes hide the truth about history, covering up what they cannot explain?

What are you supposed to think? You're neither an archaeologist nor a nuclear scientist. You may become one or the other someday, but right now you're just interested in knowing the real story behind the Great Pyramid. You want to accept what the archaeologists said, but the nuclear guy seemed so sure of himself. His conclusion suggested an undiscovered chapter of history; one that remains shrouded in the past. Could a mysterious, unknown civilization really have built nuclear facilities on Earth even before the ancient Egyptian civilization had developed?

If you feel confused at this point, do not worry. All is not lost because it is possible to decide between the two interpretations using knowledge and reason. The good news is that you don't need to be a professional archaeologist or a specialist on ancient Egypt to decide between the interpretations. You can make a reasonable decision based on a few simple skills.

This book is designed to give you the critical thinking skills to know how to decide between different interpretations. (Writing "competing interpretations" would be inaccurate because, for reasons that will become clear in this book, the interpretations do not really compete because only one of them—the archaeological one—is realistic. The other is pure fiction.) With these skills you will be able to think more clearly about the mysteries that still surround the human story. You will be able to think like an archaeologist even though you might never find yourself in the bottom of an excavation trench in Egypt or on a mountaintop in Peru. As an intelligent consumer of science and history—on television, on National Public Radio, in newspapers, on blogs, websites, and even on some media not yet invented—you will be constantly confronted with stories, articles, and videos about Egyptian and Mayan pyramids, ancient cities built with gigantic stones, the statues on Easter Island, strange underwater structures, sunken civilizations, and hundreds of other subjects put forward by professional archaeologists, untrained men and women claiming to be archaeologists, and well-meaning scientists working outside their areas of expertise. As an archaeological thinker, you will be able to disentangle the reasonable from the absurd and sort the plausible from the ridiculous. You will discover history as it was, not as we might wish it to have been.

A QUESTION OF BELIEF?

It is important to realize at the outset that this book is about critical thinking, not belief. The issue isn't what you believe. You're free to believe anything you wish. Belief does not require evidence, whereas archaeological interpretation demands it. Without concrete evidence accepted by most members of the profession, archaeological interpretations are mere pseudo-archaeology. Pseudo-archaeology, sometimes termed "cult" or "fantastic" archaeology, is the presentation of often-outlandish views about human history—and sometimes even extraterrestrial pseudo-history—backed up with misunderstood, misrepresented, or fabricated evidence. The wildest interpretations almost always lack supporting evidence.

You may believe, for instance, that the world is flat, but it doesn't change the fact that the Earth is not flat. Your flat-Earth belief doesn't change the evidence nor affect your daily life unless you are a geologist or an astrophysicist. If you were an astrophysicist, the impact of your flat-Earth belief would be huge because your findings as a scientist would constantly contradict your belief. How could you calculate the time it would take for a satellite to orbit the Earth if you thought the planet was flat? Even if you continued to hold firm in your belief, you must remain anchored, just like the rest of us, on the spinning oblate spheroid we call planet Earth. Your belief will neither affect gravity nor change its mysterious properties.

In *Thinking, Fast and Slow*, Nobel Prize–winning author Daniel Kahneman observes that "For some of our most important beliefs we have no evidence at all, except that people we love and trust hold these beliefs." So, if our father or mother was a flat-Earther, we may choose to be one, too, despite the lack of evidence. But here we see the difference between belief and science: evidence for an interpretation must exist for science; they are not required for belief. Scientific discoveries cannot be accepted without acceptable proof, and scientific experiments are no good unless others can duplicate them and receive the same results.

The topic of this book, then, is about how archaeologists evaluate evidence and think in a way that allows them *to accept* (rather than *to believe*) accounts of history that seem plausible. All scholars regardless of their fields of expertise or theoretical perspectives are constantly faced with deciding among different interpretations. Knowledge expands and interpretations change as new evidence is collected and as concepts change. All scholars, including archaeologists, accept that their interpretations will probably be modified over time. Some of the once most cherished ideas may even be abandoned altogether. This is entirely normal.

Unlike acceptance, belief is relatively fixed. The tenets of a belief usually do not change to any great degree. Religion provides a perfect example. Christians believe in the divinity and resurrection of Jesus even though no direct evidence exists. True believers don't need concrete proof (even though Biblical archaeologists often seek to provide it). In addition, Christians can believe in Jesus and accept biological evolution, a fact that makes the difference between belief and acceptance clear. Some people say that they "believe in evolution" when they really mean that they "accept evolution." Biological evolution is a well-proven fact that does not require belief.

A new and thoroughly researched book of archeological research, even one of exceptional quality, may not last forever as the ultimate interpretation. This is not to suggest that some interpretations do not stand the test of time. Some do remain the standard account for many years until enough information is gathered to permit its reassessment. For many years, archaeologists thought that they could never learn anything about the use of symbols by ancient peoples who lacked writing. In 1954, Christopher Hawkes, a well-regarded British archaeologist, even placed symbols at the highest, unreachable level in his "ladder of inference." He said that archaeologists could learn a great deal about subsistence and technology, but little if anything about symbolic belief systems. Numerous archaeologists have today demonstrated that Hawkes was completely wrong; archaeologists can and do learn about ancient symbols and symbolism.

Not all interpretations have equal merit. Archaeologists know, because of the evidence they have amassed, that some interpretations are misinformed, misguided, or simply wrong (as was Hawkes). Professional archaeologists do not mention the atomic interpretation of the Great Pyramid because without any evidence it cannot compete with the long-accepted understanding that the pyramid was planned and constructed as the eternal resting place of an important pharaoh. No matter what archaeologists learn in the future, we can be safe in concluding that the Great Pyramid was not an atomic generator.

Proposing archaeological interpretations using different perspectives is perfectly normal because highly trained archaeologists can disagree without being intellectually dishonest. Well-educated people can hold different views. New evidence can alter what archaeologists once thought they knew. You will discover once you begin to think critically that you can decide between diverse interpretations, such as those of a professional Egyptologist and a clever pseudo-archaeologist. It will be more difficult to decide between the interpretations of two professional archaeologists—who use substantiated evidence—but the process is the still same. This book teaches you how to make those decisions.

SCIENCE AND HISTORY

As a discipline, archaeology is unique because it stands midway between science and history. Today's archaeologists adopt methods, strategies, and ideas from both. Archaeology is not a hard science like physics or chemistry because archaeologists cannot recreate an ancient village and watch what the people living there do during the day. Archaeologists can only interpret the past based on their ideas coupled with the available evidence. As a result, archaeology is both one of the humanities and a social science.

If we think of science and the humanities as arranged on a continuum, we find some archaeologists describing themselves as being closer to the science end of the scale whereas others claim to be closer to the history end. Most archaeologists would be somewhere in the middle, saying that they use both science and history. Some archaeologists are very scientifically minded, and some are not. Some apply Darwinian selectionism to archaeological cultures, use highly sophisticated instruments in their research, and collaborate with hard scientists to unravel elements of human history that are incredibly complex. For example, one of the most perplexing issues facing archaeologists concerns determining exactly when and how early humans, including early *Homo sapiens*, migrated from one place to another. Scholars investigating this issue have tended to assume that the world's sea level rose and fell over time according to a global average, what is called the "bathtub model." While this model seems to make sense, when archaeologists collaborated with planetary scientists and geologists, it was clear that other processes must also be considered if the model was to provide the best possible picture of the past. These researchers realized that they needed to know about flooding after the glacial age around twenty-six thousand years ago, the histories of ice sheets, and accurate information about sea-level physics. The data used in the research is extremely scientific.

In North America, archaeologists have been intrigued by the broad, relatively rapid spread of the Clovis culture. One remarkable feature of this ancient hunting-and-gathering culture was their acquisition of far-distant chert for making their distinctive stone spear points. In a study of a 12,900-year-old Clovis campsite in northeastern Ohio, archaeologists used neutron activation analysis to document the long distance between the source of the chert and the campsite where the chipped stone artifacts were found (about three hundred miles). This research reveals that the ancient people who lived at the campsite must have been involved in a large social network that included other groups of hunters and gatherers. The inhabitants of the campsite in Ohio must have consciously sought out the distant chert because other sources of tool-making chert could be found much closer to home.

Some archaeologists pour over faded documents and decipher hieroglyphs, seldom thinking about the complex statistics and hi-tech equipment used by archaeological scientists. For instance, archaeologist John Schofield was interested in documenting the buildings constructed in the City of London following the devastating fire of 1666 that had wiped out huge sections of the city. To do this, he compiled several images of houses, shops, and warehouses and studied the floorplans made by the buildings' original surveyors. His research showed that buildings constructed after 1666 were mostly traditional in design and style, with little innovation. Schofield's in-depth research proved that historians have been too exuberant in claiming that London was a wholly new city that rose "like a phoenix" after the Great Fire. Instead, even though whole blocks of the city had new buildings, the structures tended to reflect an earlier time. In another study, underwater archaeologists investigated the remains of a ship sunken in the Gulf of Mexico. The size of the ship and the artifacts around it indicated that the vessel was either a small commercial ship or possibly even a pirate ship dating to the 1780–1820 era. This research project required the archaeologists to examine historic maps, learn what they could about the construction and design of ships of that historical period, have knowledge about the artifacts from that time (including glass bottles and ceramic dishes), and understand the construction of things on the ship, such as the cannons.

Archaeology is such a varied field of study that those on the more scientific end of the scale know that they can always use more humanistic lines of evidence if they need them. Similarly, more humanistic archaeologists understand that they have an arsenal of scientific tools available if those are required.

One study may require one kind of evidence and the next study another kind. Regardless of their field of study or the age of the remains they investigate, all traditionally trained archaeologists conduct excavations using systematic procedures rooted in scientific concepts of data collection.

The need for diligence, caution, and systematic methods is especially required during excavation because digging into the earth is a destructive process. When archaeologists conduct excavations, they disturb the soil layers, dig out storage pits, and remove artifacts. If they excavated ancient villages in a sloppy, uncontrolled manner, the evidence they acquired would be little better than that obtained by looters. As a result, today's archaeologists exercise extreme care when they excavate houses, villages, and settlements.

The science involved during excavation and the humanistic approaches often accessed during interpretation highlights the distinction between *detection* and *interpretation*. All archaeologists conducting fieldwork are equally engaged in detection. Upon approaching a village site or even an archaeological collection in a museum, every trained archaeologist should be able to detect the same things. Every individual should be able to recognize the potsherds, the arrowheads, and the pieces of metal in the same way. Their skills in detection are honed through education and experience. Where they may differ, however, is in how they interpret the meaning of the artifacts. For example, does the transition from stone to brass arrowheads at a Native American village site represent an acceptance of European culture, a technical understanding that metal is more efficient than stone, a change in spiritual beliefs, or some combination of several elements? Such questions reveal that well-trained archaeologists, detecting the same artifacts, can present different interpretations.

Some of what we will explore in this book will seem more dedicated to the science end of the scale than to the humanities end. This is because science teaches logic, reason, and evidence—all things archaeologists need regardless of their expertise. Other subjects in the book relate more to historical analysis. The presentation of ideas from both science and the humanities demonstrate that today's archaeology is a multifaceted field with room for scholars having diverse interests, talents, and perspectives.

Worth noting at this point is that this book is written from a Western perspective. Most archaeologists trained in the Americas and in Europe typically learn how to think in a tradition that extends to the European Enlightenment (ca. 1680–1790). Archaeologists working at excavations typically employ field methods that rely on Western ways of measuring space and time and their arguments are usually phrased in a linear manner. Archaeologists understand that not all cultures, in the past or the present, thought in Western ways. In North and South America, for example, many Native Indian cultures do not think in a linear fashion, nor do they necessarily accept archaeological interpretations and conclusions. Thus, this book represents one way to think like an archaeologist, but it does not claim to be the only way. Indigenous and African

American archaeologists, of which there are a growing number, may devise new ways to interpret the past using non-Western ways of thinking.

THINKING TO SOME PURPOSE

Several years ago, while I was conducting excavations in Ireland, my wife and I were invited to the home of a BBC producer living in Northern Ireland. We had met her through a mutual friend, and we were excited to visit her for several reasons, one being that she and her husband, a well-respected attorney, were renovating a late eighteenth-century house. When we arrived and were shown around, we saw that the house was a historical treasure that the couple was restoring with loving care. During the evening, our host's husband, who had an interest in my research, mentioned a book he said had changed his life by making him a more effective attorney. This book was so important to him that he'd take it off the shelf every so often and reread parts of it. When he showed it to me, I was surprised to learn that it was not a dense legal tome but a small book of logic. It was only 191 pages long, including the index, and it had been published in 1939! The title was *Thinking to Some Purpose* and its author was a long-dead English philosopher named L. Susan Stebbing. (Wikipedia reports her first name as Lizzie, but I suppose that name doesn't suit a philosopher, so she just used the L!) My interest was piqued, and I filed the information away in my mind, hoping that someday I'd find a copy of this life-altering book. To my amazement, a couple of weeks later I found a copy of the book in a used bookstore in Dublin.

According to Professor Stebbing (who died in 1943), the inspiration for the book came to her after delivering a lecture in 1936 to the annual conference of the British Institute of Adult Education. She titled her lecture "Thinking" because she believed that the average Briton's mind was turning to mush. She said it was not enough for the British people to have a parliamentary government and freedom of the press: to enjoy the full benefits of democracy they should also know how to think independently. As she stated, "Our difficulties are due partly to our own stupidity, partly to the exploitation of that stupidity, and partly to our own prejudices and personal desires" (and this was before the invention of the internet!). Although blunt, Professor Stebbing's statement perfectly grasps three of the major obstacles to clear thinking:

- admitting what we don't know,
- understanding how people take advantage of what we don't know, and
- acknowledging that we must not base our interpretations on what we may wish to be true or on our preconceived ideas.

(In his book *Idiot America: How Stupidity Became a Virtue in the Land of the Free*, published in 2010—seventy-one years after Stebbing's book first appeared—

Charles Pierce makes the same case about the lack of thought among another citizenry. This time, however, the target is twenty-first-century Americans rather than early twentieth-century Britons! Carl T. Bergstrom and Jevin D. West further the cause of logical thinking in *Calling Bullshit*, published in 2020.)

Stebbing began by discussing politics and politicians, perhaps the one place where the three obstacles might be most easily observed. She quotes the Lord Rector of the University of Edinburgh who said in 1925 that politicians and "advocates" (Americans would say lawyers and lobbyists) are more concerned with persuasion than proof. They are not necessarily dishonest, the Rector says, they simply understand that the public is unprepared to follow the average politician's arguments. As a result, the citizenry needs advocates to explain the arguments to them. (Another option is that citizens might feel so marginalized that they have stopped listening to politicians. Garry Kasparov, the chess grand master, once said that the goal of political propaganda is "to exhaust your critical thinking.") In any case, Stebbing agrees with the Rector and adds her own evidence by quoting a speech mentioned in *The Times* [of London]. In 1937, a British statesman, extolling the virtues of the gloriously complicated British Constitution, is reported to have said that one of the reasons why the British people have enjoyed continued success and happiness was because they *"have never been guided by logic in anything."* (Professor Stebbing was so stunned by this observation that she put it in italics, as I have done here.) Properly aghast, she set out to remedy Britain's widespread lack of clear thinking in her little book.

Happily, ignorance is not a terminal condition. The professor says that we can all act against it simply by training ourselves "to think effectively to some purpose" (what Bergstrom and West term "calling bullshit"). To do this, we must avoid two dangers. First, we must not rush into action without thinking. In other words, we must not accept something as a reasonable interpretation— that the Great Pyramid was made for nuclear fission—without carefully thinking it through. Second and equally important, we must not develop an intellectual distance from life itself. By this she means that we should not bury ourselves in the history of ancient Egypt to the point of ignoring everything around us. Even competing interpretations—if based on evidence and logic—may have validity even if we disagree with them. Our task—as citizens and archaeologists—is to combine the ability to think clearly with a healthy dose of skepticism. Everyone can learn to do this because, as Professor Stebbing says, we all have "some capacity to follow an argument." We can all learn to think clearly.

THE PROCESS OF CLEAR THINKING

The process of learning to think clearly begins with being puzzled about something. If we consider an explanation or interpretation to be implausible, if "it just doesn't sound right" to us, we must begin by thinking. We should not simply accept it without question. This is where skepticism is important. Once we are in a questioning frame of mind, we must seek answers to our questions. It helps to know a little something about the subject under consideration, but prior knowledge is not always essential. For instance, you probably already suspect that ancient Egypt was not the site of a nuclear energy plant. You may want to believe in this mysterious history, but you probably suspect, if you just think about it, that the atomic interpretation is pure fantasy. Still, you may not be entirely certain. You would be on firmer ground if you knew that ancient Egypt was home to a well-organized, sophisticated civilization (that it did not need foreign intervention), but you don't necessarily need this information to judge the nuclear interpretation unrealistic. You simply need to wonder why the guy promoting the nuclear interpretation did not present any physical evidence or artifacts to support his view. You might ask why don't museums with ancient Egyptian artifacts exhibit atomic artifacts? (Pseudo-archaeologists claim that the reason is because archaeologists are engaged in a worldwide conspiracy to hide the truth about human history!) The more you know, the surer you can be in your assessment. Skepticism will help you ask questions and wonder about evidence even if you do not have an abundant amount of prior knowledge at your fingertips.

Stebbing observes that no thinking person can knowingly accept two competing interpretations at the same time. We cannot decide that the Great Pyramid was both a tomb and a plutonium generator. The way forward is to recognize that the interpretations are contradictory and then puzzle our way through each. To do this, we can pose a series of questions to help us resolve our confusion. The answers we receive will allow us to reject one of the interpretations.

Stebbing relates the story of a little boy playing on the floor with an electric train. The boy puts the train on the metal tracks expecting it to move, but nothing happens. Working out a solution, he picks up the engine, goes to the cupboard, takes down a can of oil, and lubricates the wheels. He sets the engine back on the tracks, but still nothing happens. Although he has achieved no results, the little boy's actions demonstrate intelligence because he has used knowledge to oil the train's wheels when it refuses to move. Oiling has worked in the past. This time, though, his approach was unsatisfactory because oil was not the problem; the train's battery had simply run down. The boy didn't know about batteries or how they worked, so his lack of experience and knowledge failed him. His failure does not mean that he is unintelligent, only that he made the wrong interpretation because he didn't have all the necessary information. In any case, his willingness to seek a reasonable solution is admirable even though he failed to make the train move.

The same is true in the case of the Great Pyramid. How can professional archaeologists so easily reject the nuclear interpretation to the point they do not even mention it in their videos, books, and lectures? And conversely, why does the nuclear guy feel the need to mention that his interpretation differs from that of the entire archaeological profession? Is he simply trying to show that he's a bold, original thinker or does he really believe he's discovered the truth by being unconventional? The answers to these questions lie in the ability to think like an archaeologist. That an outlandish nuclear interpretation about the Great Pyramid, one of the Seven Wonders of the Ancient World, can be believed by millions of otherwise thinking people tells us that we need the guidance of people like Professor Stebbing.

A short introduction to the history of thinking in archaeology will help orient you to the subject and show that interpretations change over time as individual researchers think and learn more. The background information in the next chapter will demonstrate the importance of thinking like an archaeologist.

SOURCES FOR CONTINUED READING

GENERAL THINKING

Bergstrom, Carl T. and Jevin D. West. 2020. *Calling Bullshit: The Art of Skepticism in a Data-Driven World*. New York: Random House.

Carroll, Robert Todd. 2003. *The Skeptic's Dictionary: A Collection of Strange Beliefs, Amusing Deceptions, and Dangerous Delusions*. Hoboken, NJ: John Wiley and Sons.

Feder, Kenneth L. 2020. *Frauds, Myths, and Mysteries: Science and Pseudoscience in Archaeology*. Tenth edition. New York: Oxford University Press.

Hartley, L. P. 1913. *The Go-Between*. London: Hamish Hamilton.

Judge, Michael. 2017. "Garry Kasparov on the Press and Propaganda in Trump's America." *Columbia Journalism Review*, May 22. https://www.cjr.org/q_and _a/kasparov-trump-russia-propaganda.php

Kahneman, Daniel. 2011. *Thinking, Fast and Slow*. New York: Farrar, Straus, and Giroux.

Pierce, Charles P. 2010. *Idiot America: How Stupidity Became a Virtue in the Land of the Free*. New York: Anchor Books.

Stebbing, L. Susan. 1939. *Thinking to Some Purpose*. Harmondsworth, UK: Penguin.

ARCHAEOLOGICAL STUDIES

Bahn, Paul. 1989. *Bluff Your Way in Archaeology*. Horsham, UK: Ravette.

Borreggine, Marisa, Evelyn Powell, Tamara Pico, Jerry X. Mitrovica, Richard Meadow, and Christian Tryon. 2022. "Not a Bathtub: A Consideration of Sea-Level Physics for Archaeological Models of Human Migration." *Journal of Archaeological Science* 137:105507.

Boulanger, Matthew T., Briggs Buchanan, Michael J. O'Brien, Brian G. Redmond, Michael D. Glascock, and Metin I. Eren. 2015. "Neutron Activation Analysis of 12,900-year-old Stone Artifacts Confirms 450-510+ km Clovis Tool-Stone Acquisition at Paleo Crossing (33ME274), Northeast Ohio, U.S.A." *Journal of Archaeological Science* 53:550–58.

Horrell, Christopher E. and Amy A. Borgens. 2017. "The Mardi Gras Shipwreck: The Archaeology of an Early Nineteenth-Century Wooden-Hulled Sailing Ship." *Historical Archaeology* 51:323–450.

Piggott, Stuart. 1959. *Approach to Archaeology.* Cambridge, MA: Harvard University Press.

Robb, John E. 1998. "The Archaeology of Symbols." *Annual Review of Anthropology* 27:329–46.

Schofield, John. 2022. "Buildings in the City of London After the Great Fire of 1666." *International Journal of Historical Archaeology* 26:401–33.

Sharer, Robert J. and Wendy Ashmore. 2013. *Discovering Our Past: A Brief Introduction to Archaeology.* Sixth edition. New York: McGraw Hill.

2

A Brief History of Thinking in Archaeology

A good way to learn about the world today is to examine the past, and the same holds true for archaeology. What began as an era of speculation has grown into today's much more reasoned approach to interpreting the past. Archaeological thinking over time has become more sophisticated, inventive, and varied as greater numbers of people from different cultural, social, ethnic, and racial backgrounds have entered the field.

THE EARLY YEARS

The practice of archaeology began during the Renaissance when wealthy men and women discovered an interest in ancient things and storied places. During this era, educated elites of White European society—who were usually well versed in Greek and Latin—had the leisure time to walk among the ruins of Pompeii, to poke around the Greek islands, and to ponder the standing stones of Stonehenge and Avebury. Not being trained as archaeologists—because the profession did not exist at the time—the interpretations these amateurs made were a mixture of intuition, speculation, wishful thinking, and even pure fantasy. The earliest archaeologists seldom dug into the earth, but when they did, their excavations were usually badly planned and reckless. Even the most well-meaning and careful among them could not consult scientific archaeological journals and reports because such sources simply did not exist. As a result, the earliest archaeological thinking was characterized by two general themes: a romance for the past and an aesthetic love of beautiful objects.

In the late eighteenth and early nineteenth centuries, wealthy, educated Europeans romanticized Greek and Roman history and demonstrated their fascination with these civilizations in their architectural designs, fraternal organizations, and literature. For example, writer Edward Bulwer-Lytton used Pompeii, one of the most fabled cities of the ancient world, as a literary setting. Spectacularly destroyed by an earthquake in 79 CE, this ash-smothered city was the quintessential archaeological site of the day and it fascinated just about everyone who knew of it (figure 2.1). Bulwer-Lytton's completely

Figure 2.1. Via di Nola, Pompeii

Source: Photograph, Stephen Kay, British School at Rome. Used by permission.

fictitious book, *The Last Days of Pompeii*, published in 1834, is a romantic view of life in the city as he imagined it. Upon visiting Pompeii, he had become enthralled by what he called "those disinterred remains," so his goal was "to people once more those deserted streets, to repair those graceful ruins, to reanimate the bones which were yet spared to his survey; to traverse the gulf of eighteen centuries, and to wake a second existence—the City of the Dead!" Bulwer-Lytton was happy to offer European readers a romantic, imaginary tale that had no connection to the true history of the city.

In addition to exotic places like Pompeii, early archaeologists were also captivated by beautiful ancient objects. The red and black terra-cotta Greek vases to be found on display in the British Museum and many other museums fascinated the public with their intricate scenes of ancient life (figure 2.2). The public was so taken with the artistic marvels of the ancient world that Josiah Wedgwood, the famous eighteenth-century English ceramic manufacturer, made his first fortune by selling finely made bowls, vases, and jars embossed with Greek and Egyptian designs.

Figure 2.2. Greek terra-cotta amphora, ca. 530 BCE
Source: *Metropolitan Museum of Art, New York City, Acc. No. 63.11.6; open access image.*

A Brief History of Thinking in Archaeology   **17**

The United States, of course, had no classical Greek or Roman history, so the nation's antiquarians sought to investigate the ancient past at home. Since their earliest days on the continent, European settlers had been amazed by the earthen mounds dotting the countryside east of the Mississippi River. The great heaps of earth—some rounded, others flat-topped—were North America's pyramids. No one living at the time—immigrant European or Indigenous Native American—knew who had built them, how, or even why. The nation's early investigators became obsessed with solving the mystery of their identity.

Biased ideas about Native Americans led many of the country's earliest antiquarians to conclude that the continent's Native peoples were simply incapable of building such magnificent structures. Having discounted America's oldest inhabitants as the mounds' architects, scholars sought to identify other builders. Some named the Lost Tribes of Israel, but others settled on the Romans, the Vikings, the Phoenicians, and a host of others. One creative interpretation was that the mounds were the products of an undiscovered civilization, one completely unknown to recorded history. For them, the term "Moundbuilder" was perfect because it represented an entirely new, ancient culture unrelated to Native Americans.

America's earliest archaeological scholars were thinking but they were not thinking like professional archaeologists. They allowed their biases and preconceptions to guide their research. As Professor Stebbing observes, some people confuse logical thinking with "attempting to derive knowledge about what happens in the world by purely *a priori* [beforehand] speculation. Such an attempt is, however, thoroughly illogical; it is anti-scientific." The earliest thinkers about America's mound builders based their interpretations on speculation rather than evidence.

The trend in the United States to turn away from loose speculation and toward archaeological evidence began to change because of Thomas Jefferson's high-profile research in Virginia. Jefferson was the most famous American to express an opinion about the identity of the mounds' builders. Like many eighteenth-century scholar/scientists, Jefferson had read about the controversy, but unlike many of his contemporaries—men who were happy espousing their ideas from the comfort of their parlors—he sought to find answers through excavation. Writing in *Notes on the State of Virginia*, Jefferson recounted his investigation of a Native American mound near the Rivanna River in central Virginia, which in European fashion he termed a "barrow." (In truth, the excavation was carried out by Jefferson's enslaved African Americans.) Jefferson's account obscures the excitement he must have felt when the excavators discovered bones inside the mound. This irrefutable evidence led him to conclude that ancient Native Americans had constructed the mounds. Even he, however, left some room for doubt. In a curious footnote he wrote: "The custom of burying the dead in barrows was anciently very prevalent. Homer describes the ceremony of raising one by the Greeks. . . .

And Herodotus . . . mentions an instance of the same practice in the army of Xerxes on the death of Artachæas [Achaemenes]." Comments such as these, from one of the nation's most-revered amateur scientists, demonstrate how poorly formed was the day's archaeological thinking. Jefferson used the tangible remains found in the mound to frame his interpretations, yet he still clung to poor thinking by making reference to ancient Greek history when writing about ancient North America.

Comments by such a learned gentleman as Jefferson fueled the imaginations of many others who wanted to believe in a mysterious past, one that linked the ancient histories of the Old and New Worlds. The similarity between all earthen mounds and ancient pyramids kept alive the concept of a mysterious "Moundbuilder race." Some speculators were led to ask: if both the ancient Greeks and the ancient Americans had built earthen mounds, could they be the same people or at least have the same ancient ancestors?

Stories of an advanced, unknown "race" continued to circulate through the taverns, general stores, and parlors of the embryonic United States. Only a couple of years before Jefferson wrote his Notes, James Adair, a trader originally from the north of Ireland, published a history of Native Americans. Taking note of the controversy over the mounds, Adair observed that most of his contemporaries believed that Native Americans derived from one of three peoples: "Pre-Adamites," "a separate race of men," or the Chinese. Unlike many others who would follow him, Adair was not convinced that any of these people, even the "separate race of men," were responsible for the mounds. Instead, he believed that America's Native peoples were descended from the Jews and that they had raised the earthen mounds. He gave twenty-three reasons to support his conclusion. In 176 pages, Adair compared selected cultural elements—including the idea of tribal organization, the mode of religious observation, and the use of bodily ornamentation—to reinforce his view of a Native American-Jewish connection. His interpretation, however, rested on pure speculation because he had no concrete information to support it.

The debate about America's mounds was still alive at the start of the nineteenth century. The failure of early archaeologists to devise an agreed-upon interpretation led Caleb Atwater to compile the first systematic account of the mounds in the eastern United States. A postmaster by profession and an amateur archaeologist by choice, Atwater did not believe that Native Americans had built the mounds. His choice was the Tartars from southern Asia or possibly even "Hindoos." He conceded that Native Americans had left tangible remains on the landscape—artifacts and settlements—but said that they were "neither numerous nor very interesting." Atwater figured that one way to solve the problem of the mounds was to discover where their builders had gone. If the mounds' architects were not Native Americans, then what had happened to them? They must have gone somewhere, leaving the continent to the various Native cultures who still lived in North America. He decided that the mounds' builders must have gone to Central and South America, places where other mounds (both stone pyramids and earthen mounds) could be found.

Despite Atwater's misguided ideas about the mounds' histories, he made a lasting contribution to North American archaeology by drawing a scale map of the earthworks at Circleville, Ohio. This earthwork had provoked much speculation because it had been built in a perfect circle with an equilateral square attached to its eastern side. Atwater's scale drawing became a model for the most famous early nineteenth-century study of the earthen structures in the eastern United States: *Ancient Monuments of the Mississippi Valley* by Ephraim G. Squier and Edwin H. Davis, published in 1848.

The publication of Squier and Davis's *Ancient Monuments* was the seminal event of early nineteenth-century archaeology. It paved the way for the full-blown development of American archaeology and made modern archaeological thinking possible, despite the authors' misguided interpretations. Like many of their contemporaries, neither Squier (a journalist) nor Davis (a physician) had any archaeological training. Their faculties of detection were impeccable, but their interpretations were based on the speculation typical of the era.

THE MIDDLE YEARS

Squier and Davis's service to archaeological thinking was two-fold. First, they promoted the systematic, careful investigation of archaeological sites, and second, they executed several bird's-eye-view drawings of several mounds in the central United States (figure 2.3). Their drawings were so good that archaeologists still refer to them today. Unfortunately, the contribution Squier and Davis made to modern archaeology was purely methodological because their interpretations were speculative (and some of their measurements have been found to be inaccurate). Their field research did not lead them to the correct interpretation about America's mounds. Rather, they decided that the mounds' builders were neither the ancestors of America's Indigenous cultures nor the Jews, Tartars, or Hindus; they were a separate people altogether (the "Moundbuilders"). But, in an early indication that archaeology would eventually abandon pure speculation for a reliance on evidence, Squier and Davis observed that the earthen mounds could be used to provide conclusive proof about their creators' history and culture. The design and composition of the mounds clearly showed, they said, that their builders had developed advanced agriculture and complex decorative arts as well as organized customs and religious beliefs. They argued that without these cultural traits, their builders would not have been organized enough to design and raise the most intricate mounds. For them, ancient Native Americans could not have been the mounds' architects because the "Moundbuilders" had been industrious and settled, whereas Native Americans were "averse to labor." Squier and Davis's racially biased perception that Native Americans were lazy blinded them to the conclusion

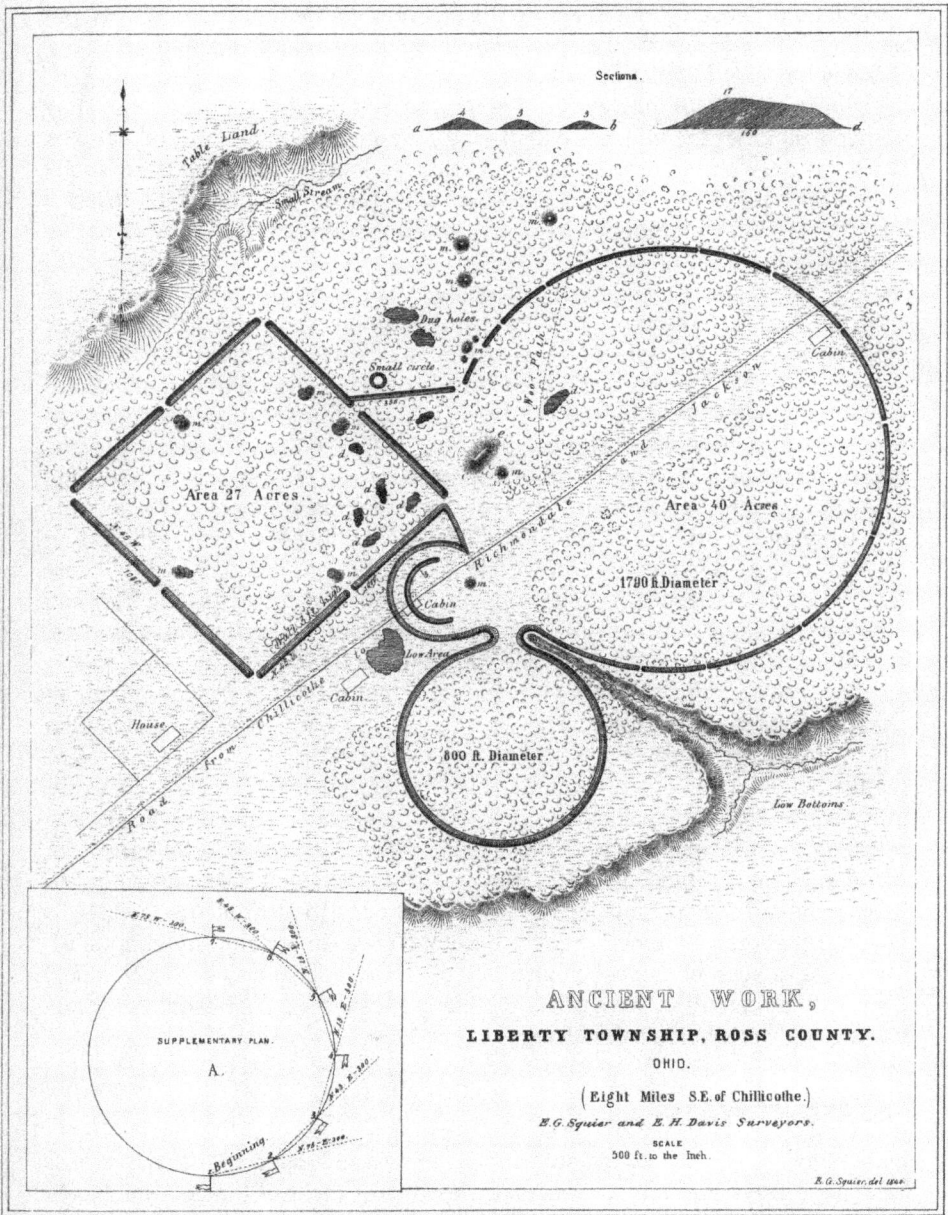

Figure 2.3. Squier and Davis's 1846 map of "High Bank Works," Ross Co., Ohio

Source: *From Ephraim G. Squier and Edwin H. Davis,* Ancient Monuments of the Mississippi Valley: Comprising the Results of Extensive Original Surveys and Explorations. *Washington, DC: Smithsonian Institution Press, 1848, facing p. 50.*

that ancient Native Americans were the builders of the mounds. Their wild speculations caused them to ignore the obvious. At the time, no one then had any physical evidence for the mysterious race they conjured up, and no one to this day has ever found any.

Squier and Davis, however, did reach some of the right conclusions. They were correct that the builders of America's mounds were agricultural peoples who had developed complex cultural features including complicated social hierarchies, religious concepts, and kinship systems. The individuals responsible for the earthen mounds of North America were ancient cultures native to the continent.

Archaeologists solved the controversy over eastern America's mounds in the late nineteenth century, with the conclusion being the most obvious one: that the ancestors of today's Native American cultures had raised the mounds. An early scholar who made this case was Cyrus Thomas, a pioneering archaeologist employed by the Bureau of Ethnology, a governmental agency dedicated to scientific, cultural, and historical research. In *Work in Mound Exploration of the Bureau of Ethnology*, published in 1887, Thomas moved professional archaeology away from mere speculation for all time. He called on archaeologists to study "the languages, customs, art, beliefs, and folk-lore of the aborigines" in addition to their ancient remains. He believed that only through comprehensive investigation could archaeologists demonstrate the obvious historical link between nineteenth-century Native Americans and the ancient stone tools, clay pots, and other remains found throughout the United States.

Thomas could not have been any clearer, but even today some untrained pseudo-archaeologists continue to espouse controversies about pre-Columbian North American history. Such speculators continue the tradition of late eighteenth- and early nineteenth-century thinking. For example, Graham Hancock, in *American Before*, published in 2019, wildly speculates about the origin and meaning of the Serpent Mound in Ohio, an ancient Native American earthwork mapped by Squier and Davis. This mound—of a wriggling snake with an egg in its mouth—is truly spectacular, but there is no need to attribute its majesty to anyone other than extremely creative ancient Native Americans (see chapter 5). The ideas of such nonarchaeologists are often outlandish and even ridiculous. Even so, they can often serve as good lessons because they represent the opposite of good archaeological thinking.

THE RECENT YEARS

By the beginning of the twentieth century, American archaeologists had begun to think in ways that are commonplace today. For most of the century, North American archaeologists used the artifacts they excavated to construct large-scale cultural histories of Native North America. It was thought at the time that these histories created with artifacts would present the entire history of the continent's Indigenous cultures once they were combined with the histories compiled with written records from more recent times.

To write regional histories, archaeologists first had to make certain that they had thoroughly and unambiguously described the artifacts from each period of the past. Only through careful description could they communicate with one another about what they had found in their excavations. Their descriptions of chipped stone arrowheads and spear points, ground stone axes, clay pots, and countless other artifacts—analyzed with scientific accuracy—were the first true steps to good archaeological thinking. Once their descriptions were agreed upon, archaeologists could employ a comparative method to piece together the history of ancient North America without having to rely on supposition. In short, they used tangible artifacts to write ancient histories.

SERIATION

The development of seriation in the early twentieth century represents one of the earliest expressions of good archaeological thinking. Seriation allowed archaeologists to use the proportions and ages of artifacts to guide their chronological and cultural interpretations. The method's quantitative aspect proved that empty speculation had no place in professional archaeology.

During the 1910s, archaeologists excavating in the southwestern United States experimented with ways of placing artifacts—mostly potsherds—into chronological sequences based on their physical characteristics. Two archaeologists in particular, N.C. Nelson and Leslie Spier, had independently found seriation to be useful in helping them work out regional cultural histories. Both sought to understand the sequence of ancient pueblo history by placing potsherds in chronological order based on the sherds' observable characteristics. Using this method, they discovered that existing pottery types disappeared over time as new styles appeared. By examining the percentages of each type, they were able to "seriate" (to arrange in a series) the various ancient potsherds chronologically.

Nelson and Spier had difficulty deciding how to present the complex information they had compiled using seriation. Percentages of pottery types reported in tables and shown in line graphs failed to display the process of historical change. The numbers were too sterile to convey the significance of cultural change. By the 1940s, however, archaeologists had discovered how to present seriation visually.

The percentages of each pottery type, as they persist through time, approximates a battleship-shaped curve. This means that when the percentage of a type's distribution is represented vertically on a graph (with time on the vertical axis), both its starting and end points are thin (when the pottery was first introduced and when it was dying out). The mid-point is thick (its percentage was high) because this is when the ware was most popular. Once an archaeologist has worked out the introduction, popularity, and demise of each pottery type (as indicated by the change in percentages over time), he or she can arrange them into a historical sequence.

A hypothetical example using Spier's pottery types shows how archaeologists illustrate the method (figure 2.4). In the example are five pottery types collected from six pueblo ruins dating between 1000 and 1400 CE. The sites are arranged vertically from earliest to most recent, and the percentages of pottery types found at each site are represented by black blocks. The pottery for each site equals 100 percent (adding from left to right). In Site 1, black-on-white pottery accounts for 98 percent of the collection and corrugated pottery for 2 percent. In Site 2, the percentage of black-on-white pottery sherds has slightly decreased and the corregated ware has slightly increased. At Site 3, corregated pottery was the most popular, and black-on-white pottery has shrunk to only 30 percent. By the time of Site 6, black-on-white pottery has completely disappeared.

Using this concept and the potsherds from 167 sites associated with the Zuñi people of New Mexico, Spier concluded that the earliest pueblo ruins were those with 96–98 percent black-on-white painted sherds and 2–4 percent corrugated wares. At later sites, the black-on-white sherds decreased to about 30 percent and the percentage of corrugated pieces increased. At this time, a new type, redware, accounted for 43 percent of the pottery collection. Corrugated wares decreased from 50–55 percent to 30 percent, and another ware, whiteware, decreased from 45–50 percent to 20 percent. At this time another new ware, called buffware, appeared.

Seriation represents a good example of careful archaeological thinking. This method can become extremely complicated when applied to large numbers of sites occupied for long periods, but by carefully observing, analyzing, and studying, archaeologists can use the physical remains along with their

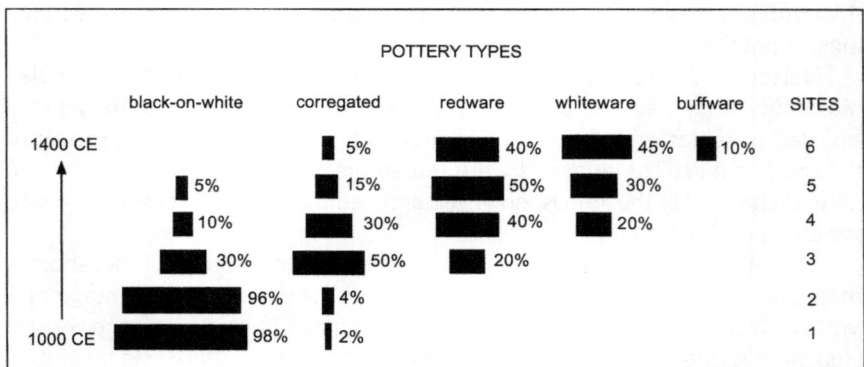

POTTERY TYPES

	black-on-white	corregated	redware	whiteware	buffware	SITES
1400 CE		5%	40%	45%	10%	6
	5%	15%	50%	30%		5
	10%	30%	40%	20%		4
	30%	50%	20%			3
	96%	4%				2
1000 CE	98%	2%				1

Figure 2.4. Hypothetical seriation of five pottery types
Source: *Drawing by author.*

knowledge of culture and history to guide their interpretations. No place exists for mere speculation.

THE CONJUNCTIVE APPROACH

The development of seriation marked an important event in the history of archaeological thinking, and in the 1940s another milestone occurred with the publication in 1948 of Walter Taylor's *A Study of Archaeology*. This book is significant because Taylor challenged archaeologists to modify how they thought about their field. He said that in their efforts to write detailed artifact descriptions and create regional chronologies—which often included complex seriations—archaeologists had gotten too far away from their anthropological roots. By being too single-minded about building chronologies, archaeologists had ceased their analyses too early. They used excavated artifacts to create reasonably reliable histories of Native American cultures as they existed before European contact, but they had overlooked the cultural dynamics experienced by people living in those cultures. They had eliminated the active lives of the people by placing their emphasis on artifact descriptions and the construction of historical sequences.

Taylor's answer to the problem, which he called the "conjunctive approach," was a six-step plan of research. His process began by identifying the research questions to be addressed. This stage involved at least two basic queries every archaeologist should ask themselves: what do I want to find out, and where is the best place to discover it? Once an archaeologist has answered these questions, the second stage involves collecting, describing, analyzing, and interpreting the amassed information. By "information" Taylor meant all pertinent factors that might have influenced a culture's history: the geology, the weather, cultural practices and traditions, historical trends, artifacts, and so forth. This stage involved both fieldwork and laboratory analysis. In the third stage, the archaeologist should create the historical chronology from the evidence collected during stage two, and in the fourth stage, they should synthesize the information. The fifth stage involves the comparative study of similar cultures to discover their broad similarities and differences. Finally, the archaeologist uses what has been learned in the preceding stages to understand the "nature and workings" of culture to help address questions about what makes us collectively human.

The conjunctive approach represented an important shift in archaeological thinking because it presented what Taylor called "a conceptual scheme made explicit in a set of goals." His central point was that archaeologists should seek to understand the dynamics of culture rather than to reduce culture to a series of historical sequences represented by a few key artifacts. For him, the creation of complex chronologies is only one step in a much larger anthropological effort to understand culture in general. Rather than viewing history as a static collection of artifacts arranged in a neat order, Taylor encouraged archaeologists to perceive past cultures as alive and active. Seriation was a tool archaeologists could use to understand ancient cultures, but it was not the end of the research process. Taylor saw archaeology as a technique anthropologically trained scholars could use to collect cultural information about the past. One notable aspect of his approach is that most of the process involved consciously thinking through a problem that archaeological research could be used to investigate. Professor Stebbing would have recognized that Taylor, and archaeologists who followed his advice, were thinking to some purpose.

Taylor's views were controversial, but they continued to percolate within the archaeological community in the late 1950s as his anthropological perspective slowly gained ground. By the late 1960s, his views were presented again in what came to be called the New Archaeology (often spelled "archeology" to show that it really was something new). In the United States, a prominent advocate of the new approach was Lewis Binford.

In an article entitled "Archaeology as Anthropology," Binford reiterated Taylor's thinking by observing that "until we as archaeologists begin thinking of our data in terms of total cultural systems, many . . . prehistoric 'enigmas' will remain unexplained." The time for Taylor's views had arrived, and the new thinking was so significant that many archaeologists dubbed it a "revolution" in the field.

The New Archaeology was also called "processual archaeology" because its designers sought to examine the processes of past daily life. Once archaeologists started thinking about past cultures as dynamic institutions, they confronted ponderous questions: how can archaeologists observe human activity in inert fragments of pottery, broken chert arrowheads, and dusty old firepits? How can they see cultural processes in action when all the people they study have long since died? How do archaeologists recreate life from inanimate artifacts and deteriorated building remains? These questions required serious contemplation and reflection because they reached into the soul of archaeological research. They were so profound that even philosophers of science began to ponder them.

The introduction of philosophers to archaeology meant that archaeologists began to explore topics entirely new to them. They started to think about creating hypotheses and to decide how they could best test them; they began to explore various methods of observation and explanation; and they started wondering whether they could discover and identify general laws of human behavior. This period of philosophical reflection was a major advance in archaeological thinking because it brought to the fore explicit ideas about logical argumentation and the need for the creation of systematic research designs.

The conscientious urge to make archaeology more overtly scientific and philosophical promoted the cause of thinking to some purpose. Twentieth-century archaeologists had left the speculation of the nineteenth century far behind as they became social scientists of the past. The transition from history to science, however, was not without difficulty.

After a few years of attempting to apply what they had learned from both philosophers of science and physical scientists, some archaeologists began to think that the strict application of the scientific method had put their research into an intellectual straitjacket. Some began to wonder whether too many archaeologists had become philosophical theorizers rather than excavators. Skeptics thought that too many of their colleagues, by turning to the philosophy of archaeological science, had given the dynamics of culture and history short shrift. In moving closer to the science end of the science/humanities continuum they had gotten too far away from the historical end.

As a result, by the 1980s, many archaeologists had begun to reassert their interests in social, cultural, and historical dynamics, saying they wanted to be archaeologists, not philosophers. What occurred, then, was a shift away from the rigid hypothesis testing of the late 1960s and 1970s, but a retention of the scientific requirement of logic and rigor. This less rigidly scientific archaeology is generally known as "postprocessual" archaeology. Professional archaeology would never return to the days of speculation, but it was clear that many archaeologists sought a thoughtful combination of logical thinking and scientific methods (from processual archaeology) and cultural sensitivity and historical awareness (from the disciplines of cultural anthropology and social history). Worth noting, though, is that throughout the evolution of archaeological thinking, archaeological fieldwork continued to rely on Western methods of measurement and a general understanding that human history proceeds in a linear manner.

The archaeology of the twenty-first century is thus perhaps best perceived as a combined anthropological and historical discipline. Today's archaeologists retain their interests in past social and cultural processes while adopting concepts and perspectives from a vast array of related disciplines, including but not limited to women's studies, political economic theory, queer theory, and postcolonial theory.

POSTMODERN THINKING

In the 1980s and 1990s, many archaeologists were drawn to postmodernism, a school of thought with roots in the 1950s. Postmodernism is a complex collection of philosophical perspectives that propose that all knowledge is culturally conditioned and often politically motivated. Postmodernists argue that the methods and perspectives of the Enlightenment—the rational, scientific philosophy of the modern age—must be overcome with new ways of thinking. Postmodern thinking in archaeology has always been controversial.

Postmodern thinking has benefited archaeology. For instance, by arguing that all perspectives have equal merit, postmodernism opened the minds of archaeologists and allowed them to consider the validity of Indigenous peoples' traditions and oral accounts. Beforehand, many archaeologists may have too readily dismissed a people's traditional histories as irrelevant to archaeological analysis. Much of the intellectual rigidity is now gone from the discipline, and today's archaeologists are likely to engage in dialogues with Native and descendant communities rather than to scorn their accounts as unimportant. Such conversations have promoted cross-cultural understandings and have led to the creation of numerous collaborative projects between archaeologists and community members (see chapter 9).

The postmodern thinking that accompanied some postprocessual archaeology also had detrimental effects. Many radical postmodernists argued that objective truth does not exist. They claim that we only fool ourselves when we think we can know anything objectively, especially where the past is concerned. They argue that objective truth is a mirage, that all accounts perpetuate an often-hidden agenda of some kind, either political, racial, cultural, or social. They propose that traditional knowledge is as valid as the findings of archaeological research and that Western knowledge is only one way of knowing.

The critics have a point because objectivity can be a knotty problem for anthropologically trained archaeologists, especially where long-held cultural traditions are involved. Common ground may be difficult to establish when a people's oral traditions conflict with tangible archaeological findings. The interpretations may be incompatible when one is based on belief and the other is rooted in empirical evidence. American archaeologists accept that beliefs are distinct from archaeological findings, but as archaeologists thinking to some purpose, they must follow the empirical evidence while simultaneously being sensitive to the traditional beliefs. Conflicts arising between belief and archaeological evidence demonstrate that archaeological thinking is still evolving.

The extreme postmodernist view that all interpretations have equal merit is especially dangerous when pseudo-archaeology is concerned. Outlandish interpretations about history lack both the validity of traditional beliefs and tangible evidence. Where the Great Pyramid of Giza is concerned, should the interpretation of someone with no archaeological training and no evidence be accorded the same weight as the entire body of professional Egyptologists?

Taking postmodern thinking to its logical conclusion leads us to imagine that any interpretation of the past is equally valid. At its most extreme, we might conclude that archaeologists need not spend all their time and money (not to mention often experiencing great personal hardships) excavating ancient sites, straining to read ancient texts, and counting huge piles of potsherds. If all interpretations are equally valid, archaeologists' time might be better spent writing novels about ancient Egypt than attempting the difficult work of serious archaeological research. To understand historical cultures, archaeologists require solid evidence, not eighteenth-century speculation modernized with tales of space aliens, nuclear energy, and antigravity flying saucers. Professional archaeologists know that much of the past can be known but accept that some of it will always be lost to history. The conversations among the enslaved laborers who slid the massive stones of the Great Pyramid into place are gone forever. This loss does not mean, however, that archaeologists should cease trying to learn as much as possible about the daily lives of those individuals and the world they inhabited.

ARCHAEOLOGICAL THINKING IN THE NEW MILLENNIUM

Beginning in the 1990s and continuing past 2000, the number of archaeological approaches to understanding the past have continued to expand. Today's archaeologists use a wide array of ideas. Most of them have a philosophical foundation in some way, with many of them being closely linked to concepts of ethical behavior and human rights. The range of perspectives is so diverse that only some can be mentioned here.

In his brief study of why anthropology is important to modern society, Tim Ingold notes that anthropology always contains a good deal of philosophy. In fact, he defines anthropology as "philosophy with the people in."

Alison Wylie, a philosopher who has spent a large part of her career pondering archaeology's inner workings, agrees with him. In *Thinking from Things: Essays in the Philosophy of Archaeology,* she observes that "Despite earthbound appearances, archaeology has always been a deeply philosophical discipline." In fact, the agreement between Ingold, writing about anthropology, and Wylie, writing about archaeology, means that one definition of archaeology might be "philosophy with the people and their material culture in."

The close agreement between archaeological thinking and philosophy was especially apparent during the rise and development of the New Archaeology, even though archaeology's link with philosophy has always existed. In the early 2000s, several archaeologists again promoted an overtly philosophical kind of archaeology.

The archaeologists espoused what they termed "symmetrical archaeology." Drawn from an array of philosophical strands, symmetrical archaeologists argue that archaeologists do not discover the past but engage in a never-ending creative process that makes archaeologists and the past what they are. They refute the artificial divisions between past and present, ideas and things, and scientific observation and perception. Advocates of symmetrical archaeology also propose that archaeological interpretation arises from a complex network that includes excavation tools, the entire material world, textual information (maps, images, documents), previous literature (reports of excavations, books), local communities, institutions (museums, universities, historical societies), specialized knowledge, and politics. In other words, they argue that archaeologists' interpretations are filtered through and influenced by a large array of factors, some of which archaeologists may not even realize. Advocates of symmetrical archaeology also say that the archaeology they promote is not new, but is just now being recognized because, for one reason, archaeologists have learned to question why they do research.

Another strand of twenty-first-century archaeology has been efforts to create an archaeology that uses theories of anarchism. The senses of anarchism archaeologists espouse are not rooted in concepts of destruction and riot, but rather in the sincere goal of understanding past societies that were politically decentralized or that had no hierarchy of leadership. Archaeologists who argue for an anarchistic perspective have investigated a range of cultures including those in the Northwest Coast of North America. These cultures had complicated displays of chiefly power and class stratification but no central political authority. Other archaeologists have used anarchist ideas to study the states and nonstates in the Pacific, including in Hawai'i and Vanuatu. Groups like the Black Trowel Collective promote an anarchist approach to archaeological research.

Beginning in the 1960s and continuing to the present, Native Americans have argued for their voice to be heard in archaeology. Much of their anger has been directed toward the looting of gravesites and sacred lands and the insensitivity shown by much archaeological research. Native Americans consider both the thoughtless looting of archaeological sites by treasure hunters and the careful excavations of archaeologists as major insults. To combat the desecration of their ancient settlements and to bring attention to their cultural traditions and contemporary lives, groups like the Indigenous Archaeology Collective—a network of Indigenous and non-Indigenous scholars engaged in archaeological research, museum studies, and heritage preservation and management—work to change the direction of archaeology, a discipline created by the colonizers of their ancestral homelands. Indigenous archaeologists and their allies work together to decolonize the profession and ensure that archaeologists respect Native peoples' rights around the world. Some archaeologists say that the practice of archaeology by Indigenous archaeologists should be distinguished from the research of non-Indigenous "scientific" archaeologists. Michael Wilcox points out, however, that separating Indigenous archaeology from scientific archaeology creates a form of racial segregation that is wholly unacceptable in contemporary archaeology.

One semantic change that has occurred in North American archaeology is that many archaeologists have ceased using the term "prehistory," substituting it with "pre-Columbian" or "precontact" (meaning before contact with Europeans). When "history" was equated with writing, as was a common practice for many years, "prehistory" simply meant "before writing." Thus, in North America, "before writing" meant the same as "before Europeans arrived." Some people, however, thought that the word "prehistory" was pejorative, because it might imply that Indigenous American cultures were without history, or in other words, that their past was unimportant when compared to the "history" of Europeans in North America. "Pre-Columbian" or "precontact" is a neutral way to refer to the past, even though the frame of reference is still Europeans.

Evidence that archaeological thinking is still evolving is provided by the protests that developed in the aftermath of the death of George Floyd and the creation of the Black Lives Matter movement. Archaeologists in the Society of Black Archaeologists have joined together to argue that the discipline of archaeology should be overtly antiracist in perspective. They seek to transform the practice of archaeology as a voice for social justice. Maria Franklin, writing with three colleagues, notes that transformations of archaeological practice have always been influenced by the changes in the wider world, and they propose that archaeology should become overtly committed to social change. For them, archaeology has emancipatory potential stemming from its ability to look beyond the written word and directly into the past using the artifacts left behind.

Many of today's archaeologists continue the work of transforming archaeology into a socially aware discipline committed to equality and an end to racism and discrimination. Christopher Barton argues that archaeology should be a realm of social activism, with the goal being to make the world a better place. This view asks the question for whom is archaeological research intended? In the past, when asked this question, most archaeologists might have responded that archaeological research adds to the greater storehouse of information about the past, and that is enough reason to do it. This is a valid argument, and archaeologists committed to social activism accept the general premise but add that the findings of archaeological research belong to everyone. Archaeology is not simply about the past and its discoveries do not belong to archaeologists alone. Rather, today's archaeologists should serve society.

Rather than denying the role of political viewpoints in archaeological research, which was commonly maintained during archaeology's overtly scientific phase, antiracist and decolonizing archaeologists merge their political perspectives with their research. They seek direct engagement with Indigenous and descendant communities. The interpretations that arise from these perspectives are offering fresh insights on the past and its connections to the present. Today's archeologists generally accept that the present influences how the past is remembered, presented, and interpreted. Archaeologists who seek to create an overtly antiracist and decolonized archaeology challenge professional archaeologists to question their research motives and goals and to engage with individuals whose pasts they investigate.

★   ★   ★

The diversity of archaeological perspectives that developed after about 1980 has created a healthy field for archaeological thinkers. Regardless of an archaeologist's theoretical perspective, methods, and analytical tools, all archaeological research requires conscious thought. Whether excavating the settlements of the earliest humans or mapping the campsites of today's homeless, all archaeologists must be clear in their arguments and logical in their suppositions. They must, as Professor Stebbing says, learn to think to some purpose. A lack of clarity of thought means that nonarchaeologists will have trouble disentangling the fictional from the well-researched. The public may not appreciate the significance of archaeological research if archaeologists cannot clearly present their findings and interpretations. Confining archaeological knowledge to a small circle of professionals would be a shame because the human story is too fascinating to be restricted to archaeology alone. After all, it belongs to all of us.

SOURCES FOR CONTINUED READING

Adair, James. 1775. *The History of the American Indians, Particularly Those Nations Adjoining to the Mississippi, East and West Florida, Georgia, South and North Carolina, and Virginia.* London: Edward and Charles Dilly.

Angelbeck, Bill and Colin Grier. 2012. "Anarchism and the Archaeology of Anarchic Societies: Resistance to Centralization in the Coast Salish Region of the Pacific Northwest Coast." *Current Anthropology* 53:547–87.

Atwater, Caleb. 1820. *Description of the Antiquities Discovered in the State of Ohio and Other Western States, Communicated to the President of the American Antiquarian Society.* Worcester, MA: American Antiquarian Society.

Barton, Christopher P., ed. 2021. *Trowels in the Trenches: Archaeology as Social Activism.* Gainesville: University Press of Florida.

Binford, Lewis R. 1962. "Archaeology as Anthropology." *American Antiquity* 28:217–25.

Bulwer-Lytton, Edward G. 1834. *The Last Days of Pompeii.* 3 vols. London: Richard Bentley.

Flexner, James L. 2014. "The Historical Archaeology of States and Non-States: Anarchist Perspectives from Hawai'i and Vanuatu." *Journal of Pacific Archaeology* 5:81–97.

Franklin, Maria, Justin P. Dunnavant, Ayana Omilade Flewellen, and Alicia Odewale. 2020. "The Future is Now: Archaeology and the Eradication of Anti-Blackness." *International Journal of Historical Archaeology* 24:753–66.

Ingold, Tim. 2018. *Anthropology: Why It Matters.* Cambridge: Polity.

Jefferson, Thomas. 1787. *Notes on the State of Virginia.* London: J. Stockdale.

Nelson, N. C. 1916. "Chronology of the Tano Ruins, New Mexico." *American Anthropologist* 18:159–80.

Phillips, Philip, James A. Ford, James B. Griffin. 1951. *Archaeological Survey in the Lower Mississippi Alluvial Valley, 1940–1947.* Cambridge, MA: Peabody Museum, Harvard University.

Spier, Leslie. 1917. *An Outline for a Chronology of Zuñi Ruins*. Anthropological Papers of the American Museum of Natural History, Vol. 18, Part 3. New York: American Museum of Natural History.

Squier, Ephaim G. and Edwin H. Davis. 1848. *Ancient Monuments of the Mississippi Valley: Comprising the Results of Extensive Original Surveys and Explorations*. Washington, DC: Smithsonian Institution.

Stebbing, L. Susan. 1939. *Thinking to Some Purpose*. Harmondsworth, UK: Penguin.

Taylor, Walter W. 1948. *A Study of Archaeology*. Memoir 69. Washington, DC: American Anthropological Association.

Thomas, Cyrus. 1887. *Work in Mound Exploration of the Bureau of Ethnology*. Washington, DC: Government Printing Office.

Wilcox, Michael. 2010. "Saving Indigenous Peoples from Ourselves: Separate but Equal Archaeology Is Not Scientific Archaeology." *American Antiquity* 75:221–27.

Witmore, Christopher L. 2007. "Symmetrical Archaeology: Excerpts of a Manifesto." *World Archaeology* 39:546–62.

Wylie, Alison. 2002. *Thinking from Things: Essays in the Philosophy of Archaeology*. Berkeley: University of California Press.

3

Archaeology and the Evaluation of Claims

In today's ultramodern, fast-paced world, it seems that science is all around us. Science is so pervasive that most of us carry around one of the recent marvels of modern science, the smart phone. Not only do we carry it, many of us also rely on it. And the smart phone is just the beginning. Enter the modern home and you are likely to see a smart doorbell, a smart thermostat, and a smart refrigerator. You may even have checked your smart watch when you arrived.

In addition to such scientific wonders, we also have access to a remarkable array of science websites, blogs, YouTube videos, and television shows. Included within the mix of science-related material available are programs about archaeology. One of the things that makes the human story as told by archaeology so fascinating is that it's still unfolding all around us, and each of us has a part to play. We each make history every day.

The almost infinite diversity contained within the human story gives archaeology its special appeal. Archaeologists explore the entire span of human history, extending from day 1 to yesterday. On any given day, a team of archaeologists can be found somewhere in the world sifting through the earth searching for information about the lives of our human ancestors. Archaeologists may be in France entering a cave once inhabited by a family of Neanderthals, and only a few miles away another team might be measuring a cement bunker used by German soldiers during the Second World War. Others may be studying ancient DNA in Ethiopia, the distribution of gravestones in a seventeenth-century English cemetery, or the trash deposits of a twenty-first-century Brazilian landfill. The diversity of subjects demonstrates archaeology's limitless possibilities. Each new research project promises endless new discoveries.

Despite the great variety of possible topics, all archaeologists are united by one common element: the way they address the questions they want to answer. Unlike the nuclear interpretation mentioned in chapter 1, professional archaeologists must develop questions that can be evaluated with tangible evidence. They cannot simply proclaim an interpretation and expect other archaeologists to accept it without proof. Untrained amateurs—pseudo-archaeologists—are free to propound any ideas they wish. As nonprofessional hobbyists not committed to the same rules of evidence and scholarship as professional excavators, they have complete freedom to propose any interpretation they can imagine. Like the armchair-bound archaeologists of centuries ago, pseudo-archaeologists do not conduct excavations (at least not legally, that is). Their interpretations thus typically rest on supposition, wishful thinking, and speculation.

A good example of using wild imagination to explain something about the past comes from the pen of Erich von Däniken, the one-time hotel manager who is largely responsible for today's ancient alien craze with the publication of *Chariots of the Gods?* in 1968. In one of his lesser-known books, *The Eyes of the Sphinx*, von Däniken writes about a man he calls "My Friend Enoch." As told in the Book of Genesis, Enoch was an ancient patriarch who lived before Noah's flood. Three books not included in the Bible mention how Enoch was taken into heaven where he met a host of angels. Von Däniken says that while he was there, Enoch was given a device that allowed him to write over three hundred sacred books (all of which have since disappeared). Von Däniken concludes from this story that Enoch "had the privilege to receive instruction inside an extraterrestrial spaceship." If we ignore the many assumptions we would have to make to accept his conclusion and concentrate on the broader question, we could simply ask how could he possibly know that Enoch had the privilege of interacting with a Biblical-era spaceship? For Von Däniken, "personal experience" is enough for him to accept the complete truth of "traditional folk tales," and as a pseudo-archaeologist he is perfectly free to do so. He does not need irrefutable evidence; supposition is enough.

Professional archaeologists have the same freedom of expression, but with far greater cost to their careers and reputations if they engage in wild speculation. A professor of archaeology who concludes that the Great Pyramid really *was* a nuclear facility, without substantial evidence, or professes that the Enoch stories are the absolute truth, may suffer professionally and lose the respect of colleagues. Unlike pseudo-archaeologists, professionals are held to rigorous standards.

As you saw in the first chapter, the amount of scientific thinking may vary from person to person depending upon their interests and the research question at hand. At the most basic level, however, all archaeologists use science when they rely on systematic concepts of observation, measurement, and evaluation. Even extreme postmodernists, when they excavate, must rely on the same scientifically based field methods as the most ardent hypothesis-testing archaeologist. A poorly conducted excavation will undoubtedly produce interpretations having little if any merit.

Fieldwork, where archaeologists collect most of their information, is an easy place to see the role of science in archaeological research. Systematic excavation involves laying out standardized excavation grids, writing detailed notes, taking photographs, drafting scale drawings and maps, and recording careful vertical and horizontal measurements. The care taken to document every step in the excavation process is a fundamental feature that sets professional archaeologists apart from nonprofessional pseudo-archaeologists. Trained professionals conduct a great deal of research and planning before they arrive in the field to conduct research. Unplanned digging is simply looting, and no professional archaeologist wants to be perceived as a looter. Archaeologists know their efforts will be wasted if they fail to be as careful as possible. Little useful information will come from a sloppy, poorly documented field project. (Worth noting, though, is that some archaeologists conduct important research without digging.)

Professional archaeologists engage in a systematic research process that involves first locating sites and then carefully planning their excavation. This process may take years of background research and field surveying. This preliminary legwork is necessary because archaeologists realize that excavation destroys. The act of turning over soil layers and disturbing the remains within them demolishes the excavated part of the site forever. Archaeologist Philip Barker once observed that excavation, no matter how carefully performed and diligently recorded, "is like cutting pieces out of a hitherto unexamined manuscript, transcribing the fragments, and then destroying them." He added that any self-respecting historian would be enraged by this act, even though archaeologists accept it as a valid research method. Knowing the destructive power of excavation, professional archaeologists undertake it with extreme caution. They know that fieldwork involves just as much paperwork as excavation. Some archaeologists are so attuned to the destructive power of excavation that they believe that some important sites should not be excavated until archaeological methods improve to the point that the destruction is minimal.

Many people think archaeology is only about finding artifacts. Artifacts are a central piece of the cultural and historical puzzles to be sure, but they only constitute one kind of evidence. Other evidence includes the location of artifacts relative to one another both vertically and horizontally as well as to all those things—hearths, storage pits, postholes, and housing remains—that cannot be removed from the ground and taken into the archaeologist's laboratory. Archaeologists can only measure and record these features as they appear in the soil. Some of the more stable remains—adobe house walls, brick hearths—can be left in place, but the more fragile features—post holes, storage pits—are lost forever when excavated.

Every archaeologist makes interpretations once they return from the field. The laboratory is where they begin to evaluate their findings and assess the initial impressions they formed while excavating. This intellectual process also relies on science to some degree because it is here that the second phase of archaeology emerges. The real work of interpretation begins after the specimens have been washed, photographed, entered into a database, closely examined, and after the maps, drawings, and site photographs have been analyzed. How archaeologists do this work provides the basis for archaeological interpretation. This detailed descriptive and analytical activity merges science and the humanities, craft and art.

SEARCHING

In their book *How to Think about Weird Things*, Theodore Schick and Lewis Vaughn present a research program they call SEARCH. Though not created with archaeology in mind, this formula provides an excellent way to envision the basic, overall structure of archaeological thinking. The acronym SEARCH stands for the various steps of the process, which Schick and Lewis present as:

State the claim.
Examine the Evidence for the claim.
Consider Alternative claims, and
Rate, according to the Criteria of adequacy, each Hypothesis [claim].

Before exploring the process itself, the obvious question is: what is a hypothesis and do all archaeologists use them?

Hypotheses can be tricky, sciencey-sounding things. The development and testing of hypotheses constituted a core feature of the New Archaeology (see chapter 2). Most archaeologists today have abandoned the explicit hypothesis testing demanded by New Archaeologists, preferring instead to think of hypotheses merely as claims, a perspective also advocated by Schick and Vaughn. During the era of the New Archaeology, the use of hypotheses was designed with good intentions to make archaeology more overtly scientific. Archaeologists today generally agree that the goals of the New Archaeology were overly optimistic in this regard because so much archaeology is interpretive.

SEARCH is one way of seeking resolution to claims. Another way to say this is: how does anyone know a claim has merit?

STEP 1: STATE THE CLAIM

The first element of SEARCH is simply to state the claim. This seems obvious but the point is that the claim must be made explicit and clear so that everyone understands what is being investigated. Archaeological research is often like opening one door to reveal two more, which in turn leads to another two, and so forth. As a result, researchers must state the exact claim they wish to address so that the goal of their research is clear.

A claim, whatever it is, must be answerable with verifiable evidence. Claims that cannot be addressed have no place in the process. For example, the claim "It takes 135 gremlins to fill up an electric Fiat 500" is not good because its validity cannot be tested with evidence. We are unlikely to find even one gremlin that we can entice into the Fiat. (If we could locate just one, we could measure its size, shape, and mass and extrapolate from there. Once we knew the interior space of a Fiat [about 75.5 ft^3], we'd then have a pretty good idea whether our claim was accurate. But alas, no gremlin, no test!) The claim "Zombies will appear at midnight tonight on the quad" is a valid (though undesirable) question because we can actually test it. We can camp out and wait to see whether any of the undead show up at the stroke of twelve. This claim may not be a serious one but it can be addressed with tangible evidence.

Thinking back to the claim presented in chapter 1—that the Great Pyramid was used as a nuclear facility—we could state this claim: "The Great Pyramid was used as a nuclear energy generator." We could also state the claim as a question: "Was the Great Pyramid used to create nuclear energy?" Either way, we have now stated a claim we would like to have answered with evidence.

STEP 2: EXAMINE THE EVIDENCE

The problem behind our use of gremlins relates to the second element of the SEARCH protocol. This step requires that we examine the evidence for the claim. For gremlins, we have no physical (empirical) evidence for their existence. We can only imagine the average size of one, but what I imagine may be completely different from what you may imagine. We'd both be right, and no one could prove us wrong. We can only be proven wrong when someone captures a gremlin and measures it. Until this happens (which is incredibly unlikely) our claims cannot be evaluated or even criticized because they spring only from our imaginations. They are merely speculative.

The claim that the Great Pyramid was used as a nuclear facility includes evidence that can be evaluated. Europeans first learned about the Egyptian pyramids through the works of French, German, and English tourists who began to write about them in the sixteenth century. The first European investigation of the Great Pyramid occurred in 1798 when Napoleon's scholar-soldiers studied it during the French invasion of Egypt (figure 3.1).

Archaeologists have been exploring Giza ever since. Throughout all this time, not a single piece of evidence has been found that even remotely suggests that the Great Pyramid created nuclear material. Instead, archaeologists have only found evidence that reinforces the most obvious conclusion: that ancient Egyptians built this ancient Egyptian monument. So, under the second step of the SEARCH process, we can consider the evidence for the nuclear interpretation. The undeniable conclusion is that no evidence exists. The nuclear interpretation is mere fantasy. It's very interesting, but it's simply wishful thinking. Realistically, we are left with the interpretations of professional Egyptologists who have spent lifetimes studying every facet of ancient Egyptian life using tangible evidence.

Figure 3.1. Napoleon's army at the Great Pyramid
Source: *From* Description de lÉgypt. *Paris: Imprimerie imériale, 1822.*

Given the real mysteries surrounding the pyramid, we should not be surprised that professional archaeologists disagree about some interpretations. Detailed archaeological studies, such as John Romer's *The Great Pyramid*, illustrate the complexities present within the pyramid's architecture. Respectable scholars have disagreed about something as basic as the size of the pyramid! For example, in the early 1880s, the famed British archaeologist William Flinders Petrie discovered that earlier surveyors had made a series of errors when measuring the pyramid's base. To correct their mistakes, he provided new measurements. The problem is that the measurement depends on where one places the measuring tape and what he or she considers to be the actual base. The rock faces are not as smooth as we might suppose, so some variation between measurements is inevitable. Archaeologists wishing to understand the Great Pyramid's inner architecture have also been hampered by the immense size of the structure and the difficulty of accurately measuring its many shafts and chambers. Thus, something as basic as measurement can be a subject of considerable debate among professional archaeologists even though measurement, by its very nature, is a technical, scientific process. (Precise measurements conducted in 2016 revealed that the base of the Great Pyramid is not exactly square. Statistical analysis of the measurements indicates that the west side is longer than the east side by 0.25 to 5.6 inches with a 95 percent probability, with an error of 2.9 inches.)

When examining the evidence for a claim, it is important to ignore wishful thinking, belief, faith, and intuition. We may secretly wish zombies would visit the quad at midnight but wishing will not make them appear. Our belief in the existence of the walking undead is discounted by the lack of tangible evidence.

Millions of people around the world believe that space aliens are piloting UFOs to our planet. This belief has sponsored a huge commercial industry, but until a spaceship lands or crashes on Earth (and is retrieved), the existence of space aliens must remain only wishful thinking (or dreadful thinking if you think they might be up to no good).

STEP 3: CONSIDER ALTERNATIVE CLAIMS

Step 3 of the SEARCH process asks us to consider alternative claims. This means that before we can accept one claim as true, we must think about and evaluate others. Perhaps an alternative claim makes more sense than the one we originally selected. To decide between them, we must compare the evidence for each of them.

To demonstrate the process, let's use the claim: space aliens are visiting Earth in a number of fast-moving vehicles we collectively term Unidentified Flying Objects. (This is step 1, stating the claim.) When we examine the evidence (step 2), we learn that:

- millions of people believe in UFOs;
- millions of people have seen lights in the sky they cannot explain as airplanes, blimps, drones, stars, weather balloons, and other Earth-made things;
- hundreds of people claim to have been abducted by aliens and many of them have told believable stories of their experiences;
- numerous TV programs and online videos show pictures of UFOs, and organizations like the Mutual UFO Network keep track of their appearances throughout the world;
- both professional and amateur pilots have reported seeing strange things in the sky; and
- many nations' air forces have been unable to explain the large number of sightings.

The Pentagon even had at least two full-blown investigations—Project Bluebook and the Advanced Aerospace Threat Identification Program—to investigate whether UFOs are real, and even they could not provide a credible interpretation.

These factors have convinced millions of people around the world that visitors from far-distant planets are among us and that they have traveled here in otherworldly aircraft using advanced technologies completely unknown to us.

Some people even believe that the US government has been reverse engineering the aliens' technology using parts from crashed flying saucers.

Numerous scientists and skeptics have offered alternative claims to account for what people are seeing in the skies. One of the most prominent claims is that people are witnessing the testing of secret military aircraft. Many UFO sightings occur near airports and military bases. Believers and Ufologists (people who specialize in studying the phenomenon) say the locations of the sightings are not accidental; they claim that aliens are checking out the state of our aircraft. This is one interpretation, but might the locations of the sightings simply have something to do with human flight?

Let's consider some evidence that will help us evaluate the alternative claim. In April 2010, the US Defense Advanced Research Projects Agency (DARPA) oversaw the flight of a prototype aircraft named the Falcon Hypersonic Technology Vehicle, or HTV-2, at Vandenberg Air Force Base in California. The amazing thing about the test flight was that the HTV-2 reached Mach 20, or about 13,000 miles per hour (mph), for about three minutes. If this plane could hold this speed constant, it could travel the 10,500 miles between London, England and Sydney, Australia, in less than an hour! (The current flight time by regular airplane is about twenty-three hours.) In 2022, the SR-71 Blackbird had reached over 2,500 mph, and the experimental NASA/USAF X-45 reached an astounding 4,500 mph. The Russian-built MiG-25 Foxbat reaches 2,190 mph and the Bell X-2 Starbuster can go 2,094 mph (Fastest Fighter Jet 2022). These speeds are significant because many UFO spotters have reported that they've never seen anything move as fast as the UFO they have observed.

Another factor we must consider is how long it would take space aliens to reach the Earth. As you might expect, physicists disagree about this because much of it rests on speculation. Nonetheless, a few truths based on the laws of physics make it possible to propose some reliable ideas.

Interstellar travel, whether by Earthlings or aliens, is constrained by distance, time, and power. Scientists know that the speed of light in a vacuum is constant at about one billion mph. Einstein famously demonstrated that space and time are relative (hence, the theory of relativity). This means that as people travel faster in space, time slows down and space becomes shorter. Mass also increases. The implications for space travel, as science writer Michael White observes in *Weird Science*, is that a person traveling at the speed of light would experience three things: "time would slow to nothing, he would shrink to nothing, and his mass would be infinite!" Thus, aliens leaving their home planet and traveling fifty light years to Earth at a speed of 95 percent the speed of light would need about 52.5 years to reach Earth. But, because time slows down, the alien crew would only age about fifteen years. Science fiction buffs know what this means. The entire trip to Earth and back would take over one hundred years for the people on the home planet, but the travelers would only have aged about thirty years. Upon their arrival they would find their friends and relatives dead or very old, their grandchildren would be older than them, they might find a new political or economic system, and so forth; the possibilities are endless.

Given the constraints of physics, some people have proposed that space aliens may have acted like the ancient Polynesians who traveled thousands of miles to colonize the South Pacific. To accomplish this monumental feat, the Polynesians sailed their canoes from island to island rather than undertaking one long-distance trek. Adopting an island-hopping method, aliens could have planet-hopped using some sort of super-advanced spacecraft. But even with advanced technology, they would need to create colonies on each planet they visited and prepare for the next hop (as the Polynesians did). Upon reaching the next planet, they would have to begin the process all over again.

Realizing that interstellar voyaging has infinitely longer distances between planets than Pacific sailing, we are justified in asking just how long would planet-hopping take? The amount of required fuel would be huge, even using the Polynesians' method. Physicists estimate that a spaceship traveling at only 10 percent of the speed of light would require about fifteen times its mass in fuel. Long-distance space travel would require extremely large ships. Even ancient alien advocate Erich von Däniken admits that a space-traveling ship would have to be the size of a modern ocean liner and have a payload of two hundred tons (with half of it being dedicated to fuel alone). Given the size requirements and the amount of energy required, planet-hopping aliens would have to establish production facilities on each of their colonized planets to replenish the fuel they would need to reach the next planet. Without planet-hopping, the amount of fuel needed to travel huge distances would make any trip unrealistic. (Wormholes seem not to be the answer, either. Physicists disagree about the theoretical possibility of using them for time travel. At present, it does not appear likely with the current state of knowledge, but as research continues quantum physics may provide a few surprises.)

Knowing all this, let's go back to our two claims about UFOs. Our main hypothesis is that space aliens visit the Earth on a regular basis and that people see them and call their spaceships UFOs. Our alternative hypothesis is that UFOs are misrecognized, top-secret planes undergoing testing near airports and other governmental facilities. According to step 4 of the SEARCH protocol, our job now is to evaluate each claim and decide which one seems most plausible based on what evidence we can amass.

The easiest approach is simply to compare the kinds of evidence presented for each claim. For the alien claim, most of the evidence is based on anecdotes, or what scientists term "testimonial evidence."

There is nothing inherently wrong with testimonies, and archaeologists use them all the time. An archaeologist excavating a farmhouse dating to within living memory may choose to speak with former residents to obtain unique insights about life on the farm. Men and women who once lived on the property can tell stories about their pastimes, they can explain how the furniture was arranged in the house, they can talk about what they ate, and they can relate what they did in the yard areas. This information may only exist in their memories, never having been written down. Historian Carl Becker famously referred to this evidence as "history people carry around in their heads."

Even archaeologists studying history before the presence of writing may ask local residents about their activities at a particular place, what they remember about artifacts they may have seen in the soil or in their neighbors' collections, and whether they know any people knowledgeable about local history and archaeology. Archaeologists have found the oral traditions of many Indigenous peoples to be remarkably reliable even though the stories they contain may be several generations old.

When archaeologists use this kind of information, they realize that people's memories can be faulty. People remember things selectively, they forget, misrepresent, and get confused. As a result, anecdotes, however interesting they may be, constitute useful but often potentially unreliable evidence. If a ninety-five-year-old former resident of a farmhouse tells you that she had internet in 1960 and that she remembers watching YouTube as a child, you can be certain that her recollections are faulty. The reliability of verbally transmitted evidence decreases when something like UFOs are the subject because verification is impossible.

STEP 4: RATE EACH CLAIM

In step 4 of the SEARCH formula, Schick and Vaughn introduce what they term "the criteria of adequacy." These criteria help us evaluate the strength of the competing claims, meaning that we don't have to make decisions based on our feelings, what we might wish to be true, or our speculations.

The criteria of adequacy has five elements:

1. testability,
2. fruitfulness,
3. scope,
4. simplicity, and
5. conservatism.

After an investigator has worked through the five criteria, he or she should have a good understanding of whether a claim makes sense.

The first criterion, testability, is exactly what it sounds like: can someone figure out a way to determine whether a claim can be evaluated by testing? If it cannot be tested (and using methods that others can copy), then the claim is worthless. This doesn't mean that it's untrue, however; it simply means it has no value as a verifiable claim. Something that cannot be tested usually falls under the heading of belief.

Of the two competing claims about UFOs, only the second one can be tested. If the military would allow it, we could arrange to have a top-secret, supersonic plane fly over two neighborhoods. The first neighborhood would be one in which the residents recently said they saw a UFO; the second neighborhood would be one that has not witnessed a UFO sighting. After the flights we could ask the residents what they saw and then we could tabulate how many thought they saw a UFO. We must remember, though, even the residents who saw the first sighting could say that what they saw during the test did not resemble "their" UFO. They may have seen a different prototype during their first sighting, the weather could have been different, their allergies may have made their eyesight blurry, and so forth. We could test the claim that the witnessed UFO was really the test flight of a super-secret Earth-bound aircraft, but we would still have several additional factors to consider.

The claim about UFOs being piloted by aliens, however, is untestable. To demonstrate this let's turn to popular television. Their boasts to the contrary, "investigative" programs cannot "unmask the truth" about UFOs. The videos they show are usually out of focus and shaky. Tests of the "best" videos by skilled technicians are either inconclusive or reveal hoaxes. No currently available video—no matter how mysterious it may seem—has been proven to provide direct evidence for alien visitation.

The second criterion of adequacy, fruitfulness, refers to what a claim can do for us; in other words, can it provide new ideas and insights, and create new questions that can be asked and tested? As Schick and Vaughn point out, most claims related to the paranormal, UFOs, and other mysterious phenomena seldom expand inquiry into new topics. One door does not lead to two new doors because the first door is never really opened. As a result, claims about mysterious phenomena have little or no fruitfulness. Ufologists, because they only have extremely weak evidence (or none), simply keep repeating the same questions:

- Are space aliens visiting Earth?
- When did they first arrive?
- What do they look like?
- What do they want here?

UFO chasers cannot progress beyond this point because they have no concrete evidence to support their views; they only have anecdotes, jumpy videos, and a handful of still photographs. On the other hand, the alternative idea about UFOs being airplanes made by Earth-bound humans can lead to other avenues of investigation. If we were allowed to witness a secret test, we could think of several questions to ask. We'd probably want to know about the effects pilots suffer at high speeds, the kind of fuel they use and what is its rate of depletion, who makes the engines and what kind are they, and a hundred other questions, all of which could be answered either by knowledgeable scientists or by our own research. The alternative claim therefore has a high degree of fruitfulness because it leads to a host of other questions.

The third criterion is scope, which refers to how many other phenomena a claim can explain. A rule of thumb among scientists is that the more a claim explains, the likelier it is to be true. If we conclude that the UFO sightings are military aircraft, we could explain why so many are seen near airports, why Area 51 and other governmental research facilities have tight security, why the Air Force never provides little or no information, and why the test pilots who fly experimental military aircraft take their knowledge to the grave. The scope of the "UFOs equal space aliens" claim is extremely narrow because it leads nowhere. It explains nothing.

Simplicity is the fourth criterion of adequacy. This criterion relies on another scientific rule of thumb: that the simplest claims tend to be correct, with "simple" referring to the number of assumptions that must be made. Scientists refer to this as "Occam's Razor" in honor of William of Occam, a medieval English friar who often used the idea in his philosophical arguments. The metaphor of the razor helps us imagine shaving off as many assumptions from our claim as possible.

The number of assumptions needed to accept the idea that UFOs are piloted by space aliens are astronomical, beginning with the two most obvious ones: that space aliens exist and that they wish to visit us Earthlings. From this follows innumerable additional assumptions concerning the nature of their fuel, the design of their engines, their advanced technology, the distances they've traveled, and how their bodies can withstand the extremely high speeds needed for space travel. And these are just a few of the assumptions we must make. Thinking about the aliens' role in building the Great Pyramid, we would have to ask this simple question: Why would aliens travel all this way in super high-tech spaceships just to build a simple pyramid, with stones, in the middle of the Egyptian desert? Why not build something as high-tech as their ships? Why would they build a nuclear plant since they obviously had a more advanced form of energy? We would have to overlook such obvious questions and simply accept the assumption that space aliens like traveling vast distances to build pyramid-shaped nuclear facilities in deserts (while leaving no other trace of their presence).

One of the most interesting assumptions that we'd have to make about the physical evidence presented in UFO videos is that psychologists are wrong about the "autokinetic effect." This is a physical phenomenon whereby people think a stationary light is moving when they see it against a dark background. Involuntary movements of the eye, which occur even when we hold our heads perfectly still, convince us that the light is moving when it's not. In the early twentieth century, psychologist Joseph Peterson set up an experiment to prove the existence of the effect. During his testing, he discovered two things that help us understand peoples' strong belief in UFOs: first, that because the autokinetic effect frightens some people, they immediately conclude that what they see must be supernatural or otherworldly, and second, that lights appear to move even when the subjects of the experiment know the lights are completely stationary. We can easily see how the autokinetic effect could figure into some claims about UFO sightings.

The final criterion of adequacy is conservatism, which refers to how well a claim conforms to what we already know. In this instance, rather than simply listing the alternative claims as we did in step 3, here we must assign relative weights to each competing claim. Here the process is simple because we have only two claims. Based on what I have presented, is it more likely that UFOs are:

a. visitations by space aliens, or
b. secret airplanes being tested by governmental agencies?

The evidence leads us to accept the alternative claim (b) as most likely based on everything we know and on the simplicity of the claim. We make fewer assumptions when we accept that governmental agencies are probably testing futuristic aircraft over our heads. The alternative claim has much greater weight than the claim about space aliens.

We can accept the alternative claim even though millions of people around the world continue to believe that space aliens are visiting Earth. This idea acquired an archaeological dimension when von Däniken proposed his claim about ancient astronauts in 1968. Since then, he and others have developed a thriving industry by claiming that the greatest archaeological sites in the world, including the Great Pyramid, are the product of alien technology rather than tangible proof of the intelligence and creativity of our human ancestors. As archaeologist Kenneth Feder states in "Help! I'm Being Followed by Ancient Aliens!" not only has no archaeological evidence ever been found for aliens— no ray guns, no phasers, no antigravity machines—we simply don't need to imagine that ancient spacemen (and women, I presume) built a pyramid in the Egyptian desert or taught the Egyptians how to build it. The very real archaeological mysteries remaining to be solved should be enough to keep us interested without having to invent wild, untestable claims.

PLAUSIBILITY

We must understand one more thing. The nature of claims is such that we can never completely prove them, especially in archaeology. All we can do is to tend to accept them. Why? Because we can never be 100 percent certain that we've collected all the evidence, even for UFOs.

The job of all serious researchers—archaeologists, historians, physicists, biologists—is to acquire knowledge about our world. Whereas physical scientists can absolutely prove a claim with evidence, archaeologists always work with partial evidence. As a result, archaeologists usually speak in terms of *probability* or *plausibility* rather than 100 percent certainty.

In *Evidence Explained*, Elizabeth Shown Mills observes that scholars who engage in historical research (including archaeologists) typically use certain words to signify their lack of complete certainty. Ranging from least to most likelihood, the tell-tale words are "perhaps" (an idea is plausible but untested), "apparently" (a scholar has formed an impression based on experience, but has not tested the idea), "likely" (the weight of evidence tilts toward the assertion), "possibly" (good evidence exists, but the claim is not yet proved), and "probably" (the assertion is more likely than not based on the evidence at hand). All archaeologists use these terms, though perhaps not with the same levels of meaning as Mills suggests. In any case, such commonplace terms indicate that no one alive today can know the past with certainty, Mills's highest level of confidence. Students reading the works of archaeologists should be on the lookout for these terms.

The need to understand that plausibility is especially important for archaeologists (and others who study the past) because the whole truth can never be known in its entirety (see chapter 4). The past is gone and all of its secrets will never be revealed. No one can recreate history in every detail. Going back to SEARCH, then, we can ask: what is the most plausible interpretation based on the evidence we have at hand right now? And "now" is key because knowledge increases with every new investigation, or in the case of archaeology, with each new excavation and analysis.

Scientists and other scholars seldom make the mistake of thinking they have learned everything about a subject. In 1950, it would have been wrong for medical researchers to state that they knew everything about the human body. Ceasing research in that year would have been an appalling idea because what they have discovered since 1950 has been astronomical. The same could be said about 2000 or 2010 because something new is always to be learned, with the COVID-19 pandemic being a perfect example. Archaeologists adopt the same view. They know their knowledge is constrained by the current state of the discipline.

In terms of plausibility, we must decide—based on our current knowledge—that it is much more likely that UFOs are secret aircraft rather than alien-powered spaceships. But can we completely discount the claim that some UFOs are space aliens? Surprisingly, not entirely.

Though extremely unlikely, it remains remotely possible that one day a spaceship may crash in broad daylight in New York City and be witnessed by hundreds of people (before the mysterious men in black can remove it!). The probability of this event ever occurring is infinitesimally small, but it remains possible. Astronomers agree that the huge number of galaxies and planets in the universe make it statistically possible for life to exist beyond Earth. Despite this conclusion, significant questions remain as to what these life forms may be like, and whether they could (or would) ever wish to visit us. The possibility of an alien visit is so tiny as to be virtually impossible, but no one knows the future. What is not plausible is that ancient space aliens built the Great Pyramid, England's Stonehenge, or any other ancient earthen or stone monument. It is pure fantasy.

THE EXETER MYSTERY

I have purposefully kept my UFO example simple to make it easier to understand the basics of the SEARCH formula. It always helps, however, to present a real incident to explain how the belief in UFOs and space aliens can rest alongside the scientific search for more plausible explanations. A real case, called "The Exeter Incident," demonstrates how long it can take for a realistic interpretation to emerge from the world of fantasy.

Just after midnight on September 3, 1965, in Exeter, New Hampshire, a police officer was driving along a road when he encountered a woman parked on the shoulder. When he stopped to investigate, he found her to be extremely agitated. She told him she had been followed for several miles by a flying object with red flashing lights. She pointed toward the horizon, where she and the policeman both saw a bright light. Not having an explanation, but seeing no danger, the cop told her there was nothing to worry about and left. About two hours later, however, a visibly shaken teenager arrived at the Exeter police station. He reported that while hitchhiking toward home he had seen a huge ship in the sky. He signed a statement and agreed to accompany an officer to the site. Upon arriving in the area of the sighting, the officer also saw the object and reported that it had five bright, red lights. Over the next several weeks, more than sixty witnesses filed similar reports about strange lights in the sky, and in February 1966 a story even appeared in *Look*, a popular biweekly magazine read by millions of Americans. Thus was born "The Exeter Incident."

True believers in the connection between strange lights in the sky and advanced space travelers quickly transformed the incident into a "close encounter." It quickly entered UFO folklore where it has prominently remained ever since.

As you may expect, a number of people offered alternative ideas about what the people may actually have seen. Some of these claims are that the lights were:

- stars or planets,
- the glare of landing lights from aircraft going into nearby Pease Air Force Base a Strategic Air Command and NORAD base,
- part of an Air Force operation,
- an advertising plane with a flying billboard,
- the corona from power lines, or
- a prankster with a lighted kite.

Skeptics presented each of these alternative interpretations, but none were ever tested. As a result, for forty years "The Exeter Incident" remained an important fixture within Ufology. It took two researchers, James McGaha and Joe Nickell, to provide the most likely alternative interpretation of what the people in New Hampshire witnessed.

McGaha, a former military pilot, realized that the light sequence the people reported seeing perfectly matched the lights on a US Air Force KC-97 refueling plane. These planes not only had a row of five red, flashing lights mounted on their fuselages, they were also based at Pease AFB in the 1960s. When a plane was to be refueled in the air, a very delicate operation at night, the KC-97 pilot would turn on the lights to tell the pilot of the other plane that the fuel boom was lowered. As the second pilot approached, the KC-97 pilot would dim the sequencing lights so as not to blind the approaching pilot. This operation would undoubtedly look strange to an observer on the ground, especially at night by someone unfamiliar with the process (as most people would be).

Most serious UFO researchers now regard this famous "cold case" as closed. The incident clearly demonstrates the importance of considering alternative interpretations, even if it takes years. Archaeologists understand the time it often takes to acquire enough evidence to be able to propose plausible claims about long-dead civilizations.

THE ONGOING BATTLE BETWEEN EVIDENCE AND PERSPECTIVE

Claims are a dry subject that seem devoid of human emotion. Perhaps in learning about the SEARCH formula and the criteria of adequacy you pictured scientists in white lab coats toiling away in the ultra-clean, white rooms often depicted in science-fiction movies. In reality, the development of claims and the decisions made about plausibility depend a great deal on the investigator's education, interests, personality, and education. This is where the art of archaeological interpretation comes into view.

In a perfectly regimented world, the process of deciding between competing claims would be as straightforward as knowing that water boils at 212°F—and just about as interesting. Thankfully, archaeology includes a process of discovery and interpretation that is anything but humdrum or rigid because human culture is infinitely complicated. Each researcher, even when strictly adhering to the SEARCH method, interjects her or his ideas, passions, and interests—combined with the traditions and practices of their discipline—into the process. And once human personality is introduced, many different perspectives can result and great controversies over interpretation can occur.

In *Reading Matter*, Arthur Berger presents a perfect example of how one's professional discipline may shape one's interpretations. In a hypothetical scenario, he envisions six scholars sitting in their individual offices in the same building. Each of them has a window that looks down on a central courtyard. In the courtyard is a picnic table with a McDonald's hamburger, an order of French fries, and a milkshake on it. The scholars are a semiotician (someone who studies symbols and their meanings), a psychoanalytic psychologist, a cultural anthropologist, an historian, a sociologist, and a political scientist. Each scholar, because of his or her perspectives, educational training, and personality, interprets the objects on the table differently.

The semiotician perceives the objects as a series of symbols. To her, they symbolize America, the efficiency of mass production, and the standardization of food preparation. She understands that the Golden Arches printed on the wrapping, the cup, and the bag as symbols recognized throughout the world. In a broad way, the symbol represents the United States and its global economic reach.

The psychologist, on the other hand, sees the objects as representing the desire for instant gratification and depersonalization. The hamburgers, fries, and milkshakes, wherever consumed in the world, all look and taste alike. A McDonald's hamburger in Dublin, Ireland, tastes just like one in St. Louis, Missouri. Individual consumers cannot decide if they want their hamburger cooked a little longer or have their fries cooked in an exotic brand of olive oil. When you go to McDonald's you get what everyone else gets (with some minor variation, perhaps).

The historian immediately sees the objects on the table in terms of the history of corporations and how twentieth-century US corporations became multinationals following the Second World War. She also envisions how the presentation of the food changed American eating and driving habits because the first McDonald's restaurants did not have tables inside them. She also thinks about how the restaurants are linked to the development of America's car culture and the creation of suburbs.

The cultural anthropologist perceives the objects as elements of a ritual. During the early years of the company, teenagers had to go into the restaurant and order food from a counter. Receiving their order, they had to leave because of the lack of tables. They ate their meals in their cars and drove around as they did so. The anthropologist interprets this behavior as part of a mating ritual, with the restaurant being a ritualized site where eligible partners can meet without their parents being present.

The sociologist thinks about how people, and perhaps especially young people, use such objects to feel part of a group and how fast-food restaurants have become places where people of all ages meet and socialize. She might also consider how places like McDonald's have become especially important to disadvantaged families as relatively inexpensive places to eat and how difficult it may be for many people to escape the low-wage service jobs fast-food restaurants offer.

The political scientist perceives the food on the table as examples of how corporations have become extremely powerful in the Western world and how they are rapidly moving into the Global South. He may see McDonald's as the worst example of globalization because it exploits its workforce while it spreads the unhealthy American diet to the rest of the world.

What is notable about Berger's scenario is that each of the scholars uses the exact same pieces of material culture—a hamburger, some fries, and a milk-shake—to frame their interpretations. The addition of more scholars—perhaps an architect, a neuroscientist, a marketing professor, and a feminist—would add to the diversity of interpretations. What is interesting, though, is that none of them would be incorrect. Their perspectives are simply different because they have examined the objects from a different angle. It is here, then, that we see the challenge of analysis, despite the power of the SEARCH protocol. Individuals simply have different ways of perceiving the world around them.

Instead of having scholars from different disciplines looking down at a picnic table, what would happen if six archaeologists examined a new collection of artifacts at a museum? What if the archaeologists included a Marxist, a feminist, an ecologist, a Darwinian, a critical theorist, and a network analyst? Archaeologists holding each perspective are active today. Each of these archaeologists, just like Berger's group of scholars in the office building, can examine the same pieces of material culture and devise different interpretations. The differences of opinion that develop and the diverse interpretations that result keep archaeology vibrant and interesting.

One of the key features of serious scholarship, especially in a discipline like archaeology, is that ideas, concepts, and interpretations change as more information is gathered and as new perspectives emerge. Some of the perspectives that develop derive directly from the concerns of society rather than specifically from scientific inquiry. For example, the archaeology of African American enslavement arose in the late 1960s in direct response to the Civil Rights movement and the growing interest in ethnic pride. When archaeologists excavated plantation sites before the 1960s, their focus was usually on the mansion and its White, wealthy residents. The civil rights and ethnic pride movements made archaeologists wonder what life had been like where most plantation residents lived, in the cabins of the enslaved. Archaeologists thus began to excavate cabin remains to satisfy their curiosity, and today throughout North and South America, the Caribbean, and even Africa they concentrate their efforts on the archaeology of the African Diaspora. The Civil Rights movement brought racism and racial discrimination to the forefront of national thinking. Minority groups, held down and ignored, have voiced their concerns about many social issues, one of which concerns how the dominant culture has attempted to separate them from their histories. Native Americans and African Americans, as well as others, demanded to have a say in how their histories are written and portrayed. At the same time, scholars in many academic disciplines have started to question their own goals, motivations, and perspectives as they pertain to the world's minorities.

The same situation occurred with pre-Columbian archaeology and the ecology movement. As Canadian archaeologist Bruce Trigger recounts, archaeologists had a long-standing interest in past economies because it was believed that material objects were a direct reflection of a culture's economic system. Archaeologists viewed cultures with stone tools as hunters and collectors, whereas they understood cultures with clay pottery as usually sedentary. In the 1960s, in conjunction with the rise of the global ecology movement, archaeologists began to make explicit connections between a culture's way of life and the environment in which they were situated. As with many things, archaeologists did not necessarily agree among themselves about the best approach to use to understand past environments, but the individual research programs, when combined, created a fresh perspective on ancient lifeways.

Archaeologists are affected by social changes because they are influenced by the things happening around them, just as is everyone else. The history of archaeology has a close connection to colonialism, but today's archaeology is striving to decolonize the profession to make it more inclusive and more respectful of the wishes of descendant communities.

*　*　*

Archaeology, like most disciplines, is constantly changing because its practitioners are always reading, thinking, and conducting research. New perspectives arise and come to prominence because they appear to offer a fresh way to conceptualize the past. Throughout the history of change, however, some elements remain the same. The tenets of the SEARCH protocol provide an important method for evaluating evidence. Archaeologists will never be able to construct a complete picture of past daily life because much that took place is lost forever. As a result, archaeologists try to present interpretations that have the highest degree of plausibility, while acknowledging that their interpretation is always going to be partial. Archaeologists know plausibility increases when more information is amassed. Shoddy research in archaeology is like shoddy research in any endeavor, whether it's interpreting the meaning of the Great Pyramid or building a bookshelf. Understanding the rules of structured thinking increases the likelihood that archaeological interpretations come as close to past reality as is possible, given what is known at the time.

SOURCES FOR CONTINUED READING

ARCHAEOLOGY

Barker, Philip. 1982. *Techniques of Archaeological Excavation*. Second edition. New York: Universe.

Dash, Glen. 2012. "New Angles on the Great Pyramid." *Aeragram* 13 (2):10–19.

Flinders Petrie, William Matthew. 1883. *The Pyramids and Temples of Gizeh.* London: Field and Tuer.

Romer, John. 2007. *The Great Pyramid: Ancient Egypt Revisited.* Cambridge: Cambridge University Press.

Trigger, Bruce. 1971. "Archaeology and Ecology. "*World Archaeology* 2:321–36.

UFOS

Flyjetify. 2022. "Fastest Fighter Jet." www.flyjetify.com/fastest-fighter-jet; accessed October 2022.

McGaha, James and Joe Nickell. 2011. "'Exeter Incident' Solved! A Classic UFO Case, Forty-Five Years Cold." *Skeptical Inquirer* 35 (6):16–19.

Peterson, Joseph. 1917. "Some Striking Illusions of Movement of a Single Light on Mountains." *American Journal of Psychology* 28:476–85.

Von Däniken, Erich. 1970. *Chariots of the Gods? Unsolved Mysteries of the Past.* Michael Heron, trans. New York: Bantam.

THINKING

Berger, Arthur Asa. 1992. *Reading Matter: Multidisciplinary Perspectives on Material Culture.* New Brunswick, NJ: Transaction.

Feder, Kenneth L. 2013. "Help! I'm Being Followed by Ancient Aliens!" *Skeptical Inquirer* 37 (2):54–55.

Jarns, Owen. 2016. "Great Pyramid of Giza Is Slightly Lopsided." LiveScience, www.livescience.com/55118-great-pyramid-giza-is-slightly-lopsided.html; accessed October 2022.

Mills, Elizabeth Shown. 2012. *Evidence Explained: Citing History Sources from Artifacts to Cyberspace.* Second revised edition. Baltimore: Genealogical Publishing.

Schick, Theodore, Jr. and Lewis Vaughn. 1995. *How to Think about Weird Things: Critical Thinking for a New Age.* Mountain View, CA: Mayfield.

White, Michael. 1999. *Weird Science: An Expert Explains Ghosts, Voodoo, the UFO Conspiracy, and Other Paranormal Phenomena.* New York: Avon.

4

Understanding and Selecting Facts

Archaeology, like any field of serious inquiry, understandably deals with facts. Most of us can accept this idea without much controversy. But when we stop and think about it, what exactly is a fact? You may have noticed that up to this point, I haven't said anything about facts even though every chapter has been filled with facts. Still, I never described anything as a fact, even though the various interpretations about the Great Pyramid and UFOs contain innumerable facts. Three of the most basic facts about the pyramid are easy to list:

- it is in Egypt,
- it is ancient, and
- it contains several chambers and shafts on the inside.

    Regarding UFOs, we can list these facts:

- people see them both during the day and at night,
- they usually appear as bright or blinking lights, and
- people often report seeing them near airports.

In Berger's example, we saw that highly trained scholars can make different interpretations while looking at the same material objects—a hamburger, a bag of fries, and a milkshake. In each case, the interpreters drew on certain facts they perceived as relevant in the process of creating their interpretations. In the office building, some of the scholars looked primarily at the symbolism printed on the bag and cup, whereas others looked at the food itself. The important point is that every interpreter, even UFO spotters, are engaged in a process known as "fact selection." Though seemingly simple, facts require careful thought because they are so numerous. The abundance of facts means that selectivity is required when using them.

FACT SELECTION

The concept of fact selection is a peculiar thing. Some people feel uncomfortable just thinking about it. After all, how can objective scholars pick which facts they wish to use in their interpretations? Doesn't the SEARCH formula make such a thing strictly out of the question?

People might become skeptical about archaeology once they discover the existence of fact selection. Once they learn about it, some people may agree with Henry Ford that "history is bunk." (He also said, "history is more or less bunk." I guess he quantified history's "bunkiness" depending upon his mood!) Most people who know what Ford said do not know his reasons for disparaging the study of history. He knew that historians, year after year, write new histories on the same subjects but with different perspectives. The publication of different histories of the same events, say of the Napoleonic Wars, made Ford skeptical to the point of dismissal. If he had known the story of the McDonald's meal on the picnic table, he might have had a better understanding of how people can employ the same facts to construct different interpretations or how they select a different set of facts from the same objects. He would also have understood that there is nothing *inherently* dishonest about the process (although there certainly can be).

At this point, it is worthwhile to discuss the urge of some people today to argue with "alternative facts." Philosophers have confirmed that facts are complex, tricky things, but when most people think of facts, they envision something that is demonstratively true. Thus, everyone should agree that $2 + 2 = 4$, and admit that this is a fact. Today's cliché that "you are entitled to your opinion" strives to give legitimacy to the idea that every person's perspective is equally legitimate and so must be respected. In *Crimes Against Logic*, Jamie Whyte argues that respecting someone's opinion, no matter how outlandish, creates a "culture of caution" that is an obstacle to truth. He believes that we can be too courteous to promoters of outrageous, ridiculous, or wrong ideas by not calling them out.

Where archaeology is concerned, facts are things about the past that can be demonstrated to have been true. For example, North American archaeologists have long been intrigued by the people they call the Mississippians, a culture that existed in the midwestern and southern United States from the eleventh to the seventeenth centuries. One of the most obvious features of this complex culture was the construction of large, flat-topped earthen mounds, one of the most remarkable being Cahokia Mound in Illinois just east of St. Louis. That the Mississippians built flat-topped mounds is an incontrovertible fact. Archaeologists may have different interpretations about the mounds, but the mounds themselves are facts. No one can reasonably debate the existence of the mounds even though the interpretations of professional archaeologists and pseudo-archaeologists may wildly differ.

Fact selection is an important element of analysis and interpretation that separates hard scientists from archaeologists. Archaeologists and others studying the past have more flexibility when it comes to facts than do biologists and chemists. A chemist who chooses to accept that water boils at 150°F will have significantly more problems professionally than an archaeologist who argues that the Mississippians built flat-topped mounds because their leaders wanted to stand above the people (and look down on them) as a reflection of the power and authority that comes with leadership. The boiling point of water is an established physical fact that cannot be refuted, whereas the reasons for erecting huge flat-topped mounds may be argued about based on the evidence at hand.

One thing that makes fact selection difficult to comprehend is that it seems to imply that every fact has the same status as every other fact; that one fact is as good as any other. This kind of reasoning, which Professor Stebbing calls "potted thinking," is just plain wrong. (In her quaint British way, she uses "potted" to mean lazy or convenient. Potted meat is meat that can be conveniently bought in a can at the grocery store rather than from a butcher, like Spam.) The professional chemist must accept that water boils at 212°F not at 150°F because the boiling point of H_2O is incontestable. The situation gets considerably murkier for archaeologists because the social sciences and humanities are not based on reproducible experiments in the same way as in the hard sciences. The past cannot be recreated in any complete way.

The idea that analysts select facts raises some interesting questions, the most obvious being: what are facts? Going back to UFOs, should we accept these two apparent facts as equal:

1. UFOs are alien spaceships, and
2. UFOs are misrecognized airplanes and other flying vehicles built by Earthlings?

These two statements obviously have different validity, but are they facts? In truth, the only true facts we have about UFOs are:

1. lights appear in the sky, and
2. people see them.

People extrapolate their interpretations from these two basic facts. Could it be that UFO spotters have left out some facts? Perhaps they failed to report that they heard sounds when they saw the lights or that they may have had too much to drink at the time of their sighting. Perhaps they were tired, had a bright streetlight in their eyes, or weren't wearing their glasses. The point is that however much they may believe in their observations, the UFO spotters were engaged in fact selection. Why? Because fact selection is inevitable.

Fact selection is a serious matter, and it has several key elements relevant to archaeological thinking. The failure to appreciate its necessity can have significant implications for archaeological interpretation.

To understand what fact selection is about, we need to go back in time just as we did to discover Professor Stebbing in chapter 1. In 1926, American historian Carl Becker presented a paper at the annual meeting of the American Historical Association in Rochester, New York titled simply "What Are Historical Facts?" He directed his comments to his professional colleagues, but his lessons are equally relevant to archaeologists.

Becker started by explaining what most people think a historian does: "He works in the past, he explores the past in order to find out what men did and thought in the past. His business is to discover and set forth the 'facts' of history." (At the time, most historians were men and their perspectives were androcentric.) Except for his dated language, Becker's description is just as apt for archaeologists as for historians.

Becker noted that the word "facts" is usually uncontroversial because people understand it to mean "what is true." Most people in the Western world are familiar with the need "to get the facts straight" and they know "that the facts are what really matter." So, Becker is correct that most people intuitively understand a fact to be what is true, or in the case of history, what *was* true; something that actually happened in the past. Viewed this way, facts are the individual pieces of the past that collectively comprise history. But for Becker, there's much more to what constitutes facts. For him, historical facts have a special meaning that historians (and archaeologists) must appreciate. He challenges his colleagues to ponder this question: when we think about it, what, after all, is a historical fact? To investigate this question, he poses two related questions: (1) where is the historical fact? and (2) when is the historical fact?

Becker began with a statement that almost every historian would consider to be a historical fact: "In the year 49 BC Caesar crossed the Rubicon" (figure 4.1). This fact is so well known that it has entered everyday speech. When we say that someone has "crossed the Rubicon" we mean that they have done something they cannot take back; they are stuck with the consequences of their actions.

Becker takes this fact and says that it's not as simple as it may appear. The fact is really a half-truth because, although Caesar did indeed cross the Rubicon (which is a small river in northern Italy), he did not go alone; he took a Roman legion with him. Once we have the image of Caesar crossing the river at the head of a Roman army, several questions immediately arise:

- How many people went with him?
- How long did the crossing take?
- Did they walk over a bridge?
- Was Caesar riding a horse?

Chapter 4

Figure 4.1. Caesar crossing the Rubicon, 49 BCE

Source: *From John Clark Ridpath,* Cyclopedia of Universal History, Volume II. *Cincinnati: Jones Brothers, 1890, p. 237.*

- Did they go in boats, and if so, where did they get the boats?
- If they used boats, what did they look like and who made them?
- Did they have to pay to use the boats?
- If they went across the river on foot, how deep was it?

These are only some questions we may wish to have answered, and you can probably think up many more with ease. For example, think about the crossing from an archaeological point of view. What questions might be posed then?

Studies show that moving the Roman army around was not such an easy matter. In her book on the Roman Army, Pat Southern directly addresses the logistical obstacles Roman generals faced as they attempted to move their armies from one place to another. She reports that some of what the Romans took with them were (1) food, (2) fodder for their animals, (3) drink, (4) tools for harvesting crops and hunting game, (5) tools for processing and eating food, (6) drinking and eating vessels, (7) weapons, (8) clothing, (9) digging tools, (10) medical and veterinary equipment, (11) one tent for each *contubernium* [a unit consisting of eight men], (12) field artillery for each century [one hundred men], and (13) a siege train with larger artillery if cities and citadels were to be stormed. This is only a partial list because each legionnaire undoubtedly carried a number of personal possessions. In any case, the list reveals that as Caesar and his men crossed the Rubicon, they undoubtedly took with them hundreds of artifacts, ranging from coins and cooking pots to pieces of artillery.

In addition to the artifacts themselves, archaeologists would be equally interested in the army's locations. If it took more than one day to move the entire legion across the river, at least two campsites—one on either side of the river—would have been necessary. Using the many techniques of site location available today, archaeologists should be able to locate the footprints of these "marching camps" to determine exactly where the crossing occurred. (The course of the river has changed since Caesar's time, so finding the exact spot of the crossing has been difficult.) But once the campsites have been found, a systematic archaeological survey could identify the legion's location on each side of the river. Everything learned from the archaeological exploration would constitute historical facts. And most excitingly, they would be entirely new facts. Each element of the crossing would exist in the past—they occurred—but they become facts only when they are brought to light in the present.

Becker's question about Caesar and the Rubicon raises an important additional question: why did it matter that Caesar crossed the Rubicon? Surely, lots of people crossed it all the time and some local residents may have crossed it several times every day. What makes Caesar's crossing so important that people around the world still use it to mean having to face the consequences of not being able to turn back?

The implications of the crossing were immense. The Roman Senate had ordered Caesar to surrender his command of the Roman army in Gaul (the ancient province that is now France) because they did not want him outside their reach with a powerful army at his command. But Caesar refused to resign his command and instead made the fateful step of crossing the river (the Rubicon) separating the Province of Gaul from Imperial Rome. Crossing the Rubicon was thus an act of treason. But having taken the fateful step, Caesar is thought to have said, "the die is cast," meaning that he had made a fateful decision from which he could not turn back. (Did he really say it? On which side of the river did he say it? Did he say it in the middle of the river?)

Crossing the Rubicon, then, is a *symbol* for thousands of related facts, some of which have tangible characteristics (artifacts, settlements, campfires) and some of which do not (Caesar's words to his soldiers about their act of treason, the soldier's own comments, and so forth). As Becker showed, the historical fact about Caesar's crossing is not as simple as it first appears. It is a shorthand way of stating the thousands of related facts bundled into this one statement. The "big" fact revolves around the political implications of Caesar's crossing, but countless "smaller" facts are grafted onto the big one. Fact selection thus involves deciding which facts to use because all of them cannot be included. Too many facts exist.

Becker observed that historical facts are not as cold and hard as many scientific facts (e.g., the boiling point of water). The dimensions, temperatures, and atomic weights of historical facts cannot be calculated despite their significance to our understanding of the past. This acknowledgment leads directly to Becker's second question: where is the historical fact?

In some ways, this is the most interesting question and the one that has captured many scholars' attention. Caesar's crossing of the Rubicon is known to have occurred on January 10, 49 BCE; it happened on that day. So where is this event now? Where does this fact exist?

At least two answers can be posited to answer this question. The first is to conclude that the event belongs entirely to the past, to the year 49 BCE. It is an event that occurred on that day in January. But where is that fact today? If we go to Italy, find the Rubicon, and using advanced geophysical equipment find the precise spot at which Caesar and his legion crossed, will we see him crossing? Of course not. The crossing is part of history; it's gone forever. But the fact of the crossing remains. So, where is it? For Becker the historical fact exists within the mind, "or it is nowhere, because when it is in no one's mind it lies in the records inert, incapable of making a difference in the world."

His last point is especially intriguing. If a historical fact actually happened, then it had been real. Historical events and practices were concrete occurrences, yet we cannot see, smell, or touch them. We can only imagine them.

We can begin to understand what Becker meant if we go back to archaeologist Walter Taylor's ideas mentioned in chapter 2. Taylor pointed out that the word "history" means different things. Becker's idea makes more sense if we recall two of these meanings. First, history is what really happened in the past. History is the sum of the trillions of things that have actually occurred during the steady flow of time; history is thus really "past actuality." If we think of human history in terms of past actuality, we can imagine the trillions of events that have occurred since the first human ancestors walked on two legs. The number of actions, ideas, and artifacts that comprise past actuality is therefore truly mind-boggling.

To get an idea of just how mind-boggling, think about your day today. How many things did you do after you crawled out of bed? Think only about the act of brushing your teeth. How many events occurred as you did so and how many objects were involved? Five, ten, fifteen? Did you floss? Did you use mouthwash, and if so, how many times did you swish it around in your mouth? What color is your toothbrush? How long is it? What brand is it? How many bristles does it have?

Each one of these things and your individual actions as you used them—no matter how insignificant they may seem—belong to past actuality because they really happened. They constitute part of human history in general and part of your own personal history specifically. They may not be important, and you may not remember them. No archaeologist will ever dig them up and no historian will ever write about them, but they occurred nevertheless.

A second meaning of history is "chronicle." To understand this meaning, how would you answer this question from a friend you met on the way to class: "What did you do last night?" How many facts should you relate? Would you recount in excruciating detail all the things that made up the past actuality of last night? Of course not. You would only relate certain things. These things, compiled together, constitute your chronicle—your story or narrative—of last night. It would be impossible for you to recount everything because, as anthropologist Alfred Kroeber observed years ago, stating everything that "really happened"—everything—would take as long as the events themselves!

So when Becker said that historical facts reside in someone's mind, he was referring to the creation of chronicle, not to past actuality. If a historian chooses not to use a fact in his chronicle, just as you decided not to tell your friend everything about last night, it doesn't mean something didn't happen. You may have slipped and fallen in front of a crowded bar. This embarrassing event is part of past actuality but not part of your chronicle because you chose not to mention it in your "history" of last night. And because you did not select it, it lies inert in past actuality. Since the history of your fall was not written down anywhere (and hopefully it didn't end up online), it recedes into the past and is forgotten (you hope). It will always have happened—you cannot change that—but it may never be part of a historical narrative.

Becker's views about fact selection are not simply interesting philosophical questions because they have real significance to archaeological thinking. One of his most interesting ideas is that facts "lie inert" if not used. Archaeologists can easily envision stone tools, clay pots, storage pits, the remains of mud walls, postholes, and millions of other artifacts lying inert in the soil until they are discovered during excavation. Each one of them is part of past actuality, but they are not part of a chronicle until they are unearthed and written about. They really do lie inert in the earth.

The difference between past actuality and chronicle was brought home to me, though I didn't realize it at the time, when I attended my very first archaeological excavation as a junior in college. The field director in charge of the project was interested in locating the remains of seventeenth-century houses inhabited by Native Americans. After eight weeks of excavation, the other students and I had uncovered numerous postholes and storage pits, many of which contained mixtures of Native American and European artifacts. The field director was pleased with our results. I, on the other hand, thought we should have found more evidence. So I asked her, "What if we missed the best house by only a couple of inches?" Her reply was "Well, we don't know, do we?"

As I look back on this experience, I realize I was experiencing the difference between past actuality and chronicle expressed archaeologically. Viewed in material terms, all the postholes, storage pits, stone tools, glass beads, animal remains, seeds, pollen, and everything else that remained at the site is part of past actuality. All these things are really there. The residents of the village had used them, and they were elements of past events that had actually taken place. But what we had collected from the site—the artifacts, the animal bones, the drawings, notes, maps, photographs, and everything else—had become pieces of the site's chronicle (including me). They became the evidence for past life at the village. This doesn't mean, of course, that the things we did not collect that summer are not part of the past, because they most certainly are. It simply means they could not be part of the chronicle developed that summer because we did not have access to them. Being undiscovered, they were inert. Archaeologists who later excavated the site were able to add the artifacts they found to the chronicle, and these additions fleshed out the overall cultural and historical picture of the village's past actuality. The chronicle compiled about the site will gain plausibility as the evidence piles up. With greater plausibility, archaeologists can have more confidence in their interpretations of life in the village, even though everything about its past can never be known (see chapter 3).

Understanding the difference between chronicle and past actuality makes it possible to answer Becker's second question: "when is the historical fact?" The answer is "the present." Becker imagined that facts are "alive" today because they exist in the researcher's head.

Becker's question of "when" is especially interesting when viewed from the archaeologist's vantage point. Archaeologists are taught to think materially about people, things, and events, and when they hear the word "history" most immediately think about the material elements that compose it. When reading documents, historians tend to focus on what the document says and what it portrays about the writer and his or her times. They usually only concentrate on a document's material characteristics when they attempt to determine whether it is authentic or a forgery. They examine the type of paper, the formula of the ink, the design of the watermark. A famous example is the so-called Hitler Diaries.

In 1983, the West German magazine *Stern* stunned the world by reporting that one of their reporters had stumbled across sixty handwritten volumes created by Adolf Hitler from 1932 to 1945. The small notebooks promised to provide extraordinary insights into the inner thoughts and secret motivations of the ruthless twentieth-century dictator. Handwriting experts and a renowned British historian judged the diaries to be authentic and the magazine bought them for a staggering $3.7 million. However, when specialists at the West German archives scientifically examined the diaries, they discovered that the chemicals in the paper, the binding, and the glue all dated after 1945, the year Hitler committed suicide. It turned out that a petty criminal had made the forgeries using ordinary school notebooks! As a saying attributed to astronomer Carl Sagan goes, "Extraordinary claims require extraordinary evidence."

Archaeologists are also interested in past ideas, and many have spent their careers attempting to discover the ideas behind the creation, use, and meaning of material objects and monuments. The conscious focus on materiality, however, allows archaeologists to expand Becker's view that historical facts exist only in the present. After all, archaeologists have physical artifacts and abandoned settlements directly in front of them all the time, just as historians have documents before them in archives and libraries. Tangible pieces of the past—potsherds, stone tools, glass bottles, brass arrowheads, letters, diaries, maps—exist both in the past and in the present. The ability of artifacts to transcend time (to be inanimate time travelers) is a special characteristic of these historical facts. Unlike most historians, archaeologists spend a great deal of time measuring, describing, and comparing artifact types and publishing their results. Historians seldom do this. I've read hundreds of histories and I've yet to find a single one that begins with a detailed, physical description of each document the historian has consulted. With some exceptions, most historians simply do not consider the material implications of the artifacts they use in their research. This may seem like a minor point, and perhaps to some extent it is. But the material point of view is a key component of archaeological thinking because all archaeological research—focused on whatever period of history and located wherever in the world—rests on the analysis and interpretation of physical things. (In truth, manuscripts are artifacts because they have been made by conscious human action. To make the point, one scholar once termed manuscripts "manufacts.")

IS FACT SELECTION DISHONEST?

Without knowing about Becker's perspective, just the mention of "fact selection" may imply something shady and unprofessional in a discipline like archaeology. Does this mean that archaeologists only use some evidence and ignore what doesn't fit their preconceived ideas? Pseudo-archaeologists are always accusing professional archaeologists of doing this, but no legitimate researcher in any field, including archaeology, should manufacture facts to suit a research outcome or to substantiate an interpretation. Anyone who knowingly disregards findings that run counter to any claim—major or alternative—or who invents "evidence" should be immediately discredited as a poor researcher (at best) and an intellectual scoundrel (at worst).

The concepts of misinformation and disinformation help to explain the distinction between poor researchers and scoundrels. "Misinformation" is the term for claims that are false but not deceptive. "Disinformation" is the term for claims that are both false and specifically designed to deceive. According to Bergstrom and West, a study completed in 2018 found that almost 3 percent of news articles published in the United States are false. Some are merely wrong—misinformation—whereas others are invented to sway public opinion, sell products, or for another reason—disinformation. The percentage seems small until we consider that 3 percent of all news readers (online and on television) equates to about eighty million readers per day.

Bergstrom and West also report that one of the most successful fake news stories of 2016 was the headline "Pope Francis Shocks World, Endorses Donald Trump for President." This disinformation was created and circulated by teenagers in Macedonia who couldn't vote in the election and didn't care who won but were looking to generate advertising revenue (which they did on a massive scale). In today's one-click world, people who range from serious entrepreneurs to get-rich-quick con artists, know that a slick, catchy title will grab the viewing audience and hopefully generate the wealth and fame that comes with it.

Scientists are not immune from the pull of fame and fortune. Predatory publishers, those who charge to publish, prey on scholars and scientists seeking to get their research to the largest possible audiences. One study showed that shady science publishers made around $74 million in 2014 by collecting publication fees. A problem with such pay-to-publish presses is that they generally do not rely on outside reviewers to evaluate the quality of the research before publication. As a result, it can be difficult to distinguish between misinformation and disinformation in what they publish. Compounding the problem is that a recent study estimates that 2.5 million scientific papers are published each year! Given this flood of information, we should not be surprised that some misinformation and disinformation sneaks in.

Some of the distrust of science can be laid at the feet of journalists. Journalism lies at the heart of a free society, but with today's minute-by-minute news cycle, speed is everything. It might mean millions of dollars in new advertising revenue if MSNBC can beat CNN with a juicy new scientific discovery. The problem with this approach is that science works slowly, with each discovery undergoing its own careful reevaluation. People lose faith in science when they read one week that coffee is bad for you and three weeks later read that drinking coffee is beneficial. But science advances slowly and carefully by constantly reevaluating evidence. Perhaps the first coffee study was flawed because the scientists, excited by their findings and eager to publish them, misread the data. Studies take a much longer time to complete than today's twenty-four-hour news cycle allows. The rush to publish or report the latest finding means that the misinformation from one study may appear as disinformation when a later study refutes its findings, even though both studies were conducted honestly.

Archaeology is no less immune to misinformation and disinformation than any other discipline. Television programs and online videos about professional excavations reinforce the idea that archaeology is an exacting field of study, and in many important ways this is true. But understanding the difference between misinformation and disinformation teaches us to be skeptical when reading about some incredible new find or interpretation. Being a skeptic doesn't make a person a cynic. It simply means that the person doesn't draw conclusions without evidence and evaluation.

The proponents of pseudo-archaeology read into the evidence what they wish to see, ignoring the vast storehouse of archaeological evidence that has been collected over the past several decades. The "ancient aliens" crowd works specifically to spread disinformation with the undoubted goal of fame and hopefully fortune. At Giza specifically, they ignore years of archaeological proof that (1) archaeologists have only found artifacts related to ancient Egyptian culture; (2) absolutely no evidence suggests that the ancient Egyptians had nuclear capabilities, knowledge, or interest; and (3) no one, professional or otherwise, has ever found anything identifiable as "otherworldly" in Egypt or anywhere else. Pseudo-archaeologists have stepped out of the realm of past actuality and into the world of fantasy. They have composed chronicles filled with speculative half-truths, misrepresentations, and even nonsense. They have created their own facts, but these "facts" have only come from their imaginations, not from past actuality.

Contrary to the efforts of pseudo-archaeologists, professional archaeologists must concern themselves with past actuality alone, understanding that it represents an immense universe of facts. Trillions of events, ideas, and actions comprise past actuality and to write about the past one must extract as much evidence as possible, acknowledging that their information will always be incomplete.

Returning to Caesar and the Rubicon helps to explain this further. If you were an archaeologist of the Roman Empire and you were writing a book about the everyday dress of the typical Roman legionnaire, you would be interested in what they wore during the crossing of the Rubicon rather than the route they took to get there. The route wouldn't cease to exist, it would simply be unimportant *for your research*. But if you wanted to write about the route of the army, you would research the specific places they stopped along the way. The soldiers' dress would have little significance to you. In any case, your selection is not dishonest, it merely reflects your research interests.

Archaeologists have always engaged in fact selection when they have described and classified artifacts. Description and classification are standard procedures that necessarily include choosing some attributes and ignoring others. Selection is simply part of the archaeological process. Two examples from widely separated periods of history demonstrate the selection process in action.

CLOVIS POINTS

The long, finely chipped-stone spear points archaeologists call Clovis points were first discovered by a road crew in 1932 near Clovis, New Mexico (figure 4.2). The first-discovered point was mixed among a mass of mammoth bones, so it was clear that the artifact was ancient. Since that discovery, archaeologists have remained fascinated by the Clovis point-using Paleoindians because they were the first recognizable inhabitants of North America, living there from around thirteen thousand to eleven thousand years ago. Archaeologists have now found over ten thousand Clovis points across the United States, from

Figure 4.2. Clovis Point
Source: *Courtesy of Briggs Buchanan, University of Tulsa.*

Washington State to Florida. Archaeologists of pre-Columbian history continue to be intrigued by the Clovis culture, wondering, for one thing, how they were able to move relatively quickly throughout the entire continent. A culture may have lived in North America before the appearance of the Clovis people, but archaeologists currently know little about it.

The Clovis point is the most distinctive tangible object left behind by the Paleoindians. The "type description"—the characteristics shared by the objects that make them recognizable—includes a number of features, including (1) overall lanceolate shape, (2) lens-shaped cross-section, (3) slight concave base, (4) slightly rounded bottom corners, (5) length ranging from 75 to 110 mm, (6) width ranging from 25 to 50 mm, (7) flutes (long flakes extending from the base upward) on both sides, covering 30 to 50 percent of the total point length, and (8) irregular flaking throughout.

Once archaeologists began to recognize the significance of these large spear points, they noticed that the points appeared to fall into two categories: those found at campsites and those found secreted in caches (tightly packed collections of objects buried at one time). The points found at the campsites and at kill sites (as was the case with the first one found) seemed to be for hunting large animals. The points in the caches, however, never appeared to have been used. Archaeologists disagree about why this was so. Perhaps the cached points were made for hunting but never used, or maybe they were intended only for ceremonies. Maybe the cached points were not spear points at all but were designed as saws. One complicating factor is that archaeologists discovered that points found at campsites and kill sites had often been sharpened or reshaped for reuse (by removing additional flakes in an ancient form

Understanding and Selecting Facts 67

of recycling!). This cultural practice meant that the shape and size of the re-chipped points had changed during the period of their use. The cached points, because they had not been used, had never been reshaped.

The broad geographical spread of Clovis points throughout North America means that points are of different sizes. Given their distribution, an obvious analytical step is to measure the points. But how to do this? It depends upon what facts we seek and how we intend to use the facts we obtain.

Archaeologists are interested in describing Clovis points, so many archaeological reports contain detailed descriptions of the points found at specific Paleoindian sites. Reporting the characteristics of the points is important because of the absence of other information. Paleoindians did not use writing, so archaeologists can only make comparisons between sites and regions to determine whether the shape of points changed over time or whether the people in one region used points that differ from those in another part of the continent. Are Clovis points in Montana like those in Florida? So, when Matthew Hill decided to measure the thirteen fluted points in a collection from Jackson County, Wisconsin, he wanted to obtain straightforward measurements. He used calipers to obtain several measurements including the base width, the overall width, and the overall length. His measurements are important because they establish the size and shape of the points from one part of Wisconsin. Archaeologists can compare his findings with Clovis points discovered outside Wisconsin.

Other times, archaeologists want to use measurements for more in-depth analyses. To investigate the difference between cached and uncached Clovis points from sites in the western United States, Briggs Buchanan and four colleagues decided on a different method of measurement than that employed by Hill. They digitized 122 Clovis points and placed 32 data points along the edges and bases of each point. With sophisticated software, they computed twelve characters. Like Hill, they obtained thickness measurements using calipers.

The two sets of measurements—one from Wisconsin and the other from the US West—provided different sets of information (figure 4.3). In other words, Hill and Buchanan's team collected different facts from the Clovis points. Which one is correct?

Without question, the archaeologists had different goals in their research. Hill simply sought to describe the points in the Wisconsin collection, whereas Buchanan's team used the measurements to test a series of predictions. For example, one prediction was that the cached points should be the same general shape but larger than the noncached points. (Based on the assumption that points from campsites and kill sites may have been resharpened because of frequent use.) Using complex statistics, the team learned that their prediction was correct: cached points were larger.

The idea that Hill and Buchanan's team had different research goals helps answer the question about which one used the correct measurements. If we

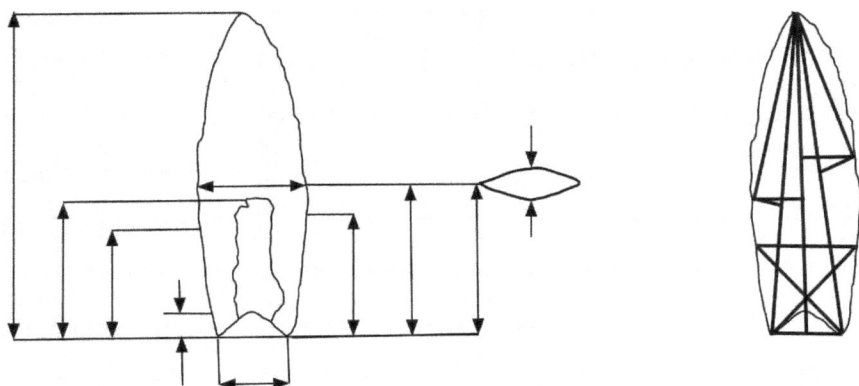

Figure 4.3. Clovis Point measurements
Source: *Drawing by author.*

keep in mind the concept of fact selection, then we know that the answer is both. The more sophisticated, statistical analyses conducted by Buchanan's team simply provide a different set of facts. It does not negate the more straightforward measurements obtained by Hill.

GLASS TRADE BEADS

In 1970, Kenneth Kidd and Martha Kidd presented a classification of colonial-era glass trade beads. Their method was so good that archaeologists still refer to their work today, and like all classification systems, it rests on fact selection.

In the 1950s and 1960s, before historical archaeology had become the mainstream field it is today, archaeologists excavating early colonial sites often discovered tiny glass beads in great quantities, sometimes in the thousands. They knew the beads had been made in Europe, shipped to North America, and traded to Native North Americans. Knowing the principles of seriation (see chapter 2), archaeologists understood that certain styles came into favor, were popular for a while, and then were replaced by something new. Beyond this they knew very little. Unknown were how many styles of beads had been produced, the precise dates of their popularity, or the geographical spread of different beads. Were the beads found at an English trading post in upstate New York like those found at a Spanish mission site in Florida? To answer such questions, archaeologists required a standard way of describing the different bead styles. Only in this way could they make comparisons between sites.

The Kidds had received a Guggenheim Fellowship and a grant from the Corning Museum of Glass to conduct a thorough study of the glass trade beads that Europeans had traded to Native American cultures beginning in the sixteenth century and lasting well into the nineteenth century. The beads produced in European workshops, including a large number from Venice, were small, remarkably durable because of their size, and easily transported great distances in ocean-going ships, small boats, canoes, and on horseback. Indigenous Americans had made and traded shell and bone beads for generations, but glass beads were new to them, so they exchanged furs and other items to obtain them. The Kidds's research indicated that European workshops had produced a huge number of trade bead styles, and that because the beads were handmade, they exhibited great variability. Given the many colors, shapes, and decorations of beads, the Kidds understood that they needed a standardized way to categorize them. As a result, they created a classification for use with colonial trade beads. Classifications, like seriations, require archaeologists to select certain characteristics as key attributes.

One of the attributes the Kidds selected as a distinguishing mark was whether a bead contained stripes (figure 4.4). Inspection of bead collections showed that some beads have one stripe, whereas others have many stripes in various combinations of colors. For instance, Type Ib beads (tubular-shaped with stripes), have several different colored stripes, including six black, three red, three white, and three black. The Kidds paid close attention to the numbers and colors of stripes, but they did not measure the distance between the individual stripes. Their illustrations indicate that the distances between stripes vary (as logically they must, given the different numbers of stripes), but they

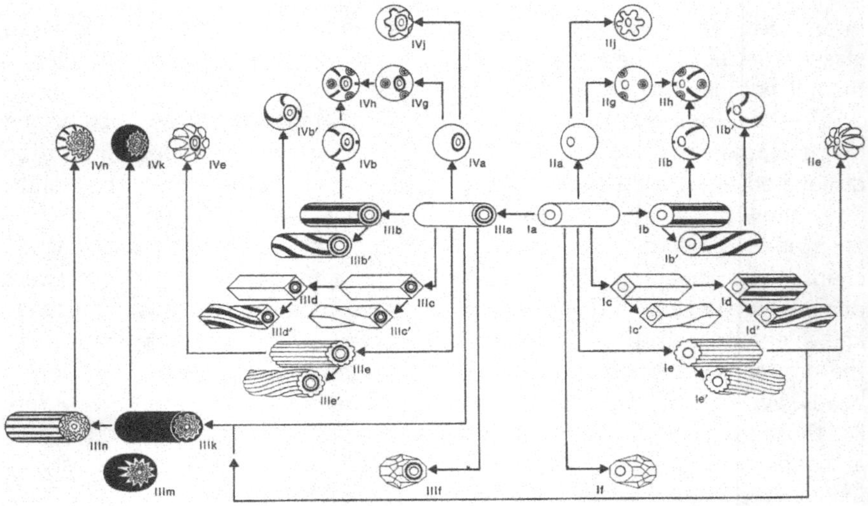

Figure 4.4. Part of the Kidd and Kidd glass bead classification system

Source: *From Kenneth E. Kidd and Martha Ann Kidd, "A Classification System for Glass Beads for the Use of Field Archaeologists," in* Canadian Historic Sites, Occasional Papers in Archaeology and History, *No. 1. Ottawa: National Historic Sites Service, 1970, p. 51. Used by permission of Parks Canada, Ottawa.*

chose to ignore this fact in their classification. Stripe distance is a fact, so why did they ignore it? The answer is that they did not perceive "distance between stripes" as a significant variable. Were they wrong? No, they simply engaged in fact selection. Their failure to choose "distance between stripes" as a key attribute does not make the distance disappear. It is still there, lying dormant until another archaeologist decides to select this measure as an attribute of glass trade beads. The Kidds's failure to include stripe distance does not negate the value of their classification.

★ ★ ★

So, it seems that fact selection is not the dishonest practice we may originally have presumed it to be. That noted, some dishonest researchers do engage in politically or personally motivated fact selection, with Holocaust deniers immediately coming to mind. But fact selection is a normal part of the research process, including for archaeologists. No archaeologist or historian, or anyone else, can ever know everything about the past. All the individual pieces of past actuality can never be collected. Some things are gone forever. Good archaeological thinkers attempt to construct the past from what they know at the time, with the appreciation that their perspectives and interpretations are likely to be modified or completely changed as more information is collected. Fact selection is only wrong when people promote knowingly false pictures of the past. Fact selection is normal when conducted honestly.

SOURCES FOR CONTINUED READING

FACT SELECTION

Becker, Carl L. 1955. "What Are Historical Facts?" *Western Political Quarterly* 8:327–40.
Kroeber, A. L. 1935. "History and Science in Anthropology." *American Anthropologist* 37:539–69.
Rentschler, Eric. 2003. "The Fascination of a Fake: The Hitler Diaries." *New German Critique* 90:177–92.
West, Jevin D. and Carl T. Bergstrom. 2021. "Misinformation In and About Science." *PNAS* 118 (15): e1912444118.
Whyte, Jaime. 2005. *Crimes Against Logic: Exposing the Bogus Arguments of Politicians, Priests, Journalists, and Other Serial Offenders.* New York: McGraw-Hill.

CLOVIS POINTS

Bergstrom, Carl T. and Jevin D. West. 2021. *Calling Bullshit: The Art of Skepticism in a Data-Driven World.* New York: Random House.

Buchanan, Briggs, J. David Kilby, Bruce B. Huckell, Michael J. O'Brien, and Mark Collard. 2012. "A Morphometric Assessment of the Intended Function of Cached Clovis Points." *Plos One* 7 (2):e30530.

Hill, Matthew Glenn. 1994. "Paleoindian Projectile Points from the Vicinity of Silver Mound (47JA21), Jackson County, Wisconsin." *Midcontinental Journal of Archaeology* 19:223–259.

Howard, Calvin D. 1990. "The Clovis Point: Characteristics and Type Description." *Plains Anthropologist* 35:255–62.

Smith, Heather L., Thomas A. Jennings, and Ashley M. Smallwood. 2021. "Do Early Paleoindian Point Blades Carry Culturally Significant Shape Information? Modules versus Complete Points Using Geometric Morphometrics." *Journal of Archaeological Science: Reports* 40:103245.

GLASS TRADE BEADS

Kidd, Kenneth E. and Martha Ann Kidd. 1970. "A Classification System for Glass Beads for the Use of Field Archaeologists." *Canadian Historic Sites: Occasional Papers in Archaeology and History* 1:45–89. Ottawa: National Historic Sites Service.

5

Archaeological Thinking and Logic

Thinking logically is an integral part of the archaeological research process, just as it is in much of daily life. So important is logical thinking that Professor Stebbing deals with it on the first page of her little logic book. In the book's prologue she asks, "Are the English Illogical?" She believes so and says that the clearest example of the English tendency for illogical behavior is in their avowed ability to "muddle through." The idea was carried through during the Second World War when a famous English slogan (which has now made a comeback in numerous ways) was "Keep Calm and Carry On." English archaeologist, Ivor Noël Hume, once the head archaeologist at Colonial Williamsburg, agreed with Professor Stebbing, writing that "archaeology is really an incredibly simple use of logic, and if you don't have that, you don't do very well." The problem facing archaeologists, however, is that what seems logical to us as twenty-first-century Westerners may not have been logical for people living in another culture or during an ancient era. Despite the difficulties, archaeologists must rely on logic to frame their interpretations, with the hope that they can get reasonably close to understanding the past.

THE IMPORTANCE OF LOGICAL THINKING

People living in Western cultures tend to admire logical thinkers. After all, the pedigree of logic extends all the way back to Aristotle, Plato, and the other philosophers who lectured in ancient Greece. Westerners generally believe that logical thinking is a trait worth acquiring. As early as 1662, Antoine Arnauld and Pierre Nicole, the authors of *The Port-Royal Logic*, referred to logic as "the art of thinking." Author Lewis Carroll (the author of *Alice in Wonderland*) described logical thinking as "mental recreation" and said that once you have mastered it, "you have a mental occupation always at hand, of absorbing interest, and one that will be of real *use* to you in *any* subject you may take up."

Clear thinking is important for archaeologists because their efforts to piece together the past from the often fragmentary remains require inference as well as the ability to make connections between things, ideas, and actions. Regardless of their theoretical orientation, logical thinking helps archaeologists strengthen their arguments and to have more confidence in their interpretations. Clear thinking increases the plausibility of an archaeologist's interpretation. Because archaeologists can never go back in time and experience the past directly, their perceptions of history rest solely on the mental images they create about it (as Carl Becker demonstrated; see chapter 4). Archaeological arguments therefore must be well conceived, properly structured, and clearly expressed.

Archaeologists use both deductive and inductive logic, though they rely most strongly on inductive reasoning. The goal of this chapter is to introduce you to the role of logic in archaeological thinking, but not to turn you into a logician. Archaeologists do not wish to become logicians, and many of the logicians' philosophical concerns are far beyond what archaeologists need to know. Nevertheless, understanding some of the basic rules of logical thinking is an important step toward developing your skills as an archaeological thinker. These skills will help you "to think to some purpose."

DEDUCTION

The first thing to appreciate about deductive logic is that it concerns the structure of arguments rather than the truth of their conclusions. Logic offers the tools for assessing the relation between statements of evidence (termed "premises") and conclusions. The term "argument" is not meant as a verbal dispute, but as a series of premises that have a conclusion.

A deductive argument is "valid" when it has the correct form and "invalid" when its form is incorrect. Deduction does not involve what is "true" or "false." Deduction concerns itself only with form, not with truth. Even so, the correct logical form of a deductive argument can guide and structure an archaeologist's thinking.

The goal of deductive argumentation is to establish true conclusions based on true premises. False premises are simply that: false. The implications of false premises in the world of pseudo-archaeology can be easily understood because its proponents present wildly speculative claims about space aliens, mysterious vanished civilizations, and other implausible interpretations of the past. They use speculation for their premises, develop arguments that defy archaeological reality, and create false pictures of the past. Today's professional archaeologists understand the pitfalls of wild speculation (see chapter 1) and avoid them by understanding logical argumentation.

In deductive reasoning, the conclusion must be true if the premises are true. A deductive argument can have a true conclusion but be invalid, just as it can have a false conclusion and be valid (as a logical argument form). A valid deductive argument cannot have true premises and a false conclusion, but it can have false premises and a true conclusion. To make sense of this, consider the following three arguments:

Chapter 5

All artifacts [a] are made or modified by humans [b] [true]
All ancient arrowheads [c] are artifacts [a] [true]
Therefore, all ancient arrowheads [c] are made or modified by humans [b]. [true]

All arrowheads [a] are glass [b] [false]
All windows [c] are arrowheads [a] [false]
Therefore, all windows [c] are glass [b]. [true]

All arrowheads [a] are stone [b] [false]
All artifacts [c] are arrowheads [a] [false]
Therefore, all artifacts [c] are stone [b]. [false]

Each of these arguments is logically valid because of its structure. Validity is determined by the form not by what the argument says, for clearly windows are not arrowheads. Given the nature of deduction, however, if the premises are true, then the conclusion must be true. A valid deductive argument cannot have true premises and a false conclusion.

Archaeologists seldom have the luxury of being able to use the logical form "All . . . are" because they can never know that all possible artifacts have been collected. Nonetheless, the above examples demonstrate how deduction works. Archaeologists, faced with the huge number of facts, can almost never assert 100 percent certainty except about the most mundane things. Archaeologists can only be certain when speaking about a finite collection of objects, such as a collection of two hundred Clovis points from one specific cache, as in,

All Clovis points in the Smith Cache [a] are obsidian [b] [true]
All fluted points in the Smith Cache [c] are Clovis points [a] [true]
Therefore, all fluted points in the Smith Cache [c] are obsidian [b]. [true]

Beyond such a simple case, archaeologists cannot assert that they can know absolutely everything about a past habitation, campsite, or village.

Much more important to archaeologists are "if/then" arguments, termed "conditional statements." Conditional statements are used in "conditional arguments," and conditional arguments have valid and invalid forms. In an interpretive field like archaeology, the structure of the argument can affect its inherent sense.

The most basic form of a conditional argument is:
If p, then q [the conditional statement]
p
$\therefore$ [Therefore] q

In this argument, *p* is called the "antecedent" and *q* is the "consequent." The above form is a valid form called "affirming the antecedent." An archaeological example is:

If arrowheads are made of brass [*p*], then they are metallic [*q*]
These arrowheads are made of brass [*p*]
Therefore, they are metallic [*q*].

In this argument, we have affirmed the first part of the conditional statement, the antecedent. A second valid argument is called "denying the consequent." This argument has the form:

If *p*, then *q*
Not *q*
∴ Not *p*

An archaeological example is:

If arrowheads are made of brass [*p*], then they are metallic [*q*]
These arrowheads are not metallic [not *q*]
Therefore, they are not made of brass [not *p*].

The two invalid forms of these deductive arguments are called "the fallacy of affirming the consequent" and "the fallacy of denying the antecedent." The first form is:

If *p*, then *q*
q
∴ *p*

In archaeology,

If Clovis points are made of obsidian [*p*], then they are stone [*q*] These Clovis
    points are stone [*q*]
Therefore, they are made of obsidian. [*p*]

This is faulty deductive reasoning because the arrowheads can be stone, but they might be fashioned from jasper or chert; they do not have to be obsidian. The second invalid form is:

If *p*, then *q*
Not *p*
∴ Not *q*.

In archaeology,

If Clovis points are made of obsidian [*p*], then they are stone[*q*] These arrow-
    heads are not obsidian [not *p*]
Therefore, they are not stone [not *q*]

As is true of the first example, the arrowheads could be made from a different
stone than obsidian.

You see in the two valid arguments that true premises lead to true conclusions, but in the two invalid forms, a false premise leads to a false conclusion.
Invalid arguments provide false conclusions because some metallic artifacts
can be made of iron, copper, or some other metal. But remember, the goal of
deduction is to create valid arguments, not necessarily to derive the truth.

We can examine the if/then argument form further by illustrating a popular
invalid argument from the world of pseudo-archaeology. It has become common for ancient astronaut theorists to argue that people who had the ability to
fly must have built all the massive ancient monuments that are best seen from
the air. They say that because Earthlings did not have the ability to see the Earth
from the sky before 1782—when the Montgolfier brothers flew the first hot air
balloon—pre-Columbian Native peoples could not have been responsible for
building the monuments. Their argument takes this form:

If large monuments are best seen in their entirety from the air [*p*],
then they must have been constructed by a culture that were capable of flight [*q*]
The biggest ancient monuments are best seen from the air [*q*]
Therefore, big monuments must have been built by a culture capable of flight [*p*].

This looks like a perfectly valid deductive argument because it affirms the antecedent. The problem, of course, is that the antecedent is based on pure speculation. Remember that if the premises are true, then the conclusion must also
be true. But in this example, and indeed in all pseudo-archaeology, the premises
are merely speculative. They derive from imagination not past actuality; no one
knows whether they are true and they cannot be verified.

Pseudo-archaeologists have made this claim about many ancient sites,
including the world-famous Serpent Mound in southern Ohio (figure 5.1).
This mound is a long earthwork resembling a curly snake holding something
that looks like an egg in its mouth. Archaeologists date the mound to about
1000 CE and associate it with the Adena Culture. Ancient astronaut theorists
argue that space aliens must have built the mound because the best view of
it is from the air. (They say this even though Squier and Davis, mentioned in
chapter 2, made a scale drawing of it—as if they had seen from the air—almost
forty years before the flight of the first hot air balloon!) Since the conclusion of
a valid deductive argument must be true if the premises are true, it becomes

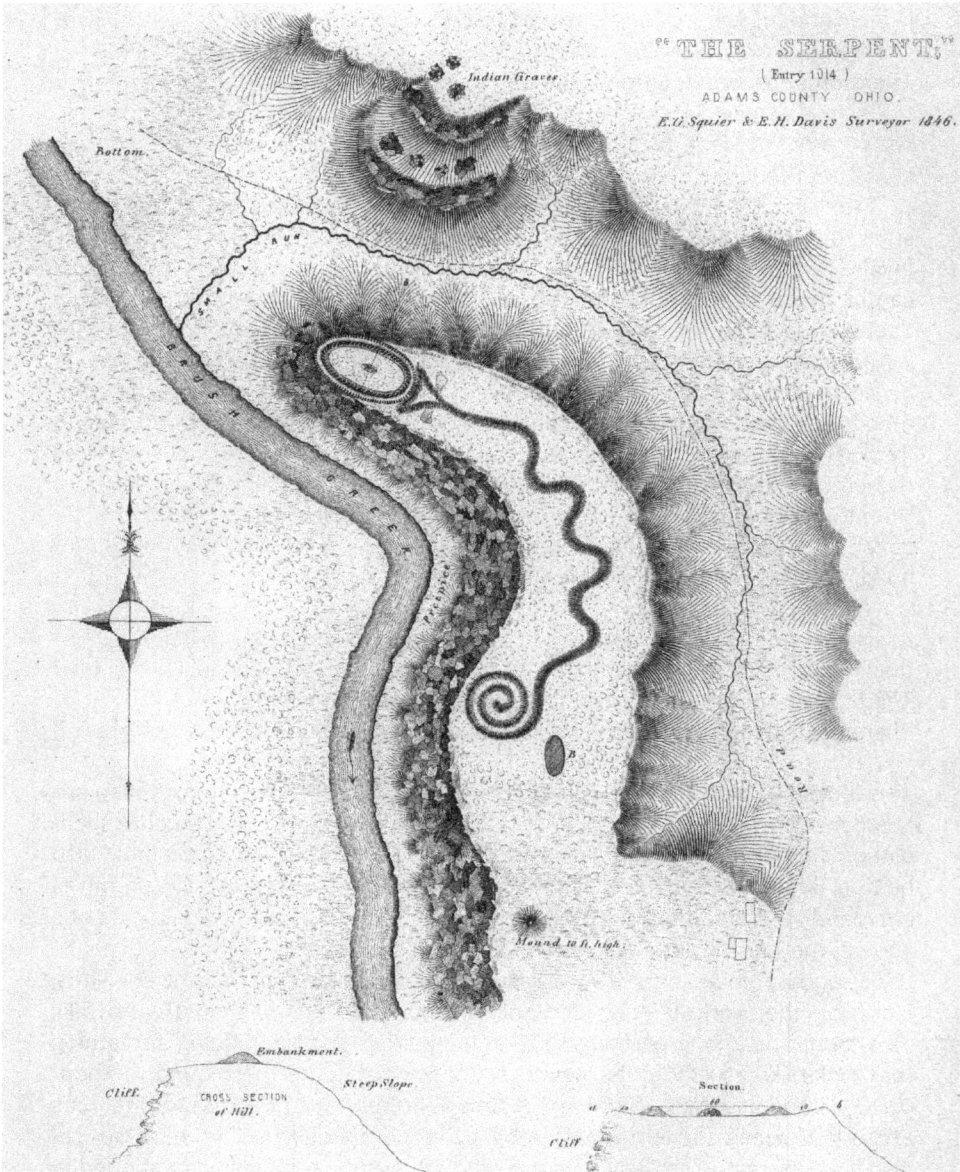

Figure 5.1. Squier and Davis's 1846 map of "The Great Serpent," Adams Co., Ohio

Source: *From Ephraim G. Squier and Edwin H. Davis,* Ancient Monuments of the Mississippi Valley: Comprising the Results of Extensive Original Surveys and Explorations. *Washington, DC: Smithsonian Institution Press, 1848, facing p. 96.*

impossible to create a valid argument with only the pseudo-archaeologist's premises. To affirm the antecedent, it would have to be true that space aliens built the mound:

If space aliens built the Serpent Mound [p], then you could see its full ¼-mile
    extent best from the sky [q]
Space aliens built the Mound [p]
Therefore, you can see its full extent best from the air [q]

Professional archaeologists cannot accept that ancient aliens built anything on Earth because no one anywhere has ever found any credible evidence for these space creatures.

In a classic study, James Deetz investigated the changing relationships between two variables—postmarriage residence (where newlyweds live after marriage) and pottery design—among the eighteenth-century Arikaras of the United States' Great Plains. This was the era the Arikaras first encountered Europeans.

Deetz's claim about Arikara culture was that greater diversity in pottery design should be explainable by a transition from matrilocality (living with the wife's family or village) to a less structured form of postmarriage settlement. The Arikaras underwent significant social reorganization after European contact because the introduction of smallpox had caused massive depopulation. Villages losing members tended to unite with others suffering a similar fate. Deetz's inference was that young girls in matrilocal settings learned pottery designs from their mothers and grandmothers, but in the absence of matrilocality (because of depopulation and village dispersal), the girls learned pottery design from women from several different villages (and thus, from unrelated kin group members). Deetz reasoned that the increase in the number of design sources (contributed by women potters from different villages) should occur as matrilocality broke down. As he stated it, "If culturally conditioned behavioral patterning is responsible for artifactual patterning, then changes in the nature and extent of behavioral patterning might reasonably be expected to affect the attribute patterning seen in the resulting objects." In plain English, this means that the normal routines of a culture, their "behavioral patterning," should be reflected in the patterns of artifacts. So, he is arguing from the culture to the artifacts.

Deetz posited that the transformation of Arikara culture should be reflected in their pottery as an increase in the number of pottery designs. In other words, if a pottery sample excavated from a site dating before European contact had ten design motifs, and a second site dating after European contact and depopulation had twenty-three motifs, then his supposition about the relationship between culture change and pottery design would seem plausible. Deetz's central claim is a conditional argument:

If residence location by women after marriage changed,
then pottery decorations should have been diversified

The only way Deetz can resolve the argument is with the fallacy of affirming the consequent:

If post-marriage residence changes [*p*],
then pottery design will become more diverse [*q*].
Pottery design becomes more diverse [*q*].
Therefore, the Arikaras experienced a change in their post-marriage residence rules [*p*].

He must make this mistake because the collection and examination of pottery sherds will determine whether the Arikaras' designs became more diverse through time. To make his argument a valid form, he would have to start with the pottery design and work toward a change in postmarriage residence.

If Arikara pottery designs become more diverse over time [*p*], then post-marriage residence will change [*q*]
The pottery designs become more diverse [*p*]
Therefore, the post-marriage residence will change [*q*].

This would have been a valid argument, but at the time Deetz was doing his analysis, American archaeologists were trying to make their research more overtly anthropological, so he wanted to make a claim about a past culture (the Arikaras) and prove it with pieces of their material culture (handmade pottery).

In truth, archaeologists seldom use pure deductive logic. The example taken from Deetz's research was not truly a deductive exercise because much of his information relied on induction. Nevertheless, his argument demonstrates the care archaeologists must take when working deductively. The use of if . . . then statements must be used with extreme caution in serious archaeological thinking.

INDUCTION

Deductive reasoning is extremely difficult for archaeologists to use because the premises must include the same information as the conclusions. The failure of archaeologists to know everything about the past (to have 100 percent confidence) shows why archaeologists rely mostly on inductive reasoning.

Inductive arguments are much more useful to archaeologists because the information they contain in their conclusions may exceed the information in the premises. Examples of inductive arguments appear in every article or book written about archaeological research. As with deduction, however, archaeologists must avoid certain pitfalls.

You will recall that in a deductive argument, if the premises are true then the conclusion must also be true. For space aliens to have built the Serpent Mound, it must be true that (1) they exist, (2) they came to Earth with the expressed purpose of building gigantic earthen monuments in the American Midwest, and (3) they left behind no other traces of their extremely advanced culture. Each of these premises are false. In an inductive argument, true premises may or may not lead to a true conclusion.

A correct inductive argument will add confidence or support to a true conclusion; it should lead to a conclusion that may be true, but in induction, true premises can lead to a false conclusion. In archaeology, this means that the premises may be true even though it has resulted in a false conclusion.

The simplest form of inductive argument in archaeology is "induction by enumeration." This is simply where a researcher infers a conclusion about all the members of a class from the observed members. For example, an archaeologist might report that "80 percent of ceramic sherds excavated at the Harris Site are pearlware" (a white-bodied ceramic popular in the nineteenth century) and use induction by enumeration to infer that 80 percent of all possible sherds at the site (those that have been collected and those that have yet to be excavated) are pearlware. This argument takes this form:

80 percent of the ceramics excavated from the Harris Site are pearlware.
Therefore, 80 percent of all ceramics at the Harris Site (including those that remain unexcavated, or "inert" as Becker would say) are pearlware.

Archaeologists make this kind of argument all the time. They conduct walk-over surveys and small test excavations to extrapolate from the collected sample to the entire site. The nature of archaeological research, and the very nature of induction by enumeration itself, however, means that true premises can lead to a false conclusion. At the Harris Site, the archaeologist may simply have excavated in the area that contained most of the pearlware at the site, perhaps a trash dump created when the site's residents threw out their old dishes and replaced them with a newer, more fashionable type of ceramic called whiteware. Given this possibility, archaeologists understand that the larger the sample size, the greater confidence they can have in their inferences. An archaeologist can usually have greater confidence in a 50 percent sample than in a 5 percent sample.

Induction by enumeration is not without problems because statistics can be manipulated. Mark Twain famously said that: "There are three kinds of lies: lies, damned lies, and statistics." (He erroneously attributed this quote to British Prime Minister Benjamin Disraeli but no one knows who first said it. Even so, the sentiment is clear!)

The most serious problem with enumeration is the "fallacy of insufficient statistics." This means drawing a conclusion from scanty evidence. An archaeologist with only a 1 percent sample would be foolish to make sweeping claims based on such a small amount of evidence. Broad claims with weak evidence are likely to lead to suspect conclusions. Consider these two examples:

1. 1 percent of the ceramic shards from the Harris Site are pearlware. Therefore, all the ceramics that exist at the Harris Site are pearlware.
2. 1 percent of the potsherds from the Harris Site are pearlware. Therefore, all Scottish settlers in the United States used pearlware.

The second conclusion is clearly the shakiest of the two, though both are based on the flimsy evidence of insufficient statistics. Still, both conclusions may be correct even if the premises are incorrect.

For many years, archaeologists have wrestled with the question "how much is enough?" when deciding whether to have confidence in the results of a survey or excavation. An archaeologist who draws conclusions from an 85 percent sample usually can have more confidence than someone who extrapolates from a 5 percent sample. Archaeologists are often forced into making claims based on limited evidence because of shortages in time, funds, and resources. It is important to realize, though, that even large samples can be biased, and that small samples can provide important information. Unfortunately, no magic number exists to indicate the "proper" sample size. Each situation is unique and archaeologists must make careful, logical decisions about how definite to be in their interpretations.

Archeologists, like all scholars, must continually be aware of selection bias. This kind of bias occurs for many reasons, but three of the most common are when a person looks in the wrong place for information, engages in pre-screening, or has too small a sample. Let's suppose that you were interested in trying to figure out who will win an upcoming election. You decide that the best way to get an answer is to interview people. Selection bias would result if you (1) ask only Democrats, (2) ask them first if they are Democrats and if they say yes, ask them questions, but if they say they are Republicans, you walk away, and (3) if you only ask five people. The answers you get will constitute a "weighted" or "skewed" sample, one that cannot be trusted. In their book *Calling Bullshit*, Carl Bergstrom and Jevin West note that many social psychology professors, in an effort to discover the universal elements of human cognition, rely on the most available and cheapest sample subjects: college students. They say that such selection bias has caused some researchers to call this population WEIRD: Western, Educated, Industrialized, Rich, and Democratic. The acronym may be somewhat strained, but their point is well made: someone would need a huge, unbiased sample to obtain a true picture of universal human cognition. Only asking college students provides a skewed sample worth little beyond the sample group.

Two inductive argument forms are more prevalent in archaeology than is enumeration. They are also more problematic. The difficulties arise from assessing whether the conclusions reached are justified or based on personal bias.

The first argument is called the "argument from authority." This argument form is straightforward:

X says p
$\therefore p$.

Converting this to English, we might say:

Dr. Miller says I have an ear infection,
Therefore, I have an ear infection.

All scholars, including archaeologists, implicitly use this argument form every time they cite someone else's research. In doing so, they assume that the cited person is a legitimate authority on the subject being explored. In the above case, we accept that Dr. Miller has a degree from an accredited medical school, holds a current and legitimate license to practice, and knows an ear infection when she sees one.

Archaeologists regularly make the same assertions in their research. In fact, relying on the works of prior authorities is an important characteristic of all scientific and scholarly research. For example, in a publication of mine, I wrote:

> Maritime archaeologists are conducting serious and important research around the globe and diligently working to convince the public that maritime archaeological sites are as important to the world's cultural heritage as land- based remains (e.g., Adams 2002; Corbin and Rodgers 2008; Flatman and Staniforth 2006; McConkey and McErlean 2007; Richards 2008; Staniforth 2003; Staniforth and Nash 2006; Van Tilburg 2007; Webster 2008; Williams 2007).

In this statement, I regard all the cited men and women as authorities on maritime archaeology. I assume that each of them has extensive knowledge of and experience in the field, so I feel completely comfortable mentioning their names and publications to support my assessment about maritime archaeology. Since this is not my area of expertise, I am willing to rely on the authority of others.

In truth, an argument from authority has a premise that actually comes before the premise "X says p." This initial premise is something like "X is a recognized, reliable authority on subject p." This means that the prestige of X (in my case, Adams and the other archaeologists I cited) is secure enough in the field of p (maritime archaeology) to be referenced as an authoritative scholar on maritime archaeology.

Arguments by authority, however, have an inherent problem: how do we know that someone is an authority on something? Should we accept X as an authority on p?

Celebrity product endorsements are an easy place to see the problem. The reputation of famous actors, sports figures, and politicians often transfers beyond their areas of expertise. For example, the basketball great Michael Jordan was well-known for his promotion of a certain brand of men's underwear. Advertisers are clever enough to know that most people recognize his name and that they are therefore likely to associate him with something special. Advertising executives thus exploit the transfer of prestige from basketball to underwear. But if we stop and think about it, we must ask ourselves: is Michael Jordan really a reliable authority about underwear? To put this question in the form of a comparison: should we have greater confidence in someone who works in the underwear industry but is unknown to the world at large, or Michael Jordan who, though unique in the world of basketball, is just like millions of other men who wear underwear?

We can return to the world of pseudo-archaeology to explore the problem further. Consider these three authors and their famous books: Erich von Däniken, who jump-started the current fascination with ancient aliens with *Chariots of the Gods?*; Barry Fell, who, in *America B.C.*, argued that ancient Celts and other Old World peoples visited North America thousands of years before Columbus; and Gavin Menzies, who developed an entirely new line of speculative inquiry with *1421: The Year China Discovered America*. Each of these authors is a talented and engaging writer, and their books, though frustrating for professional archaeologists, can be fun to read as pure speculation. Should we conclude, however, that each man is an authority on archaeology and ancient history? One way to answer this question is to examine their archaeological training. Before finding fame as writers, none of these men had any experience in archaeology. Von Däniken was a hotel manager, Fell was a professor of invertebrate zoology at Harvard University, and Menzies was a lieutenant commander in Her Majesty's Royal Navy. If I wanted advice about hotel management, information on fossil sea urchins, or to learn about daily life onboard a submarine, I would judge each of these men as expert authorities. I could assume that each man knew more than me about each subject.

Unwary readers might be led to conclude that Fell is a reliable authority because he was a Harvard professor or that Menzies's military credentials add credibility to his interpretations. The key point to remember, however, is that both men are dabbling in realms outside their areas of expertise. They write about archaeological subjects but without the professional background or experience. Each man's interpretation of human history is seriously flawed (by professional standards) and illogical (by nature). Neither Menzies, Fell, nor von Däniken can be considered a legitimate archaeological authority regardless of how much each has written or how believable readers may deem their fantastical accounts. Their economic success cannot diminish or erase the fallacies in their interpretations.

Another difficulty of determining who is a proper authority is caused by the way pseudo-archaeologists often misuse the work of scientific authorities. For example, in *Underworld*, Graham Hancock, in attempting to substantiate the distant age of huge stones in the Bay of Bengal, India, cites a geologist as an authority. The geologist apparently told him that during the last nineteen thousand years, the level of the sea has been continuously rising. A look at the geologist's faculty webpage indicates that he is indeed a recognized authority on the world's sea levels. Hancock uses the geologist's statement to argue that "common sense" indicates that something located in seventy-five feet of water must be older than something located in six feet of water. Thus, since the structure that has piqued his interest is in deep water, it must be very old. But is his conjecture really a matter of common sense or has he misused or perhaps misunderstood what the geologist told him? As a group, geologists know that measuring the sea level is an intensely complicated process because regional sea levels vary, based on the location of glaciers, gravitational forces, and other factors. As a result, the world is not like a bathtub; the oceans' water rises and falls unevenly, something a trained and well-respected geologist undoubtedly knows.

Determining who is an authority can be difficult because someone may be formally untrained in a subject but still knowledgeable about it. Unlike civil engineering or accounting, archaeologists are not required to pass certification tests. Myriad television programs and internet videos demonstrate that almost anyone can claim to be an archaeologist without any training at all.

The difficulty in determining expertise is made even more complex because professional archaeologists often rely on nonprofessionals for information. Most residents know a great deal about their local areas and many are conversant with local and regional histories and traditions. Amateur archaeologists or avocationalists can be extremely knowledgeable yet professionally untrained; they can be self-taught experts. A powerful but unique example comes from the personal history of Ivor Noël Hume, mentioned at the beginning of this chapter as an archaeological pioneer and a world-renowned authority. He started his professional life as a stage manager for a London theater, not as an archaeologist. He began in archaeology as an untrained volunteer while waiting for his big break on the stage. His opportunity never came and luckily for archaeology, he fell into a job with a museum in London. At the time of his death in 2017, he had decades of experience, had written several well-received books, and had won many awards. Despite his background, no one in his or her right mind would consider him anything but a true archaeological authority. He learned through dedication, self-education, and on the job.

Given the difficulties, how do we decide who is an authority on a particular subject and who is a pretender? In his book *Logic*, Wesley Salmon offers clues to assess whether someone is an authority. Putting these clues in the form of questions helps to clarify them:

1. Is the person making a statement so famous they experience a "transfer of prestige"? (Does Michael Jordan's fame as a basketball great translate into knowledge about underwear? In other words, is his fame in one area simply migrating to another area? Has he spent time in the underwear industry learning its ins and outs?);
2. Is the person making a statement about something speaking outside his or her area of expertise? (Should Barry Fell have stuck with his sea urchin research and left ancient history to scholars better trained in the subject?);
3. Has the person received enough training outside his or her area of expertise to make them an expert on something? Should we accept their expertise in the absence of formal education? (Ivor Noël Hume has proved his expertise despite not having an advanced degree in archaeology); and
4. Is the person making a statement about something for which they could not possibly have any information? (How can Erich von Däniken know that space aliens exist when no one else has been able to prove it and no physical evidence exists?)

Answers to these questions will clarify whether we can justifiably consider someone an expert in a particular subject. Unfortunately, the resolution of the questions may never be wholly satisfactory. Most readers are willing to accept the word of authors who write authoritatively and seem credible. For example, Menzies's expertise as a naval officer suggests that he knows a great deal about ocean currents, and he probably does have this knowledge. But the key question is: should we allow his knowledge of the ocean to transfer to ancient history and archaeology? Is his knowledge great enough for us to accept that Ming Dynasty Chinese sailors visited North America seventy years before Columbus?

An additional difficulty with assessing whether an argument from authority is legitimate stems from the problem that true authorities can disagree. Archaeologists, like all scholars, are perfectly free to change their opinions as they acquire more information and rethink things. Because archaeologists can never know the past with certainty, they must often hedge their bets and make inferences based on sample size, their knowledge of the works of others, and their own research.

Sincere differences of opinion by committed, knowledgeable scholars create dissenting camps that can cause hard feelings lasting for years. The processual archaeology of the late 1960s (see chapter 2) created two opposing camps: "new-style" processual archaeologists and "old-style" culture historians. The disputes between the groups were often ill-tempered, as each struggled to demonstrate they were right and the other side was misguided at best and terribly wrong at worst. As Wesley Salmon points out, what often happens in these situations is the development of an "argument by consensus." As dissenting camps form, the entire group, rather than a lone individual, is regarded as an authority. This approach, however, also has problems. It can take years for a single individual going against the consensus (but ultimately correct in their interpretation) to get their views accepted by most authorities within a specific field.

Since the 1930s, archaeologists argued that the only way the first inhabitants of North America could have arrived on the continent was by crossing the Bering land bridge and traveling through an ice-free corridor in the middle of the Alaskan peninsula. (The first person to make this suggestion was a sixteenth-century Jesuit priest!) In the 1960s, a few archaeologists began to question this "mid-continental hypothesis," and instead suggested a coastal route. In 1979, writing in *American Antiquity*, American archaeology's premier journal, archaeologist Knut Fladmark made a strong case for considering an entryway along the Pacific coast. His interpretation failed to take hold as the consensus view. Brian Fagan, the best-selling archaeologist-author, did not even mention the idea in his *The Great Journey: The Peopling of Ancient America* (published in 1987). But the idea of a coastal migration route never died out, and research conducted by a team of archaeologists and geologists showed in 2012 that ecological conditions would have made a coastal migration route entirely possible. As a result of this and other findings, archaeologists are now less inclined to dismiss the coastal route outright, even though reaching this point has taken over forty years of analysis, argumentation, and reinterpretation. That Fagan mentioned the coastal route in his *The First North Americans* (published in 2011) demonstrates that mainstream attitudes have indeed changed. (Recent DNA evidence adds further weight to the idea that at least some people came across the Bering land bridge. The controversy about other routes rages on.)

The nature of archaeological research, like all scholarly endeavors, mandates that changes in interpretation can occur slowly. It may take years to establish one's credentials as an authority in a particular field and once accomplished, it may take even more time for a new interpretation to become the consensus view. This process, however, characterizes how knowledge grows over time.

The creation of intellectual camps around a particular subject, such as the introduction of humans into North America, can lead to a kind of inductive argument called "the argument against the person" (or an Ad Hominen Argument; older books call it "the argument against the man"). This argument takes the form:

X says *p*
∴ not *p*.

This argument maintains that whatever *X* says about *p* should be disregarded because *X* is known to be consistently wrong in his interpretations. This argument is a difficult one to sustain except in the most extreme circumstances. For instance, someone who insists the sun will rise in the west tomorrow morning cannot be trusted as an authority on astronomy. Being consistently wrong about the sun, day after day, has created a lack of confidence in that person's judgment.

The argument against the person must relate specifically to the matter at hand. It would be unwise to reject something someone says simply because we do not like their political affiliation, religious beliefs, organizational memberships, or even education level (and in some cases where a person obtained their education). People are biased in this way all the time, but it is logically unwise. Individuals may wish to discount what a politician says about nuclear safety simply because his or her position on gun control is unpopular. In his book on archaeological method and theory, Guy Gibbon mentions that some archaeologists immediately reject the ideas of individuals lacking a PhD. He is referring to amateur or avocational archaeologists, not to the more intellectually questionable pseudo-archaeologists. Many women and men with sincere interests in archaeology can be incredibly knowledgeable about a particular region or past culture. The same is true of many Indigenous people who have abundant traditional and place-based knowledge. Today's archaeologists have developed better relations with both Indigenous men and women and avocational archaeologists, so what Gibbon terms an "appeal to pedantry" is becoming less of a problem. It remains likely, however, that the fallacy will never entirely disappear.

We humans have the right to think illogically when it comes to the mundane circumstances of daily life, but a lack of logic in archaeology carries the consequence of affecting how the history of the world and our place within it is perceived and understood.

Wesley Salmon points out the difficulty of labeling someone an "antiauthority." Affixing the label can be tricky because no one can ever be 100 percent certain that the person has *always* been wrong. Salmon observes, though, that scientific cranks are one instance where the label can be applied without undue danger. Cranks:

1. usually reject all established knowledge or some area of it,
2. tend to be ignorant of the knowledge they reject, generally believing that it's just wrong on a gut level, but not being able to provide concrete details,
3. have no access to recognized publication outlets for scientific research and are not invited to scholarly conferences,
4. think the opposition they receive from the professional community is based on the bias and close-mindedness of scholars, and
5. oppose science because of a belief or beliefs based on religious or political views.

To Salmon's five characteristics, we can add a sixth one specific to archaeology:

6. belief that archaeologists are engaged in a conspiracy to cover up the true history of humanity.

It's easy to find evidence of Salmon's claims in the books of pseudo-archaeologists. For instance, Von Däniken writes in *Chariots of the Gods?* that "It took courage to write this book . . . Because its theories and proofs do not fit into the mosaic of traditional archaeology, constructed so laboriously and firmly cemented down, scholars will call it nonsense and put it on the Index of those books which are better left unmentioned." In their book *Forbidden Archaeology: The Hidden History of the Human Race*, authors Michael Cremo and Richard Thompson complain about a widespread archaeological conspiracy to keep their interpretations out of the scholarly press. Whether such writers are true cranks or simply misguided history buffs is a judgment call, but true cranks are known in the history of archaeology.

One of the most famous cranks in American history with a connection to archaeology was a man named Ignatius Donnelly. Donnelly, who was born in 1831 and died in 1901, initially gained fame as a politician, having run for and won several state and federal offices. A friend of Abraham Lincoln's, Donnelly served as lieutenant governor of Minnesota and was a member of the US Congress. His real claim to fame, and the reason he is today widely regarded as the Prince of Cranks, was his speculative writings, especially *Atlantis: The Antediluvian World*, published in 1882. Just about everything people believe today about Atlantis comes from Donnelly's imagination rather than from Plato, the only original source on the lost civilization. *Atlantis* was a major best seller when it first appeared, and the book is still available today.

In keeping with the spirit of the late nineteenth century, Donnelly embraced science with gusto, realizing he could use the public's optimistic belief in it to exploit their gullibility.

Today's cranks have learned to be more sophisticated, and rather than openly accepting science as Donnelly chose to do, they have decided to tap into an undercurrent of suspicion about science and intellectual scholarship. Like Donnelly, though, they still use knowledge selectively, letting their imaginations do most of the work.

ABDUCTION

Before leaving logic, another set of concepts is worth mentioning. In the late nineteenth century, an American philosopher named Charles S. Peirce explained what he called "abduction." Rather than having anything to do with space aliens, Peirce identified abduction as a kind of reasoning. His views, though controversial among philosophers, have relevance to archaeological thinking.

Peirce understood that not every claim that can be dreamed up is equally suitable to providing reasonable interpretations. Proposing that not all claims are created equal, he concluded that a proposition that is more "economical" than any others is most likely the best one. In his sense, "economical" means the simplicity and conservatism of the SEARCH formula presented in chapter 3.

Philosopher Cameron Shelley has directly applied abductive reasoning to archaeology by exploring "visual abduction." This form of inference is common in archaeological research.

Archaeologists use mental frameworks and pattern recognition to identify specific classes of objects. Field surveying is the easiest place to see visual abduction. When archaeologists walk a field looking for artifact scatters and other evidence of past settlements, they do not know precisely what artifacts they're looking for because they've never actually seen them before. They won't see them until they find and handle them. They know the basic shapes of the artifacts they're likely to find but they don't know how the individual pieces will look. Will the chert flakes be gray or brown? Will the bottle glass be clear, brown, blue, yellow, or green? They know the patterns that fit the various mental pictures of "arrowhead," "scraper," "bottle neck," "dinner plate," and so forth, but that's all. They know that things called "arrowheads" should have pointed ends (if not broken), that they will be made of chipped stone (at pre-metal sites), and that they will conform to certain designs common for the cultural traditions of the region. Archaeologists have a framework for "stone tools" in mind and they will pick up objects that have those general characteristics. Anything that does not fit into the mental image of "artifact" will not be picked up during the survey. A professional with a well-honed mental image of "arrowhead" can easily distinguish the real thing from a pointed rock. The lack of a well-developed mental framework for artifacts, in fact, is one reason why so many people email pictures of rocks and other nonartifacts to museums and universities for identification, thinking the rocks are ancient artifacts.

Even well-developed mental pictures can be fooled, however. While excavating colonial-era sites I have sometimes mistaken white cigarette butts for the stems of white clay smoking pipes. From a distance, a cigarette butt visually fits the mental picture of "pipe stem": they are white in color, tube-shaped, and approximately 1.5 inches (4 cm) long (figure 5.2). Only when the butt is picked up is it clear that it violates an important feature of the mental framework: it must be made of kiln-fired white clay (not paper).

An artifact's shape is one of its most recognizable visual properties. Archaeologists conduct abduction when they infer the shape of an entire object from a single fragment. For instance, an archaeologist given a broken bottle neck and lip (the lip is technically called a "finish") with a rectangular shape in cross-section would immediately know that the piece is likely to have come

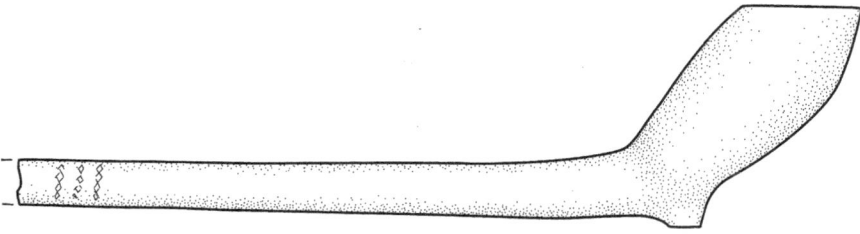

Figure 5.2.   Idealized white clay smoking pipe
Source: *Drawing by Tina Ross.*

from a nineteenth-century patent medicine bottle. Makers of patent medicines typically put their concoctions in rectangular bottles so that they could affix a colorful, eye-catching label on the front and the back. The flat sides often carried the embossed name of the product and where it had been made.

One advantage of this kind of recognition is that archaeologists can reasonably identify other pieces of the bottle because the shape (and color) of the undiscovered pieces can be inferred from the shape of the finish. The archaeologist has no need to find every piece of glass to construct a mental image of the whole bottle. The mental framework—developed through knowledge and experience—will do most of the work.

Archaeologists also regularly use visual abductive reasoning when they reconstruct buildings using the often-minimal evidence left behind, such as postholes and soil stains. Lines of postholes and the locations of wall trenches and hearths help them construct visual representations (often as computer models) that then can be constructed if desired. A number of experimental archaeologists have built life-sized models of ancient houses and then burned them down to assess how well the remains of the modern building conform to excavated physical remains. For example, archaeologists in the American Great Plains had the opportunity to compare the burned remains of a Native American earthlodge (like the kind in which the Arikaras studied by Deetz lived) excavated in Nebraska with a replica built in 1990 by the Mills County (Iowa) Historical Museum. When weather damaged the replica beyond repair, the museum decided to burn down its remains and construct a new one. The builders of the original replica had based it entirely on archaeological remains of lodges excavated in the region (a case of visual abduction). Once the replica was burned, archaeologists were able to compare its charred remains with those of the burned archaeological example in Nebraska.

The final form of an inductive argument with archaeological importance is "the argument by analogy." This form of argument is so widely used in archaeological thinking that it is the subject of the next chapter.

SOURCES FOR CONTINUED READING

LOGIC

Bergstrom, Carl T. and Jevin D. West. 2020. *Calling Bullshit: The Art of Skepticism in a Data-Driven World*. New York: Random House.

Carroll, Lewis. 1896. *Symbolic Logic: Part I, Elementary*. London: Macmillan.

Salmon, Wesley C. 1973. *Logic*. Second edition. Englewood Cliffs, NJ: Prentice-Hall.

Shelley, Cameron. 1996. "Visual Abductive Reasoning in Archaeology." *Philosophy of Science* 63:278–301.

Twain, Mark. 2010. *Autobiography of Mark Twain, Volume 1*. Harriet Elinor Smith, ed. Berkeley: University of California Press.

ARCHAEOLOGY

Bleed, Peter, Jerry Renaud, and Luis Peon-Casanova. 2009. "Burning Issues: Observations on Old and New Burned Earthlodges." *Plains Anthropologist* 54:19–25.

Borreggine, Marisa, Evelyn Powell, Tamara Pico, Jerry X. Mitrovica, Richard Meadow, and Christian Tryon. 2022. "Not a Bathtub: A Consideration of Sea-Level Physics for Archaeological Models of Human Migration." *Journal of Archaeological Science* 137:105507.

Deetz, James. 1965. *The Dynamics of Stylistic Change in Arikara Ceramics*. Urbana: University of Illinois Press.

Fagan, Brian M. 1987. *The Great Journey: The Peopling of Ancient America*. London: Thames and Hudson.

———. 2011. *The First North Americans: An Archaeological Journey*. London: Thames and Hudson.

Fladmark, K. R. 1979. "Routes: Alternative Migration Corridors for Early Man in North America." *American Antiquity* 44:55–69.

Gibbon, Guy. 2014. *Critically Reading the Theory and Methods of Archaeology: An Introductory Guide*. Lanham, MD: Rowman and Littlefield.

Misarti, Nicole, Bruce P. Finney, James W. Jordan, Herbert D. G. Maschner, Jason A. Addison, Mark D. Shapley, Andrea Krumhardt, and James E. Beget. 2012. "Early Retreat of the Alaska Peninsula Glacier Complex and the Implications for Coastal Migrations of First Americans." *Quaternary Science Reviews* 48:1–6.

Noël Hume, Ivor and Henry M. Miller. 2011. "Ivor Noël Hume: Historical Archaeologist." *The Public Historian* 33:9–32.

Saraceni, Jessica E. 1996. "Redating Serpent Mound." *Archaeology* 49 (6): 16.

PSEUDO-ARCHAEOLOGY

Donnelly, Ignatius. 1882. *Atlantis: The Antediluvian World*. New York: Harper and Brothers.

Cremo, Michael A. and Richard L. Thompson. 1993. *Forbidden Archaeology: The Hidden History of the Human Race*. San Diego: Bhaktivedanta Institute.

Fell, Barry. 1976. *America BC: Ancient Settlers in the New World*. New York: Demeter.

Hancock, Graham. 2002. *Underworld: The Mysterious Origins of Civilization*. New York: Crown.

Menzies, Gavin. 2002. *1421: The Year China Discovered America*. New York: William Morrow.

Tyree, J. M. 2005. Ignatius Donnelly: Prince of Cranks. *The Believer* 3 (6): 5–14.

Von Daniken, Erich. 1968. *Chariots of the Gods? Unsolved Mysteries of the Past*. Michael Heron, trans. New York: Berkley Medallion.

6

Analogy and Archaeological Thinking

Analogies are so commonplace that most people don't even realize that they use them. Professor Stebbing observes that "analogy forms the basis of much of our thinking," and Carl Bergstrom and Jevin West agree that analogies help people to evaluate a claim by using something familiar to comprehend something less familiar. They use an analogy to explain to a vaccine skeptic the value of the flu vaccine by reference to seatbelts.

The analogies we make often without realizing it can be puzzling. A personal experience brought that home to me in a surprising way.

Like millions of people around the world I've always been fascinated by modern and contemporary art. But perhaps unlike connoisseurs, what has intrigued me the most is the artists' combination of skill, creativity, and sometimes even audacity. One of the things I've found especially fascinating when thinking about contemporary art is the bewildered public's frequent question: "why is *that* art?" I sometimes think what is accepted and admired often says more about the viewer than the artist. An artist's creativity can mean that decisions about what constitutes art may take a curious turn. This was exactly what happened to me based on an analogy I made.

A few years ago, while visiting a large art museum, I was confronted by what looked like a heavy wooden chair. It fit my mental framework of what a chair should be. It had four legs, a seat, and a back—nothing odd there. But I found its location confusing because it was placed in the middle of a room in the modern and contemporary art wing. This made me wonder if the chair was art or was it merely a chair? The object was not discreetly placed in a corner as a guard's chair might have been. Instead, its position suggested that the object was more than just an ordinary place to sit.

My mind raced. The object had all the characteristics of what I know a chair to be, but its placement in the gallery made it seem like art. So, is it a chair, or is an artist using its contradictory solidity and emptiness to reference some muted desire in the human spirit? I wondered what Berger's five scholars (see chapter 3) would have made of this situation.

What exactly was happening? My problem was that upon entering the gallery and seeing the chair, my brain immediately and unconsciously made a simple analogy. The analogy, which took nanoseconds to compute but which resulted in confusion, was a calculation between my mental picture of "chair" (what I knew a chair to be) and "art" (what I suspected a piece of art could be).

As Professor Stebbing tells us in *Thinking to Some Purpose*, analogies are one of the most widely used forms of inductive argument. Everyone uses them every day. Most of us usually make them so quickly and effortlessly that we don't even realize we're doing it. For example, when you walk into a classroom for the first time, your brain rapidly makes a simple analogy between what you know to exist elsewhere (chairs and desks in other classrooms) and what you see for the first time in the new setting (new chairs and desks in a different classroom). As you sit down, you are confident your experience with similar objects in other places means you can safely sit on the new chairs without having them crumble beneath you. The context also helps you decide that the chairs can be sat upon. In a classroom your analogy is justifiably strong, but in the context of an art museum I could not have the same confidence in my analogy. The "chair" I saw may have been made of papier mâché. I would have made a fool of myself, and probably been arrested, had I attempted to sit in the "chair." (I never discovered if the "chair" was art.)

In logic, an analogical argument takes the form:

Objects of type X have attributes a, b, and c.
Objects of type Y have attributes a, b, and c.
Objects of type X have attribute d.
∴ Objects of type Y have attribute d.

At the art museum, I was trying to make this analogical argument:

Chairs (X) have four legs (a), a seat (b), and a back (c).
The object in the gallery (Y) has four legs (a), a seat (b), and a back (c).
Chairs (X) can be sat upon (d).
Therefore, the object in the gallery (Y) can be sat upon (d).

This is the same analogical argument you make every time you sit in a chair you have never seen before. If it has all the characteristics of a chair, it fits your mental picture of what a chair is, and so you decide you can safely sit on it. One pitfall, though, as Professor Stebbing says, is that we humans are often willing to accept any analogical comparison that seems to make sense without having to think too much about it. If it sounds good, we may accept it without evaluating its details. As we saw with my museum experience, such assumptions could have serious consequences!

ARCHAEOLOGISTS AND ANALOGY

Analogies are extremely useful in archaeological thinking. Untrained amateur archaeologists used analogies when they first contemplated the monuments of ancient Egypt, Italy, and Europe. Many of their analogies were misguided and fanciful, and they would be easily discounted once archaeology was professionalized. But simple analogies constituted a significant element of early archaeological research.

When, in 1873, silver tycoon Heinrich Schliemann pulled out of the ground what he called "Priam's Treasure" at Troy (in today's Turkey), he described individual finds with the words "shield," "cup," "sauceboat," and "knife." These ancient objects may never have functioned in the ways Schliemann envisioned, but his analogies allowed the public to grasp their general shape and form. In fact, simply reading the words forces your brain to create an instantaneous visual image that makes each meaning (and thus function) clear. When we hear "shield" each of us quickly creates a mental image of how we think a shield should look.

While excavating the ancient ruins at Knossos in the early twentieth century, Arthur Evans used analogical reasoning to identify the "Grand Staircase" and the "Throne Room." The stairway and the room had the appearance of these things, so he interpreted them that way, and his analogies helped others understand his interpretations. A big chair in one room looked to him like a throne, so its location became the "Throne Room." You probably have already created a picture of the room in your mind based on how you imagine a throne room should look. Evans did the same thing.

Archaeologists continued to employ such informal analogies until the 1960s. Since then, archaeologists have spent a great deal of time thinking about the importance of logical reasoning, and analogy has been a topic under consideration because of its wide usage.

When archaeologists started to think about it, they realized they make two kinds of analogies: *artifact analogies* and *ethnographic* or *cultural analogies*. Artifact analogies involve examining the attributes of an artifact and associating it with something known from another source, either past or present. This is what Schliemann did with the artifacts from Troy.

Philosophers sometimes refer to Schliemann's kind of analogy as a "single analogy" because only one source is used. An ethnographic analogy is considerably more complex than an artifact analogy because being "multiple analogies" they contain evidence from many sources. Ethnographic analogies are also complicated because they refer to cultural traditions and practices rather than to a single piece of material culture.

ARTIFACT ANALOGIES

One of the most interesting features of artifact analogies is that they often include an implicit cultural analogy. This means that the similarities between two objects from different cultures can imply a similarity between the cultures themselves. A good example comes from one the earliest recorded archaeological analogies.

In 1699, Edward Lhwyd, the second Keeper of Oxford University's Ashmolean Museum, used an artifact analogy when he proposed that chipped stone artifacts found in prehistoric Scotland were used in the same way Native Americans employed similar-looking objects in seventeenth-century New England: as arrowheads. The residents of the rural Scottish Highlands, where Lhwyd's artifacts were found, believed that arrowheads were charms created by elves and fairies, but Lhwyd used an analogy to dispute this interpretation:

Stone artifacts (X) found in Native New England are made of stone (a), they are chipped (b), generally triangular in shape (c), and pointed (d).
Artifacts found in the Scottish Highlands (Y) have the characteristics (a), (b), (c), and (d).
The artifacts in North America (X) are employed as arrowheads (e).
Therefore, the artifacts in Scotland (Y) were used as arrowheads (e).

In this example, Lhwyd infers the artifact's *function* from its *form*. The Scottish artifacts looked like those used in North America as arrowheads, so they probably had the same function. The link between form and function is common in archaeological analogies.

Archaeologists studying non- or preliterate societies from the past face a problem noted by philosopher Marilee Salmon: "There is obviously no opportunity to question the makers of these artifacts about their purposes in designing them." Archaeologists cannot see these objects being put to use, so they must use analogies to infer their use from their form. Archaeologists know, for instance, that an arrowhead cannot be used to carry drinking water. But difficulty comes from attempting to decide whether an arrowhead may have had a purely symbolic meaning or was simply used in hunting or warfare (like the Covis points in chapter 4). Form relates to function, but not necessarily in every case. An example from a common artifact helps to make the point.

The straight pin is so ordinary that it seems uninteresting and unworthy of much serious thought, but both Adam Smith and Karl Marx commented on their manufacture in their famous works on political economy. Despite their mundanity, straight pins have ancient history. The first straight pins were sharpened bones made by people alive during the Paleolithic era (which ended twelve thousand to ten thousand years ago). The Romans made pins, and artisans made straight pins in every epoch since then. Native Americans made and used bone pins at least as early as six thousand to five thousand years ago.

We understand that straight pins are simple, usually temporary, fasteners. So, when an archaeologist finds something that resembles a pin, they usually determine that its function was for holding something, usually clothing, together. (Though before the widespread use of machine-made staples, people often used straight pins to hold papers together.) So, the analogy between straight pins today and straight pins found in an archaeological excavation seems straightforward. Accordingly, the analogy employed by Stanley South during the excavation of Brunswick Town, North Carolina (burned in 1776) is as follows:

Objects used today to fix clothes together (X) are straight (a), pointed (b), and have a neat, round head (c)
The artifacts found at the Public House and Tailor Shop in Brunswick Town (Y) have attributes (a), (b) and (c)
Objects (X) are pins (d)
Therefore, artifacts at Brunswick Town (Y) are pins (d).

This is straightforward because we view the pin as a completely ordinary artifact and one that we know well. But do we really understand straight pins? Simply deciding that a straight pin was used to fasten clothing together is too simple. Actually, for most of Western history, straight pins had magical uses.

In the early French version of Little Red Riding Hood, for example, when the wolf meets the girl in the forest, he asks her whether she will take the path of needles or the path of pins to her grandmother's house. As anthropologist Mary Douglas reveals, in early nineteenth-century France, when the tale was first making its rounds, peasant women had created an informal system of age-classes, and women used the symbolism of pins and needles to indicate life stages. Girls of marriable age would throw pins into wishing wells and receive gifts of pins from suitors. Pins have no opening, whereas needles have an opening, one that Douglas contends has a sexual connotation. She says that the mention of pins and needles in the Red Riding Hood story alerts French listeners to expect a tale with a sexual content and one that makes distinctions between young unmarried girls and older married women.

Witch bottles provide another intriguing case in which a simple analogy will not provide the whole story. A witch bottle can be any kind of container, but the most famous are Bellarmine jugs, also called "bearded-man," "Bartmann," and "greybeard" jugs. These heavy stoneware jugs are distinguishable by their globular bodies and the unmistakable face of a bearded man on their necks. These jugs, generally produced in German workshops, were immensely popular throughout Western Europe in the late sixteenth and seventeenth centuries.

The name "Bellarmine" is generally believed to refer to the Roman Catholic Cardinal Robert Bellarmine, who was universally despised by early modern English Protestants. In reality, the earliest Bellarmine jug dates to 1550; at the time, the cardinal was only eight years old. At last count, over two hundred examples have been found in England and several in the eastern United States.

Colonial-era English men and women afraid of being bewitched put fingernail clippings, human hair, thorns, their urine, and other items in the bottles and buried or otherwise concealed them as protection against witches. Bent straight pins are a common object found in witch bottles, meaning that pins were thought to have had a symbolic (nonfunctional) usage (figure 6.1).

Figure 6.1.   Witch Bottle found at Holywell Priory, London, England
Source: *Used by permission, Museum of London Archaeology. Photo: Andy Chopping.*

Pseudo-archaeologists make artifact analogies to increase the plausibility of their highly questionable interpretations. Their outrageous examples are instructive because only common sense is required to evaluate them. For example, in *America, B.C.*, Barry Fell makes an analogy between a form of ancient writing called "ogham" and various scratches found on rocks in North America. Ogham is an ancient Irish writing system dating to the first millennium CE. Instead of appearing as a script, ogham is composed of a series of lines extending from or crossing over a vertical line. A few examples can still be found in rural Ireland, where their presence makes perfect sense (figure 6.2). Fell, however,

Figure 6.2. Rathglass Ogham Stone, Ireland
Source: *Image courtesy of Nora White, Ogham in 3D Project (https://ogham.celt.dias.ie).*

Analogy and Archaeological Thinking

identified scratches found on rocks in the United States as ogham writing and argued that Celtic people from the Emerald Isle must have visited the eastern United States long before Columbus. His analogy is:

Ogham writing (X) consists of a vertical line [a] and several horizontal lines [b] scratched onto rocks [c].
Rocks (Y) with characteristics a, b, and c appear in the eastern United States.
Ogham writing (X) was the product of ancient Irish Celts [d].
Therefore, the scratched rocks (Y) in the US were made by ancient Irish Celts [d].

This analogy is extremely weak, and most professional archaeologists would say ridiculous. To evaluate his analogy we only need to ask a few simple questions:

1. Do the scratch marks in the United States date to the first millennium CE?
2. Is there any concrete archaeological evidence for Celtic presence in pre-Columbian America?
3. Does any evidence exist to prove ancient Celts knew about the Western Hemisphere? and if so,
4. Does any evidence show they had an interest in visiting it?

Without archaeological evidence, Fell's analogy rests strictly on supposition. It is the weakest kind of artifact analogy because what could be simpler than comparing scratched lines?

ETHNOGRAPHIC ANALOGIES

Ethnographic, or cultural, analogies are usually "multiple analogies." These analogies can often be more difficult to evaluate than artifact analogies. They require more information because the greater the information, the greater the strength of the analogy. At the same time, cultural information extracted from widely different cultures can weaken an analogy and leave it open to criticism.

Archaeologists use two kinds of ethnographic analogies: *historical* and *comparative*. Both have been around for a long time, and both continue to serve archaeologists as they struggle to interpret the past.

As noted in chapter 2, early nineteenth-century scholars constructed analogies to interpret the earthen mounds of North America. Assuming Native Americans were incapable of building such massive structures, authors created analogies using the barrows of Europe and the pyramids of Egypt. By the end of the nineteenth century, and certainly by the start of the twentieth century, most archaeologists had abandoned the use of extremely weak, speculative analogies. Out of this interest developed what American archaeologists call "the direct historical approach," a kind of historical analogy. (Europeans call it "the folk culture approach.") Later, archaeologists developed more sophisticated comparative ethnographic analogies.

THE DIRECT HISTORICAL APPROACH

The idea underlying the direct historical approach maintains that archaeologists can infer characteristics of the unknown (an ancient, undocumented archaeological culture) from the known (an observable or historically documented culture). The direction of analysis thus extends from the ethnographic present (the date of a written account or observation) to the archaeological past (the dates of the settlement being studied). Using attributes compiled as "trait lists," the analyst simply compares the elements of the ethnographic culture with those of the next-most contemporary archaeological culture, moving step by step backward in time until an entire culture history is constructed.

The direct historical approach can be further explained with a hypothetical example (table 6.1). In this example, the culture in the ethnography wears shell beads, cooks in red pots, lives in round houses, uses iron scrapers to prepare hides, and travels on rivers with canoes. The date of the fictional ethnographic account is 1770–1775 and its author was a Jesuit missionary. The first archeological site (A) in the example dates to 1650–1700, or before the priest reached the village and wrote about it. The excavation of Site A unearthed shell beads, red pots, and postholes for round-shaped houses. The archaeologists found no evidence of canoes and no iron scrapers. They did find chipped stone scrapers, however. Based on the history of the long-term European presence in the region, the archaeologists conclude that European traders must have introduced the iron scrapers after 1700 and before 1770–1775.

The culture living at site B (1500–1600) had the same artifacts as culture A, except that they used black pots in place of red ones. In culture C

Table 6.1. The Direct Historical Approach in Action

	Ethnographic	Archaeological Sites			
		A (1650–1700)	B (1500–1600)	C (1400–1500)	D (1300–1350)
	1770–1775				
Attributes					
shell beads	x	x	x	x	
red pots	x	x			
round houses	x	x	x		
metal scrapers	x				
canoes	x				
stone beads					x
black pots			x	x	x
square houses				x	x
chert scrapers		x	x	x	x

x indicates presence

Analogy and Archaeological Thinking

(1400–1500), the archaeologists discovered that the people had much the same material culture as culture B, except that they had lived in square houses. In culture D, the excavators learned that about one hundred years earlier (1300–1350), the people wore stone beads, used stone scrapers, made black pottery, and lived in square houses.

Two key elements are important in this simple example. First, the process allows archaeologists to move steadily and systematically backward in time, to frame analogies between each of the individual cultural expressions, beginning with the one visited by the missionary. A second thing to note is that the artifacts of culture D (1300–1350) look entirely different from the ethnographic culture (1770–1775) even though the ethnographic culture may be the descendant of culture D. Using the direct historical approach, archaeologists can make direct connections between the two cultures, even though they are distant in time, often for hundreds of years. Even one hundred years is a long time, but we can still see culture change in the artifacts over time.

The direct historical approach, though a useful form of ethnographic analogy, has two major weaknesses. First and most significant, the approach appears to reduce the cultures to stationary, snapshot images rather than constantly changing social organizations. All cultures adapt and invent, and no single picture can capture the richness and diversity of any culture throughout its entire history. Therefore, archaeologists study several sites hoping to learn something about culture change over time. The direct historical approach provides this level of analysis, but only by appreciating that gaps in time may occur between the occupational periods represented by each site. In the example, culture change continued to occur during the time gaps between each site's period of occupation even if the archaeologists were unable to see it.

A second problem with the direct historical approach is that it works best in places where the cultures have not moved around too much. A lack of migration increases the reliability of the between-site analogies. Archaeologists may not be able to establish connections between an ethnographic observation and earlier archaeological remains when a great deal of migration has occurred in a region. In the example, it may be that culture D is not culturally related to the ethnographic culture at all or perhaps even to cultures A, B, or C. Perhaps the people in culture D faced a draught and moved hundreds of miles away from their homeland, and between 1350 and 1400 another culture occupied their former territory. This would account for the difference between the material expressions of cultures C and D; the remains represent two distinct cultural traditions rather than an example of cultural change.

MORE RECENT COMPARATIVE ETHNOGRAPHIC ANALOGY

Archaeologists face considerable challenges when attempting to use comparative ethnographic analogies because they usually involve several complex variables. Greater sophistication in archaeology since the late twentieth century means that archaeologists cannot investigate cultural change with trait lists alone as in the direct historical approach. No longer can they simply list two cultures' material traits, check the traits against one another, and conclude a historical connection existed between the cultures. Today's ethnographic analogies require amassing a body of reliable information that will help archaeologists interpret complex cultural and historical traditions. The pitfalls also increase with the addition of more sources because the archaeologist must ensure the reliability of each source (see chapter 3).

A well-known archaeological example of an ethnographic analogy is Lewis Binford's "Smudge Pits and Hide Smoking: The Use of Analogy in Archaeological Reasoning" published in 1967. This study was largely responsible for creating increased archaeological interest in the use of analogies, while at the same time exposing the need for extreme care when doing so.

While excavating at the pre-Columbian Toothsome Site in central Illinois, Binford discovered fifteen pit features, each with the same general characteristics. Each was slightly oval in shape and only about twelve inches in length and width. The bottom of each pit was filled with charred twigs, corncobs, and other fibers. The people who dug these pits had placed them at random around the site's three former buildings.

Reading the reports of fellow archaeologists, Binford learned that many others had discovered similar pits in their excavations. These archaeologists had usually described the pits as "caches" or "corncob pits" and said little else. Binford wanted a more culturally sensitive interpretation, one that would provide insight into the daily lives of the people who had lived in the small village whose remains he had excavated. He wanted to know what caused them to make and use the pits. To provide a culturally relevant interpretation, Binford created an analogical argument to understand the pits' past functions.

Binford's ethnographic survey revealed that at least four Native American cultures in the American Southeast, five from the Great Plains, and three from the Great Lakes region had used shallow pits to tan hides. Various observers had seen Native peoples lighting smoky fires in pits and then stretching hides over them. The Indigenous people knew through experience that smoking hides would darken them and help preserve them from insects. The visitors' descriptions of the pits generally matched those found at the Toothsome Site, so Binford concluded, based on this evidence, that the fifteen pits he found had probably been used in the hide-smoking process. Even though Binford started with the archaeological evidence, his ethnographic analogy can be written as:

Pits identified in various ethnographic accounts (X) are small [a], oval [b], and contain charred materials [c].
The fifteen pits found at the Toothsome Site (Y) are small [a], oval [b], and contain charred materials [c].

The ethnographic pits (*X*) functioned to darken hides [*d*].
Therefore, the Toothsome Site pits (*Y*) had been used to darken hides [*d*].

This is a straightforward analogical argument made between ethnographic descriptions and archaeologically discovered remains. It allowed Binford to infer an otherwise unrecognized cultural practice (hide smoking) from excavated physical remains (fifteen simple pits).

EVALUATING ANALOGY STRENGTH

Binford's article was an immediate sensation among archaeologists, and it quickly brought the subject of analogy to the forefront of archaeological thinking. But it was controversial. Only two years after the article appeared, archaeologist Patrick Munson offered another interpretation of the pits. Using a different set of ethnographies to create his own analogy, Munson demonstrated that the residents of the Toothsome Site may have used the pits for smudging the insides of clay pots rather than for (or perhaps in addition to) smoking animal hides. Archaeologists excavating Native American village sites in the American Southeast—the only region from which Munson drew his ethnographic information and the area archaeologists considered most closely related to the people who had once inhabited the Toothsome Site—had found potsherds with blackened interiors. Munson thus presented an alternative claim: that Native potters produced blackened pot interiors using the small, shallow pits.

The ethnographic information Munson presented raised important questions about the archaeological use of analogy: How do archaeologists know which analogy is best? To put it more formally: how do archaeologists determine the *relevance* or *applicability* of an analogy? Is it the right one for the situation or has the archaeologist stretched the analogy too far? In the effort to "make the case," did the archaeologist choose only ethnographic examples that suited their interpretation? Was the archaeologist guilty of selection bias?

Some questions can be answered by taking a closer look at Binford's sources, by evaluating them based on what I call the T-S-T test: the time, space, and technology test. The relevant information to consider is how well the ethnographic sources match the archaeological case along these three dimensions.

Regarding time, the Toothsome Site residents were Mississippians (see chapter 4), whose culture in Illinois existed from about 900 to about 1450 CE. The villages in the region of the Toothsome Site date to around 1000–1450 CE. If these historical dates are placed alongside Binford's sources, we can see the problem immediately (table 6.2). The dates of his ethnographic sources are hundreds of years later than the Toothsome Site dates. The minimum mean dates are 402 years apart, with the maximum discrepancy between the dates

Table 6.2. Date Differences between the Toothsome Site and the Ethnographic Sources

Toothsome Site (CE)	Ethnographic Dates (CE)	Minimum Difference (years)	Maximum Differences (years)
1000–1500	1700–1750	250	850
	1900–1950	450	1,050
	1900–1950	450	1,050
	1900–1950	450	1,050
	1850–1900	400	1,000
	1800–1850	350	950
	1800–1900	400	1,000
	1800–1850	350	950
	1900–1939	450	1,039
	1850–1860	400	960
	1800–1890	350	990
	1930–1940	480	1,040
	1900–1920	450	1,020
Mean		402	996

being a whopping 996 years. Even if we accept the minimum discrepancy of just over 400 years, we must still resolve several cultural implications because of the many assumptions we would also have to make.

The most serious assumption is that the ethnographic cultures Binford used did not experience any significant changes in how they prepared hides for at least 250 years, or between about 1450 (the final date when people lived at the Toothsome Site) and 1700 (the date of his earliest written source). This is a huge assumption to make considering the significant technological and ecological changes Native North Americans experienced because of the presence of Europeans among them.

Regarding space, if we compare the location of the Toothsome Site and those in Binford's sample of ethnographic cultures, we can also see large discrepancies (table 6.3).

None of the cultures lived especially close to the Toothsome Site. None of them lived in Illinois except the Menominees, who lived in northern Wisconsin, about five hundred miles north of the Toothsome Site.

In terms of technology, the strongest analogies derive from comparing cultures that exploited the environment in roughly similar ways using comparable technologies. For example, it would make little sense to use an industrial market economy in an analogy with a culture of hunters and collectors, even if

Table 6.3. Place Differences between the
Toothsome Site and the Ethnographic Sources

Culture	Place
Toothsome Site	south-central Illinois
Natchez	Mississippi, Louisiana
Creek	Alabama, Georgia, Oklahoma
Choctaw	Mississippi, Oklahoma
Seminole	Florida, Oklahoma
Omaha	Nebraska
Dakota	Minnesota, South Dakota
Blackfoot	Montana, Alberta
Crow	Montana
Arapaho	Colorado, Nebraska, Kansas
Iroquois	New York State
Ojibwa	northern Michigan, Ontario
Menominee	northeast Wisconsin

the criteria of time and space could be managed. The cultural practices in such wildly diverse cultures may allow for the creation of an analogy that initially may seem reasonable but is misguided.

Technology is a much more difficult variable to assess because many of the ethnographic cultures Binford used in his analogy were horticultural peoples just like the residents of the Toothsome Site. A major deficiency appears, however, when considering the dates of the observations in conjunction with technology. Except for the Natchez, the dates of all the ethnographies belong to eras long after the Native cultures had adopted many Western ways. For example, the Creeks, Choctaws, and Seminoles were members of the so-called "Five Civilized Tribes," cultures forcibly evicted from their homes in the American Southeast and moved to the Oklahoma Territory in the 1830s. Nineteenth-century Americans referred to them as "civilized" because they had begun to accept many European ways, including Western styles of dress, animal-powered agriculture, log cabins, and a form of enslavement. A creative Cherokee man even invented a written transcription for their spoken language, and the people used it to print a Cherokee newspaper. Writing about the Seminoles living in Oklahoma, anthropologist Richard Sattler noted that "Western Seminole culture in the nineteenth century generally conformed to pre-Removal Seminole and Creek patterns, but twentieth-century conditions produced profound changes." The accounts of these cultures Binford used date to 1900–1950, decades after they had been removed to Oklahoma. The source he used, Alanson Skinner's 1913 report among the Florida Seminoles—those who had not been removed—indicates that members of the eastern band had maintained many of their traditional practices. While this seems to strengthen their presence in Binford's analogy, Skinner did note that many of the band regularly visited Miami and Fort Lauderdale to trade. Thus, while the Seminoles were indeed located in a remote area, they were not unconnected to or uninfluenced by Western ways. By the same token, when other ethnographers made their observations, some of the cultures (namely, the Dakotas, Blackfoots, Crows, and Arapahoes) were not horticulturalists at all, but horse-riding hunters. Their nomadic way of life was dramatically different from the sedentary lives of the Toothsome Site residents.

Based on the T-S-T test, Binford's analogy ascribing the Toothsome Site's pit features to the process of smudging hides appears shaky. So, how might we improve it? The ideal situation, of course, would be to find eyewitness accounts from the first literate visitors, individuals who could have observed the Native cultures before the impacts of foreign interference. Such information would provide greater confidence along the dimension of space. We would have less confidence in the technological dimension because of culture change, but the analogy would still be strengthened. The dimension of time would present a problem, but the difference in years would roughly match that of the Natchez in the original analogy. We might be able to accept this time span, but it would always be problematic.

Archaeologists investigating ancient cultures will always have difficulty along the temporal dimension when they attempt to devise analogical arguments. So, how might we create stronger analogies, ones that include a closer agreement in time? One answer comes from the archaeology of more recent history.

While considering the importance of analogy in archaeology, Robert Schuyler presented the case of three iron artifacts archaeologists had excavated at the eighteenth-century Fortress of Louisbourg in Nova Scotia, Canada. French colonists had begun to build a small village on the site in 1713, and when they were finished, they had constructed a fortified city much like those that dotted the landscapes of continental Europe. The thick, stone walls of the city made a political statement that was difficult to misinterpret: Louisbourg was an important outpost of France's colonial North American empire and the French took its defense seriously. Appreciating the strategic importance of the location, the British—France's long-time enemy—attacked the city twice. They finally destroyed the fortress in the 1760s after they had defeated France in the Seven Years' War. Archaeology at the fortress, begun in 1959, is one of the world's flagship examples of French colonial archaeology.

The Louisbourg archaeologists realized that the three iron artifacts had been designed to be affixed to wooden handles like a broom or a rake. This interpretation made sense, but the form of the objects was unusual: each one appeared as a set of twisted, fork-like tines. Their archaeological contexts made it clear that they were eighteenth-century French artifacts, but how they had been used was a mystery.

Figure 6.3. Tirebourres from Fortress Louisbourg, Nova Scotia, Canada

Top: 1B16C3-141; center: 1L1X3-5, 51L3H2-5; bottom: 1B1E11-456. Source: Courtesy Parks Canada/ Heidi Moses/9298E. Photograph by Heidi Moses.

Seeking to find an answer, Schuyler checked a source called *Encyclopédie* written in 1762 by French scholar Denis Dedirot. He discovered that these objects, called *tirebourre*, were well known in the eighteenth century (figure 6.3). They were fixed to long wooden handles as the archaeologists had surmised, but they had a specialized function, one that would be unknown to most people alive today.

In the eighteenth century, artillery soldiers shoved tirebourre down the mouths of cannons to extract the cotton wad they had pushed down the muzzle to fire the previous cannonball. When a shot misfired, the soldiers had to unload the cannon, an operation that included removing the wad of cotton as well. For the next shot, they were afraid to use the old wad because if still smoldering it could explode and kill them all. Thus, they had to carefully extract it using a tirebourre.

The case of the tirebourre shows that the construction of a perfect analogy is possible in archaeology. Schuyler's analogy between Diderot's encyclopedia and the three Louisbourg artifacts meets the challenge of the T-S-T test. The analogy is perfect in terms of time (both the objects and the source belong to the eighteenth century; in fact, they are contemporaneous), space (cultural rather than geographic space; France and a colonial French outpost), and technology (they are part of the same European society). Such one-to-one analogies, what Schuyler termed "historic analogs," are the tightest analogies archaeologists can construct.

WHAT IS THE PURPOSE OF ANALOGY IN ARCHAEOLOGY?

Not all archaeologists have accepted the application of analogical reasoning in archaeology. Some who study extremely ancient societies believe that the time gap is simply too great between the cultures they study and the accounts written by much-later observers. They say that cultural change is too prevalent a force in human history to give the analogies much merit when so much time has elapsed.

These archaeologists are correct, and their position can be appreciated by thinking about the fast pace of change in our own time. Only a few years ago the idea of a handheld computer existed only in science fiction. Today, we take these things for granted. They are so familiar we don't even call them tiny computers; we call them smart phones. Just think about the changes these little tools have brought about in our daily lives. Our digital age might be a wholly unique example because of the speed of change, but anthropologists know that all cultures constantly change wherever they are (in space) and whenever they lived (in time).

As noted in the hypothetical example of the direct historical approach, the contacts that may have occurred between different cultures raise problems when equating the ethnographic present with the archaeological past. The influence of cultural change caused by outside influences may have trans-formed the ethnographic culture in ways completely inconsistent with the archaeological culture. Some archaeologists worry that selecting only a few comparative attributes from a multicultural complex may provide misleading analogies. Years of research into the complex variability of cultural change has led some archeologists to conclude that ethnographic analogy is just too simple a method to explain complicated cultural history.

Many archaeologists, however, continue to think that analogy must play a role in archaeological thinking. After all, even though Munson showed that the pits at the Toothsome Site may have been used for darkening pots rather than hides, Binford's basic point—that the pits were probably used for smoking *something*—stands up. Without analogy, archaeologists may not have recognized the ancient practice of pottery smudging at long-abandoned village sites for many years. Skeptics may counter that a clever archaeologist may have devised this interpretation without using an analogy, and that may well be true. But one important value of the analogy is that it helps humanize the pits by allowing analysts to envision real people using them. The addition of ethnographic writings, made by observers watching people practice their cultural lives, helps to breathe life into dry archaeological specimens.

One of the most controversial aspects of the archaeological use of ethnographic analogies concerns whether they are useful for devising new ideas to test or whether they are best used for testing ideas that have already been formulated. In other words, do analogies help archaeologists think up new propositions or are they only good for testing the ones they already have?

Archaeologists have had trouble answering this question. A consensus is that analogical reasoning is fine when archaeologists use specific historical analogies rather than general comparative ones. Regardless of how they choose to use analogy, archaeologists must always be careful not to make bad analogies. These are often far too easy to create, and the thoughtful archaeological thinker must always be on the lookout for them.

Another problem exists with poorly framed analogies. To understand this, let's return to the artifact analogy Lhwyd presented in 1699.

Implicit in Lhwyd's analogy is the idea that the similar use of arrows (and thus bows) suggests that the cultures of seventeenth-century Native New Englanders and ancient Scots might have been similar as well. Hidden within his artifact analogy is a subtle cultural analogy. To appreciate the significance of this, we must understand the historical context of the late seventeenth century.

New England, the American region most familiar to Lhwyd, was the scene of unresolved conflicts between its Indigenous residents and its European newcomers. In 1699, the Pequot War, the first sustained English-Native American armed conflict on the continent, had occurred only about sixty years earlier, and King Philip's War was only about forty years in the past. The English-Native conflicts that occurred during King William's War (1689–1697) were only two years distant.

Alliances between French Canadian colonists and their Native American allies to the north kept the British in New England worried and up at night. In addition, a continent full of Native peoples lived west of the mountains that defined the original English colonies. Many of these cultures would have their own battles with British and American settlers in the future.

At the same time, relations between Scotland and England were also tense, and the political union between the two would come only eight years after Lhwyd made his analogy (in 1707). Tensions between England and Scotland were still strained one hundred years later. The Highland Clearances, the eviction of rural families from their land to "improve" them, occurred during the eighteenth and nineteenth centuries. During this long history, many English men and women believed the Scots to be culturally backward, and that the only way to help them "better" themselves was to make them more English. Most English men and women had the same attitude about New England's Native peoples; they simply needed to be more English.

With this cultural and historical backdrop, it may be that Lhwyd's analogy carried with it a concealed message. He may have thought that Highland Scots and American Indigenous people, both of whom were in direct, long-term contact with English men and women, were equally "savage." And being so, each needed to be brought under the civilizing umbrella of the expanding British Empire. Equating an ancient European people (the ancient Scots) with living American cultures also implied that Native Americans were stuck in a time warp. People who thought in such biased ways believed that seventeenth-century Native Americans lived just like ancient European cultures, or in other words, that they had not "advanced" to the same cultural level as the "highly cultured" English.

The idea that Lhwyd's analogy may contain a hidden message proves Professor Stebbing's point that we must proceed cautiously when accepting any analogy, particular one equating cultures. Like everything else in archaeological thinking, the use of analogies requires thought and consideration. An interpretation about the past can be smashed to pieces with a weak, misleading, or just plain bad analogy. Part of the difficulty of assessing the relevance of an analogy arises because, as Wesley Salmon notes in *Logic*, the strength of an analogy cannot be determined with formal logic alone. Once we understand the proper form of an analogical argument, the rest is up to us. We must use our knowledge to create sensible analogies just as we must use care when evaluating the analogies of others. We must be on the lookout for bad analogies as we learn to think like archaeologists.

SOURCES FOR CONTINUED READING

ARCHAEOLOGICAL ANALOGY IN THEORY

Binford, Lewis. 1967. "Smudge Pits and Hide Smoking: The Use of Analogy in Archaeological Reasoning." *American Antiquity* 32:1–12.

Lyman, R. Lee and Michael J. O'Brien. 2001. "The Direct Historical Approach, Analogical Reasoning, and Theory in Americanist Archaeology." *Journal of Archaeological Method and Theory* 8:303–42.

Munson, Patrick J. 1969. "Comments on Binford's Smudge Pits and Hide Smoking: The Use of Analogy in Archaeological Reasoning." *American Antiquity* 34:83–85.

Salmon, Merrilee H. 1982. *Philosophy and Archaeology*. New York: Academic Press.

Schuyler, Robert L. 1968. "The Use of Historic Analogs in Archaeology." *American Antiquity* 33:390–92.

Shelley, Cameron. 1999. "Multiple Analogies in Archaeology." *Philosophy of Science* 66:579–605.

Stebbing, L. Susan. 1939. *Thinking to Some Purpose*. Harmondsworth, UK: Penguin.

Wolverton, Steve and R. Lee Lyman. 2000. "Immanence and Configuration in Analogical Reasoning." *North American Archaeologist* 21:233–47.

Wylie, Alison. 1985. "The Reaction Against Analogy." In *Advances in Archaeological Method and Theory, Volume 8*. Michael Brian Schiffer, ed., pp. 63–111.

ARCHAEOLOGICAL ANALOGY IN PRACTICE

Diderot, Denis. 1993 [1751–1772]. *Diderot Pictorial Encyclopedia of Trades and Industry*. 2 vols. New York: Dover.

Evans, Arthur. 1921. *The Palace of Minos: A Comparative Account of the Successive Stages of the Early Cretan Civilization as Illustrated by the Discoveries at Knossos, Volume 1.* London: Macmillan.

Sattler, Richard A. 2004. "Seminole in the West." In *Handbook of North American Indians, Vol. 14: Southeast*, Raymond D. Fogelson, ed., pp. 450–64. Washington, DC: Smithsonian Institution Press.

Schliemann, Heinrich. 1875. *Troy and Its Remains: A Narrative of Researches and Discoveries Made on the Site of Ilium and in the Trojan Plain.* Philip Smith, ed. London: John Murray.

Skinner, Alanson. 1913. Notes on the Florida Seminole. *American Anthropologist* 15:63–77.

WITCH BOTTLES AND STRAIGHT PINS

Douglas, Mary. 1995. "Red Riding Hood: An Interpretation from Anthropology." *Folklore* 106:1–7.

Hoggard, Brian. 2016. "Witch Bottles: Their Contents, Contexts, and Uses." In *Physical Evidence for Ritual Acts, Sorcery, and Witchcraft in Christian Britain*, edited by Ronald Hutton, pp. 91–105. Basingstoke: Palgrave Macmillan.

Jefferies, Richard W. 1997. "Middle Archaic Bone Pins: Evidence of Mid-Holocene Regional-Scale Social Groups in the Southern Midwest." *American Antiquity* 62:464–87.

Longman, E. D. and S. Loch. 1911. *Pins and Pincushions.* London: Longmans, Green.

Merrifield, Ralph. 1955. "Witch Bottles and Magical Jugs." *Folklore* 66:195–207.

Orser, Charles E., Jr. 2019. "Rethinking 'Bellarmine' Contexts in 17th-Century England." *Post-Medieval Archaeology* 53:88–101.

South, Stanley. 1977. *Method and Theory in Historical Archaeology.* New York: Academic Press.

7

Thinking with Things

One thing almost everyone seems to know about archaeology—except those who think that archaeologists study dinosaurs—is that it involves artifacts. Most people may think, perhaps because of blockbuster movies and thrilling novels, that archaeologists routinely scramble after golden idols and chests full of jewels. Indeed, archaeologists sometimes, though rarely, find such remarkable objects, but in general most of the artifacts archaeologists find, analyze, and interpret are common, everyday objects. And many of these artifacts are broken into fragments. One reality of archaeological research is that mundane artifacts usually provide most of the information available about past daily life. Since most people who have lived on Earth are not wealthy or famous, it follows logically that most archaeological artifacts will be mundane when viewed through the lens of the unique and magnificent.

Artifacts—anything made or modified through human action—are the essence of archaeological research. In fact, it is the discipline's concentration on artifacts (or more broadly, material culture) that makes archaeology a unique field of study unlike any other. Norwegian archaeologist Bjørnar Olsen has described archaeology as "the discipline of things," stating that "things constitute a fundamental and persistent foundation for our existence." Michael Schiffer agrees that "Whether their interests are in prehistoric, historical, industrial, classical, or modern societies, archaeologists are preoccupied with discerning how people and artifacts interact." Accordingly, archaeologists spend most of their time studying artifacts—the physical remains from the past. These objects range in size from the tiniest flint chip to the largest industrial factories.

A curious fact about the artifacts excavated by archaeologists is that in most cases the objects were never intended to be found. A brief comparison with written documents will help explain this idea. When someone sits down to write a letter, compose a report, or record legal information, the composer expects the document to be read and understood by whomever receives it. In many cases, the written material is intended to be saved for posterity. Legal documents are preserved in courthouses, reports are housed in libraries and similar repositories, and personal letters often find themselves curated in archives. Archaeologically discovered artifacts are different because their makers and users treated the objects differently. Chert arrowheads and clay pots were intended to be used and discarded when they were no longer useful. Glass bottles were often thrown away or recycled when their contents were gone. Most people in the past probably never imagined that their castaway objects would interest anyone, much less future scholars. Some artifacts may have been thrown away with the hope that they would never be found. When she excavated a Prohibition-era (1920–1933) speakeasy in Detroit, Michigan, Krysta Ryzewski and her crew discovered a hidden tunnel filled with debris from the period, including liquor bottles. They also found the dirt piled up during the construction of the tunnel!

That artifacts constitute a central topic of archaeological research is thus undeniable. The question, however, is: how do archaeologists know how best to study them? This question has been a central issue for archaeological thinkers since the earliest days of the profession.

The daunting task archaeologists face when attempting to unravel an artifact's past function, cultural meaning, and use can be appreciated by thinking about the artifacts held today by the world's museums. The British Museum in London owns around eight million artifacts, but only displays about 1 percent of them. When we imagine the huge number of artifacts in all the world's museums and add that number to all the artifacts that archaeologists have yet to find, we can grasp the immensity of the difficulty. Given the size and variety of the artifacts from the past—extending from the earliest days of humanity to yesterday—it should come as no surprise that individual archaeologists may interpret artifacts in distinctly different ways.

When opting for one theoretical approach over another, archaeologists must adhere to the principles presented in the earlier chapters. Archaeological interpretations must be based on logic as well as on a detailed knowledge of the cultural and historical contexts of the era under study. The interpretations must be as plausible as possible given the current state of knowledge.

Resolving the most appropriate way to interpret artifacts is the most difficult challenge facing archaeologists. Different perspectives have played a large role in most of the debates within the discipline as the various theoretical camps have staked out their intellectual territory. The debates, though sometimes causing rancor, have advanced archaeological thinking by challenging archaeologists to consider alternate ideas and to ponder new approaches.

The different views expressed by archaeologists are far too immense to present here. As such, the goal of this chapter is to present only five ways that archaeologists have chosen to interpret artifacts. The examples are not necessarily representative of the entire field of archaeology but are only presented to suggest the variety of perspectives archaeologists can use to analyze and interpret the artifacts they have excavated or have studied in existing museum collections. That other archaeologists might choose other examples is perfectly fine, because their selection would further prove that numerous approaches exist within today's professional archaeology.

A CULTURAL SYSTEMS APPROACH

One of the most prominent voices for the creation of processual, or New Archaeology, was Lewis Binford. In a classic study, he argued that archaeologists should use the artifacts they unearth from the soil to explain cultural processes rather than using the artifacts to reconstruct history before the development of writing.

One of Binford's central points was that archaeologists should learn to recognize how the many artifacts within a "cultural system" fit into the various subsystems within that system. He identified three subsystems—technological, social, and ideological—within every cultural system. For him, the archaeological goal should be to determine the roles artifacts played within each subsystem. In this way of thinking, technomic artifacts were those whose primary function was to help people cope with the natural environment. Sociotechnic artifacts were those items like a king's crown that function within the social subsystem, and ideotechnic artifacts were those that work within the ideological realm and appear as symbols, like a clan's motif.

As an example, Binford used artifacts associated with what archaeologists refer to as the Old Copper Complex, a people who lived in the Great Lakes region for thousands of years beginning around 4000 BCE. One of their characteristic cultural features was the use of the region's native copper to fashion axes, spear points, knives, fishhooks, harpoons, and other items.

Binford noted that archaeologists typically viewed the use of native copper in the Great Lakes region as an example of cultural devolution. During the Old Copper Complex's Archaic Period (ca. 4000–500 BCE) the people used native copper to make useful tools, but during the later Early and Middle Woodland eras (ca. 500 BCE–500 CE), they used copper to fashion nonutilitarian objects. Binford observed that archaeologists had often assumed that artifacts primarily functioned as technomic tools, meaning that they helped the people cope with the natural environment. Archaeologists also usually thought that metal tools (in this case made of copper) tended to be more efficient than stone tools. When viewed this way, the production of nonfunctioning objects (like necklaces) may be perceived as nonadaptive (because they don't help people mediate between them and the environment). So, the archaeological idea was that objects having no use in the natural environment was a cultural step backward, even though the claim about the efficiency of metal tools over stone tools was totally based on an assumption. The problem was that archaeologists were seeing the artifacts in one way only.

Binford countered the older interpretation by asking whether copper tools were more efficient than stone or bone tools. After all, most Old Copper artifacts are not found near the sources of native copper, meaning that significant expenditures of time and effort were needed to acquire the raw material, carry it back to the village, and produce a functional or appealing object from a lump of copper.

Binford also questioned why so many copper tools were discovered within burials. For him, the appearance of native copper artifacts in graves indicated a shift in the use of artifacts from the technomic subsystem to the sociotechnic subsystem. He then proposed that the Old Copper people may have established a relationship between social status and artifacts because copper objects found in graves can never have been intended to be functional artifacts. They are no longer available for use once they are buried in the earth. In past societies with differing levels of social status, it seems plausible that some artifacts would have been used to signal social position. In addition, some artifacts might have been used in a purely symbolic manner as ideotechnic artifacts.

Ultimately, Binford observed that thinking about artifacts as positioned within subsystems answered many questions that archaeologists had once posed about the Old Copper Complex. The presence of copper artifacts within burials alone helped to dispel the idea that all Old Copper artifacts were designed and used to help people survive in their environment. It also showed the illogical assumption that the production of artifacts with no practical use in the environment reflected an example of cultural devolution. The way of perceiving artifacts as operating within different spheres of cultural life opened up new lines of inquiry and got archaeologists thinking more broadly and more creatively about the past. Ancient life in the Upper Great Lakes was undoubtedly harsh, but members of the Old Copper Complex undoubtedly were also able to think beyond mere physical survival.

A BEHAVIORAL APPROACH

The behavioral approach for interpreting artifacts is part of a larger program of research termed behavioral archaeology. One of its prominent advocates has been Michael Schiffer.

Behavioral archaeology developed as a refinement of processual archaeology as practiced by people like Lewis Binford. Unlike processual archaeologists, who tend to examine broad-scale cultural patterns, behavioral archaeologists usually take a closer look at the behaviors practiced within cultures. Behavioral archaeologists share with processualists the view that past cultures lived in cultural systems and have as their goal the discovery of laws of human behavior as revealed in archaeological remains. In Schiffer's view, a law is a statement that involves two variables that interact without respect to time or space. Dry grass hit by lightning and bursting into flames might be considered a law because the relationship between the grass and the lightning strike are unaffected by the date or the region; flames are produced when lightning strikes dry grass wherever and whenever it occurs. An important aspect of such laws is that they can be repeatedly tested. In the example above, someone could stand in a dry grass field and wait for lightning to hit the ground and then watch the fire start (although this is not recommended!). Or, a creative scientist could build a device that mimics lightning, take it to a dry field, strike the grass, and observe what happens (this would also probably be a bad idea).

One of the hallmarks of behavioral archaeology is that it includes a special set of terms and several formulas related to the study of artifacts. Behavioral archaeologists perceive artifacts as "distorted reflections" of "the structure of material objects in a past cultural system." This means that the patterning of artifacts in the present (how they appear today when revealed through excavation) may not necessarily reflect their patterning in the past (how they appeared then). This means that the patterning of remains at an archaeological site (where things are found in three-dimensional space) does not perfectly reflect the past activities at the site because of changes in the structure of the "archaeological record"—the material objects, features (pits, postholes, cellars), and residues (including botanical and animal remains) over time. Behavioral archaeologists identify the era in which the artifacts were made and used as the "systemic context" (the sociocultural system in which the artifacts existed) and the artifacts' place of disposal and eventual discovery as the "archeological context."

The differences between an artifact in the systemic context (when it is made and used) and the archaeological context are caused by "transformations." In the jargon of behavioral archaeology, C-transforms are cultural actions such as chipping a stone to make a hand axe or sharpening a stick to make a digging tool. N-transforms are natural processes such as erosion, weathering, and rusting. Behavioral archaeologists maintain that archaeologists must be aware of the roles played by natural action and human activity on archaeologically discovered artifacts in both the systemic and the archaeological contexts. Before the idea of the N-transforms was made explicit, most archaeologists tended to downplay or disregard nature's effects on artifacts as they lay in the ground. Behavioral archaeologists like Schiffer have presented numerous studies demonstrating just how much artifacts could change while lying in the soil. A straightforward example is an iron knife blade. When buried it may have been sharp and shiny, but when excavated many years later, it might be a lump of rust. In addition, all buried archaeological remains are affected by the actions of groundwater, earthworms, roots, and several other natural actions.

To help explain the significance of the systemic and archaeological contexts, Schiffer devised a model (figure 7.1). The model is designed to illustrate how any "durable element" (such as a tangible artifact) can be viewed as involved in certain processes while in use and before being discarded. Using

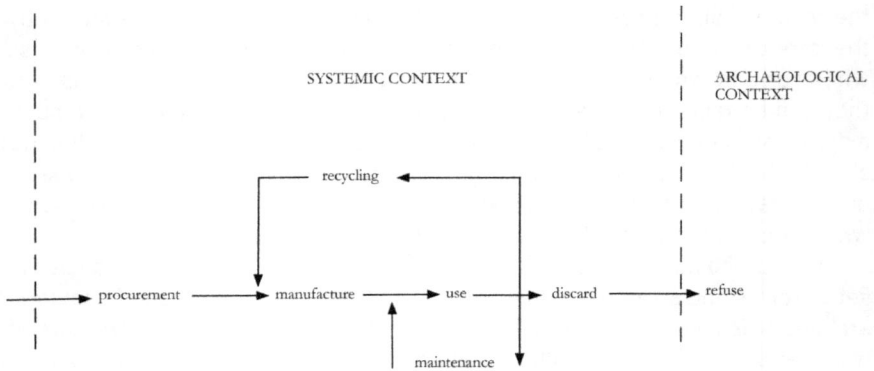

Figure 7.1. Simplified version of Michael Schiffer's Flow Model
Source: *Adapted from Michael B. Schiffer,* Behavioral Archaeology, *New York: Academic Press, 1976, p. 46. Drawing by author.*

a chipped stone tool in the systemic context as an example, the procurement process begins by acquiring chippable rocks from a natural source (like the obsidian needed for making Clovis points). After the raw material is found, an individual manufactures a tool from it, and once finished, the tool is used by someone. (The "someone" could be the person who made it, a person to whom it was given, someone who traded for it, or perhaps even someone who had found it.) During the tool's period of use, its user maintains it in working condition, periodically removing a few flakes from its surface to keep its edge sharp. The tool's user might occasionally decide to recycle it. Perhaps its frequent use as a knife to cut animal hides has reduced its size so much that it can no longer be easily used, so its user decides to return it to the manufacturing stage and reshapes it as an arrowhead. In this new shape, it enters a second stage of usage. Finally, the user discovers that the arrowhead has become cracked and, since it is no longer useful, the user decides to throw it away. The cracked arrowhead then enters the archaeological context where it awaits its eventual discovery by an archaeologist.

This hypothetical example demonstrates that the systemic context is extremely complex because numerous processes may occur during the life of even one stone tool. Every action within the systemic context may result in objects entering the archaeological context. Waste materials might be created from the quarrying activity, obsidian that can no longer yield useful flakes might be tossed aside, and some tools might have been broken during the tool's initial manufacturing.

A distinguishing feature of behavioral archaeology is the attempt to quantify the processes involved in the interaction between artifacts and people in both systemic and archaeological contexts. Behavioral archaeologists like Schiffer maintain that the formulas they devise demonstrate that several quantitative laws already exist and are regularly, albeit unknowingly, in use by archaeologists. They also argue that the act of quantification provides new insights and implications that can further advance archaeological thinking. One of the first formulas Schiffer presented is:

$$T_p = F_p t.$$

The formula means that a given process (p) occurs at a rate (F) and acting through time (t) involves a total number of elements (Tp). Using stone tools as an example, quarrying stones to make tools (p) occurs once every spring (F), and over ten years' time (t), involves the creation of unused flakes, hammerstones (for making flakes from raw chert), broken tools, food remains, campfires, and everything else (Tp).

Given the complexity of daily life even within a small village over time (the systemic context), it is easy to see how numerous formulas may be created to quantify past human behavior. These formulas are intended to replicate the many C-transforms (cultural actions) that might occur in any living society.

Schiffer used chipped stone artifacts excavated from an Ancestral (pre-Spanish-contact) Pueblo site in east-central Arizona to demonstrate his method of analysis. His specific goal was to reconstruct the specific activities related to chipped stone tools, as well as to assess their rates of performance (how many times an activity occurred). As an initial step, he devised a classification of chipped stone tools based on three "dimensions": potential use, manufacturing stage, and raw material. He used raw material as a dimension because two identical stone tools made of different material (obsidian vs. chert) might have been used for different activities.

A feature of behavioral archaeology, like the New Archaeology that preceded it, involves testing hypotheses. Hypothesis testing is, of course, central to the hard sciences. Archaeologists realize that their hypotheses can never be as rigorous as those used by physicists or chemists because of the huge variations in human behavior. People don't act as uniformly or consistently as do the elements. Nevertheless, the use of hypotheses constituted a key characteristic that helped transform archaeology into a more scientific (less speculative) field of study beginning in the late 1960s (see chapter 2).

One of the hypotheses Schiffer sought to answer with his excavated chipped stone collection was the idea that stone tools made from material that is difficult to obtain are used more intensively than tools made of easily accessible material. (Remember, people collected the raw stone material during the procurement process in the systemic context.) He tested this idea by developing an index number from the tools' used edges. His assumption was that a high index number would indicate a high usage of the tool. The stone materials in his collection were chert, quartzite, and chalcedony, with the last being the rarest material. When he examined the results of his test, it was clear to him that the chalcedony tools yielded the highest index value, meaning that they had indeed been used more frequently than either the chert or quartzite tools. Thus, his hypothesis appeared to be confirmed.

Schiffer divided the stone tools into "use-potential categories," and examined four of their attributes: tool size (with the assumption that the larger the tool, the greater its potential uses), the angle of the working edge (because some angles can only be used for a certain range of tasks), specific modifications (meaning that the tools may have been altered for a new use), and degree of modification and finishing (with the idea that tools that have had a great deal of time expended in their manufacture were probably expected to last a long time or were intended for a specific task.) Schiffer examined his chipped-stone tool sample and created a series of complicated flow charts for the four categories of chipped stone artifacts: those modified on one edge only (unifacial retouch), those modified on two edges (bifacial retouch), those modified by use, and those that were unmodified. Schiffer figured that these attributes would allow him to learn more about the systemic context (the cultural situation when the artifacts were in use).

One of the things Schiffer thus needed to know was how long stone tools would last, which he termed "uselife." With his belief in the power of quantification, he decided to calculate the potential uselife of the stone tools found at the site. Based on his findings, and the formula he created for this variable, he determined that a useful chert flake should have a uselife of about eleven days.

A COMMODITIES APPROACH

Commodities are things that have been intentionally made to be sold. Commodities have been around for thousands of years, but with the full development of the Industrial Revolution beginning around 1750, entire factories were involved in the mass production of objects intended for the consumer market. Great Britain was a major manufacturer of commodities, but so was China.

By the thirteenth century, China was on the verge of becoming the world's most powerful nation because it had achieved an unmatched level of technological development, including a vast marketing network. One of their most profitable commodities was blue-and-white porcelain (thus, the origin of the general term "China" to mean ceramics). At first, Chinese factories made porcelain specifically for Muslim buyers, and during the Ming Dynasty (1368–1644), as European nations began their voyages of exploration and colonialism, Portuguese and Dutch consumers increasingly desired the beautiful, exotic plates, bowls, and jars brought home from the East. Seeing the intense demand, Chinese factories shipped hundreds of thousands of porcelain dishes, now called Chinese Export Porcelain, to Europe. The immense volume of ceramics shipped out of Asia can be grasped by understanding that in 1636, six Dutch ships sailed from the port of Batavia in Indonesia carrying 259,000 pieces of porcelain in their holds. Archaeologists who excavate underwater often find huge collections of Chinese export porcelain on ships sunken while engaged in the export trade. As an example, the *Witte Leeuw* (*White Lion*), owned by the Dutch East India Company, sank in 1613 after a battle with the Portuguese. It and an accompanying ship carried over thirty-eight thousand porcelain dishes onboard.

The historical importance of Chinese export porcelain in colonial Australasia led maritime archaeologist Mark Staniforth to wonder about the impact of these commodities on colonial societies. In 1977, SCUBA divers had discovered a shipwreck on the ocean floor off the west coast of Australia lying in around twenty feet of water. Historical research revealed that the ship was the *Sydney Cove* that had sailed from Kolkata (formerly Calcutta), India, and had sunk in 1797 while carrying three chests of "China ware." Its destination had been the British Colony of Port Jackson, New South Wales. The discovery and analysis of the porcelain cargo revealed what had been contained within the three chests. The collection contained twelve sets of toilet wares (wash bowls, chamber pots, water bottles), dinner wares (soup bowls, warming dishes, and at least 182 dinner plates), and tea wares (cups, saucers, tea bowls). Almost all the dishes had been painted by hand with blue pigment and most pieces had been broken during the wrecking of the ship (figure 7.2).

Figure 7.2. Porcelain plates from the Sydney Cove shipwreck
Source: *Image courtesy of the Queen Victoria Museum and Art Gallery, Tasmania.*

Staniforth realized that the porcelain objects, like most commodities that have been sent around the world since the eighteenth century have acquired numerous complex meanings within the cultural contexts of their use. The artifacts begin as simple commodities embedded within capitalist and consumerist environments. Thinking about teacups alone opens up a multicultural, transnational world because tea drinking requires tea and (often) sugar in addition to the cups, saucers, and teapots. In the eighteenth century, the cultivation of tea and sugar involved the enslavement of laborers in Asia and the Americas. Staniforth observed that most archaeologists who find teacups in their excavations often equate the objects with status, such that during colonial times only the wealthy could afford porcelain place settings. Historical records indicate that the *Sydney Cove* carried forty-eight chests of tea in addition to the porcelain. The presence of these chests suggests that Australian settlers continued the eighteenth-century British practice of drinking tea. Staniforth took this idea further and argued that most Westerners had accepted tea drinking by this time, meaning that this pan-European behavior, though locally experienced, was part of an emerging global economy. This is essentially the economy most of us experience today.

Staniforth suggested that Australian settlers made a pragmatic decision to use Chinese export porcelain. The route of the *Sydney Cove* showed that if British merchants were reluctant to ship delicate ceramic articles all the way to the small colony, then the Australian settlers would obtain ceramics from any source, including British merchants living in India. Australians continued to use Chinese porcelain in the colony long after consumers in Great Britain had started using English-made earthenware dishes (often imitations of Chinese porcelain). Rather than reflecting a kind of conservative thinking, Staniforth reasoned that settlers in faraway Australia were probably unaware of the changing ceramic fashions in the homeland. In other words, late eighteenth- and early nineteenth-century Australians continued to rely on trusted commodities.

A SEMIOTICS APPROACH

One of the key characteristics of the postprocessual era (see chapter 2) includes different ways to see material culture. Before the rise of processualism, archaeologists tended to perceive material objects as mute reflections of society. To many of them, a clay pot with lines around the neck was simply an interesting and possibly unique cultural trait. With postprocessualism, archaeologists began to see the rigid hypothesis testing of the processualists and the codification of cultural processes by behavioral archaeologists as overly mechanical. Some believed that the formulas created by behavioral archaeologists, though often profoundly interesting, tended to reduce humans to automatons whose routines were so predicable that a formula could explain them.

In reaction to such perceptions, some archaeologists charted a new path, one that urged their colleagues to envision artifacts as objects actively engaged with the world around them. Rather than perceiving artifacts as mute objects simply put to use, these archaeologists sought to understand how artifacts engaged with people and, in some cases, even influenced human action. According to Robert Preucel, this perspective includes at least three key perspectives. The first perspective involves objectification. This means that when a person makes an artifact, the process of shaping the artifact also creates the person. The manufacture of a chipped stone arrowhead becomes part of its maker's personal history, just as does a work of fine art by a famous artist. This view might even be extended to the act of purchasing things. The saying "The clothes make the person" exemplifies this idea. On a more profound level, this perspective merges dualities like subject and object and individual and society and, in doing so, reflects the interconnected complexities of cultural life, meaning that in the real world it is virtually impossible to separate a person from society or an artifact from its context. A second perspective is materialization. This is a process whereby physical objects are employed to control and manipulate. Monumental architecture, usually massive stone structures like the pyramids of Giza, are symbols intended to project the power and authority (and in many cases, the deity) of the ruling elite. A third perspective relies on an approach called the "social life of things." This is a view that artifacts have biographies, or life histories. An example might be a pair of scissors. When new, the scissors were used as intended, to cut paper or cloth. In middle age, after the screw holding the two pieces together wore out, one blade of the scissors might be used as a letter opener. Now that almost everyone uses email, the old blade becomes a way to prop open a window on a nice spring day. Eventually, the old scissors blade will probably be put in the trash and end its days in a landfill. The scissors, although ordinary, thus has a life history. (Worth noting is that behavioral archaeologists have formulas to replicate the periods of an artifact's life!)

Before delving into archaeological semiotics—the study of signs—some background information will help explain why it was so revolutionary in archaeology. In a much-referenced article published in 1954, distinguished British archaeologist Christopher Hawkes expressed the rationale behind the idea that deciphering past beliefs, such as those that may lie behind signs, may be beyond the archaeologist's grasp. His views were rooted in how archaeologists then conceptualized culture.

Today, most archaeologists view culture as an intricate network of interconnected parts that work together to sustain human life. Some of the components in each culture's network concern economics, some relate to social behavior, and others involve the sacred world. The number of parts depends upon a culture's complexity and population size, but all cultural systems are complicated in their own unique ways.

The network concept is easy for us to grasp today because so much of our daily life revolves around networks and networking. Christopher Hawkes and most of his colleagues living in a precomputer age, however, tended to see culture more like a layer cake than an interconnected network. On the bottom layer were the processes and skills humans needed to master life on Earth. Research on this layer meant that an archaeologist's main task involved figuring out how chipped stone axes and clay pots had helped humans survive during different periods of history. Research often meant spending long hours of boredom measuring the thicknesses of clay potsherds or calculating the cutting angles of sharpened stone knives. Even today, such painstaking analysis lies at the heart of most archaeological research regardless of one's theoretical views (e.g., as can be seen in behavioral archaeology).

Hawkes's next level concerned the connection between subsistence and economics. He said that on this level an archaeologist seeks to tie the information obtained from stone tools, pottery, and other artifacts to their economic purposes. This research might include collaborating with geologists and wildlife biologists because of the natural environment's role in most economic activities. Sitting above the economic layer were the sociopolitical institutions that allowed societies to maintain equilibrium through time. Hawkes argued that if an archaeologist excavated an ancient village and discovered that one hut was bigger than all the others, then it might stand to reason that the society had a social ranking system, one that equated house size with social authority, so that the bigger the house, the greater the residents' influence in society.

In the upper layer of cultural life were religious institutions and spiritual life, the realm of signs. Hawkes believed that deciphering abstract signs and symbols used by a long-deceased culture requires far too much speculation and too many inferences. Researchers know that the greater the number of inferences, the weaker the argument. (Readers will notice that Lewis Binford used Hawkes's model of culture but with newer, more scientific-sounding terms.)

With the arrival of postprocessual archaeology in the 1990s, archaeologists had largely discarded the layer cake model of culture. The use of semiotics was one element of the postprocessual era that openly rejected the idea that understanding ancient signs was beyond the archaeologist's reach.

Semiotics provides an innovative way to envision artifacts as signs. The roots of semiotics lie within linguistics and philosophy, and a central figure in the development of semiotics was American philosopher Charles S. Peirce. Many archaeologists who have employed semiotics in their research have used Peirce's ideas.

Peirce created pragmatism. One thing pragmatists propose is that research into the past can never be divorced from the present. Archaeologists spend their entire professional lives engrossed in studying the past, even though they excavate, classify, and interpret in the present. The questions they ask in their research—regarding race, class, gender, cultural traditions, and many other things—often arise because these issues have significance today. Pragmatism pushes critical reflection to the forefront of archaeologists' minds, forcing them to think about the past, the present, the myriad connections between past and present, and how archaeological research is forever imbedded within its own time. In short, pragmatism is a way of thinking to some purpose.

Peirce worked on the theory of signs throughout his life and created an immense collection of writings in which he performed an in-depth analysis of signs and their meaning. In its simplest sense, a sign is something that stands for something else. A red, octagonal sign in the United States is a good example. Even without the word STOP, we would know that a blank red, octagonal sign signifies "stop." Other countries have adopted the red sign but with their own language for "stop," so that tourists driving around can still know to stop at that point in the road. In this case, the stop sign is literally a sign meaning "stop."

The interpretation of signs is enormously complex because a sign's meaning exists in someone's mind, like Carl Becker's concept of facts (see chapter 4). Three relations must be recognized to understand a sign: the object being referenced (the stop sign), the sign (the requirement to stop), and the person interpreting the sign, called the interpretant (the driver). Going back to the five scholars looking down on the hamburger, fries, and milkshake from their office windows (see chapter 3), we can see that each scholar (the interpretant) sees an object (a hamburger), and from it creates a sign (of exploitation, of the need for instant gratification, and so forth). This example demonstrates the difficulty scholars face when attempting to interpret a sign and its meaning because of the unique perspective each scholar brings ready-made to the situation. The difficulty increases exponentially the further back in time one goes. Controversy accompanies the difficulty of interpretation because of the unique perspective each archaeologist brings to the analysis.

Robert Preucel used Peirce's perspective to interpret pottery used at the community of Kotyiti, New Mexico, a pueblo involved in the 1680 Pueblo Revolt. In August 1680, the Puebloans, along with Navajo (Diné) and Apache allies, staged an armed rebellion with the intent of driving Spanish colonists from their ancestral homeland. The revolt was successful, and the Native peoples involved in it were free of Spanish interference for the next twelve years. Throughout this era and for the next eight years, the Native peoples of the region were free to relocate without Spanish meddling.

Working with a colleague named Patricia Capone, Preucel sought to understand whether the pottery used in the Kotyiti Pueblo reflected the ideology of the revolt. Archaeologists in the American Southwest have long used pottery to identify social groups, population movements, and trade relations, but at the time of Preucel's research they had conducted far fewer studies into past belief systems.

The people who lived at the Kotyiti Pueblo used two main kinds of pottery, a glazed ware and a painted ware in two-color and multicolor varieties.

Pots with two colors were decorated with red, yellow, tan, or white. The multicolor variety is identical to the two-color variety except that the makers of the pottery filled in the empty spaces with red matte paint. The painted wares consisted of a black-on-white version and two multicolor versions. The question that Preucel and Capone had was whether the variations in the designs had any ideological significance.

To assess the ideological role of the pottery, Preucel and Capone conducted an analysis of the design elements found on the pottery sherds. They identified thirty-one designs on 103 pieces of pottery. One of the most common was the "doubleheaded key motif." This is a design that appears on far older pottery, so Preucel and Capone argued that the increased use of the motif during the Pueblo Revolt provided evidence that the potters of Kotyiti (who were women) revived a traditional design while the pueblo was attempting to throw off Spanish influence and revitalize their traditional society. Another popular design was the "hooked triangle." This is also an ancient motif that women potters painted on pottery during the era of rebellion (figure 7.3).

Figure 7.3. Symbols studied by Robert Preucel
Source: *Adapted from Robert W. Preucel,* Archaeological Semiotics, *Malden, MA: Blackwell, 2006, pp. 236–38.*

Potters also used other ancient designs on pottery and even experimented with new designs. A pyramid-shaped design, called the "sacred mountain" motif by Preucel and Capone, is one such design. Another design is the "shield" motif. This design appears to be a reproduction of an actual war shield complete with eagle feathers. The symbolism included in this design is easy to appreciate, given that the Puebloans were in open revolt against the invading Spanish.

Semiotic analysis, although its conclusions are open to interpretation, offers an exciting way for archaeologists to delve into the minds of past peoples. The research is extremely complex, but the intricacies only mirror the complexity of the human mind.

A SOCIAL ACTIVISM APPROACH

In recent years, as the discipline of archaeology became more inclusive and sensitive to the world at large, several archaeologists have begun to think that the connection between the past and the present should become the focus of social action. As Jeremy Sabloff states in *Archaeology Matters*, "archaeologists can play helpful roles in broad, critical issues facing the world today." Sabloff was thinking about the world's major problems like the relationships between climate change and mass migration and the population pressures resulting from the creation of cities, but the logical next step, once the the huge problems facing humanity are recognized, is social activism. In other words, once archaeologists recognize a social problem, what can, or should they do about it? Or is archaeological research strictly an esoteric exercise?

Archaeologists engaged in social activist research argue that archaeological research has tremendous social value. Christopher Barton, in his edited volume, *Trowels in the Trenches*, has made the case that "no matter where in the world, no matter what time period is being studied or what methods are being used, archaeology can be used as social activism." As noted in chapter 2, many of today's archaeologists are using their research to advocate for the disenfranchised and overlooked in history as they actively seek to transform the discipline. Many archaeologists thus see their discipline as a medium for contesting social injustice by bringing to light the often-harsh realities of the past.

Archaeological social activist perspectives can take many forms, but some archaeologists have directed their attention to the use of artifacts for teaching mores and attitudes. Teaching children through play has been an important means of socialization in most of the world's cultures.

To investigate the reproduction of racial and class-based discrimination, Christopher Barton and Kyle Somerville choose to examine toys and games marketed to White American consumers between 1880 to 1930. This period of American history was the Jim Crow era, when African Americans were abominably treated throughout the United States, but particularly in the South. Other peoples—notably Chinese, Native Americans, and Irish—were also widely discriminated against by White America. Toys are an interesting way to investigate racism and class-based prejudice because children learn through play but also because mass consumerism increased during the 1880–1930 era. The mass marketing of racist toys and games is one way to instill racists attitudes in susceptible children.

The methodology Barton and Somerville employed in their study was not archaeological per se, although their focus was on artifacts. They created a database of 103 toys from antique collector websites, advertisements, patent records, and museum collections. They focused their attention on cast-iron mechanical banks, toys widely available during the late nineteenth and early twentieth centuries. During their era of study, only a few companies—mostly in New York, Connecticut, and Pennsylvania—made mechanical banks. The general way that banks worked was that a child would put a coin in, for example, a dog's mouth, press a button, and the dog would leap forward, pushing the coin into the bank's slot. Some banks were made in harmless ways, but a surprisingly large number were fashioned into racist images.

Irish and Chinese immigrants were caricatured as racist figures in some banks because many White Americans perceived them as laborers who were willing to work for lower wages than Whites were willing to accept. Makers of mechanical banks were willing to use such images to promote sales. In 1882, the J. and E. Stevens Company of Cromwell, Connecticut, produced a mechanical bank called "Paddy and the Pig." At the time, non-Irish Americans often indiscriminately referred to all Irishmen as "Paddy," and the face of the man on the bank, who holds a pig in his lap, has the appearance of a monkey, a common racist caricature of the Irish in the nineteenth century. Chinese immigrants in the United States also faced tremendous levels of discrimination, with one prominent slogan being that Chinese immigration must be stopped "by the ballot or the bullet." Playing on this theme, the Ives Company of Bridgeport, Connecticut, sold a "Chinese must go" cap pistol in the late 1870s. Such toys were commonplace, but those caricaturing African Americans were especially widespread.

Of the 103 toys in the sample amassed by Barton and Somerville, over 80 percent depicted African Americans. Ten of the toys showed African Americans as menial laborers, such as porters, washerwomen, and sharecroppers. One such toy was "Tip the Bell Boy," a game where the young man was shown as a racist caricature. The goal of the game was to shoot a ball into one of the two trays the bell boy holds. In another toy, called "Old Nurse," a stereotypic racist figure of a Black nanny holds a White child in her arms. The description of the toy in the promotional ad calls it "comical," a racist way some Whites used to refer to the "childlike" characters of African Americans. Many of the toys depicting African Americans in racist ways were made to dance or play fiddles or banjos.

Many African American figures were used in mechanical banks. One example was called "Always Did 'Spise a Mule." Marketed as "most amusing," this cast-iron bank showed an African American riding on a mule. When a coin was put in the mouth of the rider and a spring was touched, the mule would kick, the rider would be flung over its head, and the coin would be deposited into the bank's slot. The rider's head would then strike the ground. The advertisements for almost all of these toys used racist language wholly unacceptable today.

One goal of studying racist toys is not to glorify them or to shock the contemporary senses. Rather, the idea of bringing them to light is to show the harm they could do and to ensure that such toys are never again available. Another goal is to highlight the idea that artifacts—in this case toys and games—are not necessarily neutral. They can be made to promote and to sustain biased views. Toys are powerful tools, artifacts that contain messages as culturally embedded as the Kotyiti motifs examined by Preucel and Capone. Social scientists have long known that the home is a central place for learning and personal growth. Children learn attitudes and worldviews from those around them, and toys with racially motivated themes are designed to teach racial perspectives. As Barton and Somerville note, mechanical banks and other toys are one way to observe the socialization process of children living in an environment where White supremacy is a theme. They recognize that studying racism in toys is a small example of social activism, but what their study demonstrates is that artifacts contain messages, and that one goal of archaeological activism is to highlight these messages and to correct them.

★　★　★

This chapter demonstrates that archaeologists have used numerous ways to analyze and interpret artifacts. As is true in most disciplines, older views get replaced by younger, more innovative ways of understanding. Archaeologists use artifacts as one of the most accessible ways to investigate the past, so it is inevitable that ways of interpretation will continue to change with time. The creation of innovative, new ways to analyze and interpret archaeological remains helps keep the discipline fresh and exciting.

SOURCES FOR CONTINUED READING

Barton, Christopher P., ed. 2021. *Trowels in the Trenches: Archaeology as Social Action.* Gainesville: University Press of Florida.

Barton, Christopher P. and Kyle Somerville. 2012. "Play Things: Children's Racialized Mechanical Banks and Toys, 1880–1930." *International Journal of Historical Archaeology* 16:47–85.

Binford, Lewis R. 1962. "Archaeology as Anthropology." *American Antiquity* 28:217–25.

Fischell, Rosalind. 1987. *Blue and White China: Origins, Western Influences.* Boston: Little, Brown.

Hawkes, Christopher. 1954. "Archaeology Theory and Method: Some Suggestions from the Old World." *American Anthropologist* 56:155–68.

Olsen, Bjørnar. 2010. *In Defense of Things: Archaeology and the Ontology of Objects.* Lanham, MD: AltaMira.

Pijl-Ketel, C.L. van der. 1982. *The Ceramic Load of the "Witte Leeuw" (1613).* Amsterdam: Rijksmuseum.

Preucel, Robert W. 2006. *Archaeological Semiotics.* Malden, MA: Blackwell.

Ryzewski, Krysta. 2022. *Detroit Remains: Archaeology and Community Stories of Six Legendary Places.* Tuscaloosa: University of Alabama Press.

Sabloff, Jeremy A. 2008. *Archaeology Matters: Action Archaeology in the Modern World.* Walnut Creek, CA: Left Coast Press.

Schiffer, Michael Brian. 1976. *Behavioral Archaeology.* New York: Academic.

Schiffer, Michael Brian with Andrea R. Miller. 1999. *The Material Life of Human Beings: Artifacts, Behavior, and Communication.* London: Routledge.

Staniforth, Mark. 2003. *Material Culture and Consumer Society: Dependent Colonies in Colonial Australia.* New York: Kluwer Academic/Plenum.

8

Deceitful Archaeological Thinking

Throughout this book, I have stressed the importance of critical thinking in archaeological research. One of the prime reasons why archaeologists must frame plausible interpretations stems from the difficulty of understanding another culture, especially one that existed in the past and is no longer available for direct observation. Interpreting the past from the remains left behind contains numerous pitfalls, but what happens when thinking about the past is consciously clouded by prejudice and the willful misuse of archaeological information?

Today's professional archaeologists understand the power of the past to influence the present, and as a result, they appreciate their responsibilities to the present. In 1984, prominent Canadian archaeologist Bruce Trigger observed that archaeological research can generate passionate responses from people. An example is the ancient alien theorists' impassioned claims that professional archaeologists nefariously hide evidence of past extraterrestrial contact from the public.

To make a point that deceitful archaeology can be performed even by professional archaeologists, Trigger identified three types of what he termed "alternative archaeology." Each one can pervert the way that an archaeologist interprets the past. Trigger's first type was nationalist archaeology. He noted that most archaeological traditions are nationalistic, or at least started that way. Much of the early archaeology performed by eighteenth-century British scholars, for example, was designed to glorify a past that was often overly romanticized. Early research into the history of King Arthur falls under this category. Nationalist archaeology could also be used to identify an ancient homeland in another country to stake a claim on its territory. Colonialist archaeology, Trigger's second type of alternative archaeology, occurred in places where European settlement had replaced or overwhelmed an Indigenous population. A key feature of this kind of archaeology is that its practitioners have no historical connection to the archaeological cultures under study. Another feature of colonialist archaeology is that because the archaeologists belong to the conquering culture, they have no reason to praise Indigenous history. The history of American archaeology provides an example of this archaeology (see chapter 2). Imperialist archaeology, Trigger's final type, occurs when one nation-state is powerful enough to exert its cultural, political, and economic wishes on a smaller, less powerful state. Colonialist and imperialist archaeologies can be linked, such that the former appears first. As the power of the colonialist state grows, the archaeology may become increasingly imperialist in design. Imperialist archaeology would become worldwide if its advocates claimed that its approaches and perspectives are the preferred way that all archaeology should be practiced. Trigger notes that the New Archaeology (see chapter 2) can be perceived as an archaeological expression of post–Second World War American imperialism because it sought to downplay cultural histories in favor of broad-based generalizations about humanity.

More recently, some archaeologists, linking Trigger's three kinds of alternative archaeology with the continuation of racism in society, have argued for the need to erase racism from archaeological practice and interpretation. Maria Franklin and three colleagues have urged archaeologists to follow the lead of the Society of Black Archaeologists and to remove all traces of anti-Blackness and racism from the field. American archaeologists now recognize that racist thinking has been a significant problem since the earliest days of archaeological thinking, going back as far as the "Moundbuilders," when White Americans simply could not imagine that the ancestors of the Indigenous Americans around them were responsible for constructing the mounds (see chapter 2). Even today, pseudo-archaeologists regularly recycle a century's-old claim that the builders of America's mounds were Egyptians, early Christians, or some other Old World people.

Today's professional archaeologists are extremely mindful of their responsibilities to interpret the past as fairly as possible without relying on outmoded, biased, and even racist thinking. Unfortunately, the same cannot be said for much of the pseudo-archaeology that appears in websites and on television. Most of the time, careful critical thinking can expose the undercurrent of racism that is contained within these pseudoscientific programs.

Articles and books about Atlantis, the world's most fabled lost continent, offers an example of how racist ideas can be quietly inserted into the outlandish interpretations of pseudo-archaeologists. In one well-known case, American psychic Edgar Cayce learned through his many trances that two races had developed on Atlantis from the original five. With the destruction of the island, one of the races (the spiritual and creative one) traveled to Egypt and established the famous library at Alexandria. The other race (the self-centered and materialistic one) journeyed to North and Central America, just those places that the Mayas and the builders of earthen mounds had lived. Later, English occultist Murry Hope transformed Cayce's races into a triad that included a "red or copper-skinned people" that were like Native Americans, a shorter,

Figure 8.1. Gate of the Sun, Tiahuanaco, Bolivia
Source: *Public domain image, Wikimedia Commons.*

dark-haired people, and a "tall, white, gentle, bearded" people who were "the bringers of knowledge, law, science, and medicine." Such views reached a new level of absurdity in the hands of David Hatcher Childress, one of today's most vocal pseudo-archaeologists. He argued, without any evidence, that the ancient site of Tiahuanaco, in today's Bolivia, could only have been built by the "Atlantean League," a cadre of seafarers who "sailed the world spreading a megalithic culture and wore red turbans over their blond hair" (figure 8.1).

The racial element in these accounts is obvious—and wholly unnecessary. Plato is the only original source for the Atlantis tale, which he wrote around 355 BCE. Everyone who has written about the fabled lost island ever since, and has expanded on what Plato wrote, is quite simply making it up. Plato never mentioned different skin colors, blond hair, or an Atlantean League. All of this nonsense came much later than Plato and is pure fiction. Scholars today disagree whether Atlantis was a real place or whether Plato was using the story as a morality tale. Worth noting, though, is that even Plato's students didn't think Atlantis was real. (Interestingly, another "lost continent," Mu, created in the mind of James Churchward, is almost an exact duplicate of Atlantis, including its racial aspects. The only difference is that Mu was located in the Pacific Ocean.)

Pseudo-archaeologists are of course free to make up whatever fantasies they wish, just like novelists. The problem is that when we read a novel, we know the story originated in the author's imagination. The stories presented

Deceitful Archaeological Thinking 135

by pseudo-archaeologists often ring true because they rely on actual archae-ological sites and artifacts, even though their fantastical interpretations come from their imaginations.

Shoddy thinking by pseudo-archaeologists has profound implications for understanding human history because willful distortions can cause significant harm. Many of the most outlandish interpretations—such as the nuclear pyra-mid idea presented in chapter 1—are harmless. The nuclear reactor idea does violence to history to be sure, but information about ancient Egypt is so readily available that anyone can easily discover how professional scholars understand the history of Egypt's many ancient dynasties and the monuments they built. Even the most basic knowledge about ancient Egyptian culture should quickly allow anyone to disregard the nuclear hypothesis as totally unrealistic. Addi-tionally, the idea that some unknown advanced culture made a nuclear pyramid denigrates ancient Egyptian culture because it covertly decrees that the Egyp-tians lacked the intelligence to build a stone pyramid.

Unfortunately, interpretations conducted by individuals not thinking clearly have extended far beyond the world of fringe archaeology. Most professionally trained archaeologists have decided either to ignore pseudo-archaeology alto-gether or have chosen, as I have done in this book, to confront the silliness of their interpretations because of their illogical thinking. This means in a practical way that pseudo-archaeology has no impact on the practice of archaeology or on the history of humanity. The views of pseudo-archaeologists will continue to pervert history and frustrate professional archaeologists, but anyone with a sincere interest in history and archaeology—and who has learned to think to some purpose—will quickly understand the many fallacies in their interpreta-tions and the outlandish nature of their perspectives.

Archaeologists know that their research can have powerful social impli-cations because people with influence have often been able to misrepresent history because of biased, racist, and even bizarre views of the human past. Examples from pseudo-archaeology appear throughout this book because the errors committed by untrained archaeologists are easy to spot, mostly because their interpretations are based on speculation, just like Cayce's pronounce-ments about Atlantis. But more serious interpretations, also using shoddy thinking, also exist. These more developed interpretations of the past, using archaeological findings, have distorted, misrepresented, and ignored important pieces of human history. Even professional archaeologists have been occasion-ally involved in promoting bizarre interpretations.

The most dangerous and poorly thought-out interpretations in archaeol-ogy have been used to silence, erase, or misrepresent the past and its peoples. Some examples rely on fringe ideas, and these can be dismissed without much effort. More dangerous, however, have been the advancement of harmful ideas in professional archaeology, containing ideas and interpretations that were accepted, or at least tolerated, for some time. Without question, ideas, concepts, and interpretations change as new information is made available and this is how good science and scholarship advance. Sadly, the effects caused by damaging distortions of history (or other things for that matter) may last for many years. Here it is useful to recall the internet adage called "Brandolini's Law": "the amount of energy needed to refute bullshit is an order of magnitude bigger than that needed to produce it." Scientists overwhelmingly agree that the effort is worthwhile, even though it may seem like the message is difficult to get through to people.

Two examples will suffice to illustrate the danger of deceitful archaeological thinking. The first comes from a site called Great Zimbabwe, and the second involves the archaeological efforts of German archaeologists during the Nazi era. In both cases, powerful people used distorted thinking to deform history and erase culture. These are extreme examples, but they aptly demonstrate the negative effects that may occur when archaeological thinking is ill-advised and harmful.

GREAT ZIMBABWE AND SILENCING THE AFRICAN PAST

The story of Great Zimbabwe stands as a prominent example in the annals of archaeology on the dangers of misguided archaeological thinking. Located in the Republic of Zimbabwe in southern Africa, Great Zimbabwe is sub-Saharan Africa's largest and arguably its most dramatic ancient site. Zimbabwe means either "houses of stone" or "venerated houses." Both names are accurate.

The site lies among gently rolling hills and is composed of a series of oval-shaped, dry-laid stone walls between four and seventeen feet thick and about thirty-four feet tall at their highest. The site covers almost 198 acres and incorporates a complex of stone walls encircling stone houses, raised platforms, and stairways (figure 8.2). A few nonstone buildings, made from a mixture of clay and fine gravel, appear among the stone structures. Rounded bastions are situated along walls here and there, and some sections have stone slabs arranged in decorative chevron patterns. Narrow alleyways meander between high stone walls. Two spectacular buildings are the Elliptical Building (figure 8.3) and the Conical Tower, a solidly built turret eighteen feet around and thirty feet tall (figure 8.4). Great Zimbabwe is a marvel of architectural engineering, and in 1986 the United Nations recognized it as a World Heritage Site. Archaeologists have determined that the original inhabitants built the site in the ninth century CE, abandoned it in the sixteenth century, and reoccupied parts of it in the nineteenth century.

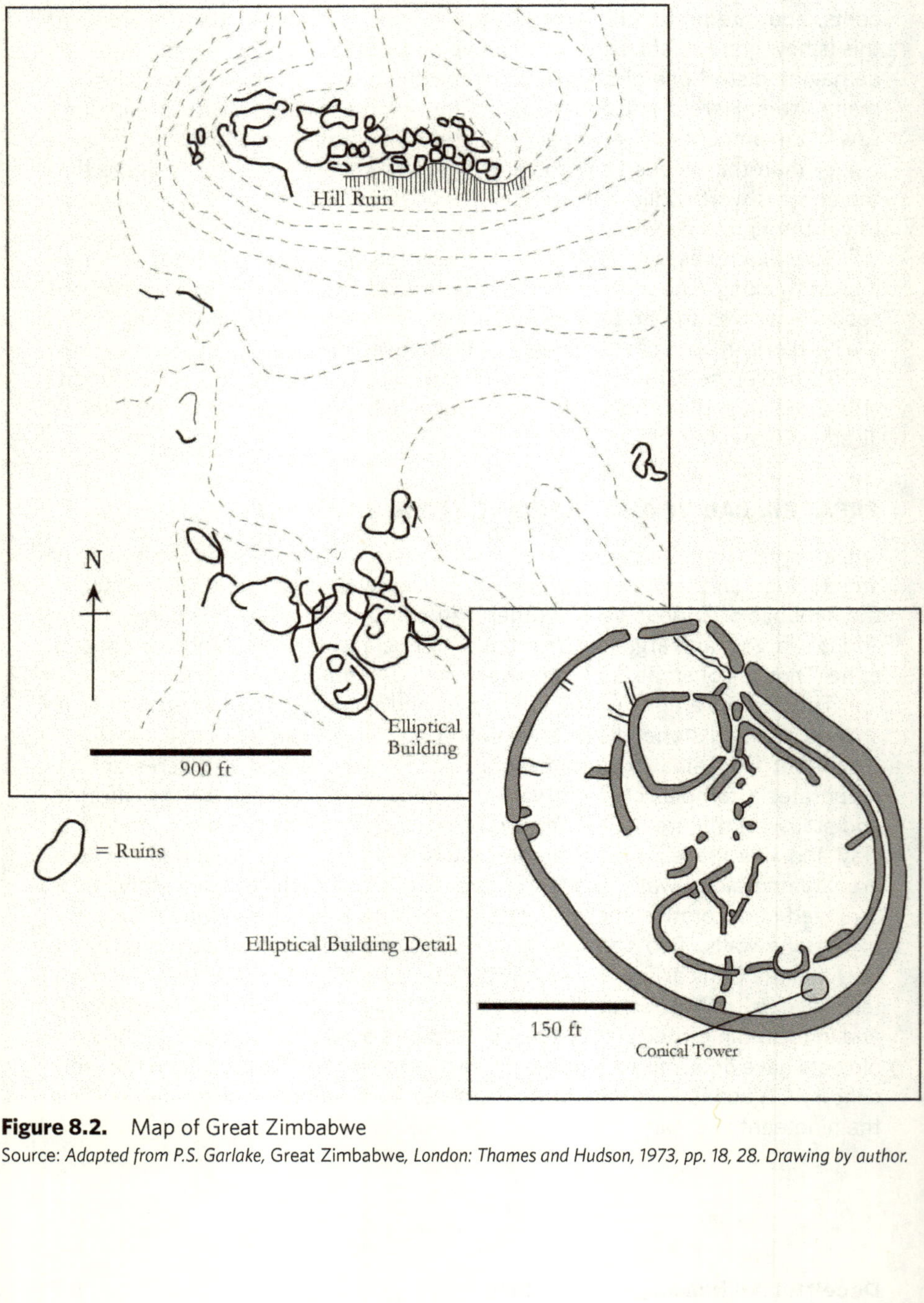
Hill Ruin
N
Elliptical
Building
900 ft
= Ruins
Elliptical Building Detail
150 ft
Conical Tower

Figure 8.2. Map of Great Zimbabwe

Source: *Adapted from P.S. Garlake,* Great Zimbabwe, *London: Thames and Hudson, 1973, pp. 18, 28. Drawing by author.*

Figure 8.3. The Elliptical Building and other ruins at Great Zimbabwe
Source: *Photo by Innocent Pikiyari. Used by permission.*

Figure 8.4. The Conical Tower at Great Zimbabwe
Source: *Photo by Innocent Pikiyari. Used by permission.*

Colonial Portuguese visitors, who were the first Europeans to mention the site in writing, called it a "fortress." Despite its remarkable appearance, they showed little interest in it. The site's archaeological history began in September 1890 with the occupation of the region by Cecil Rhodes's powerful British South Africa Company. Rhodes was an immensely wealthy mining tycoon as well as a committed advocate for the British Empire. Thus, he was prepared to do whatever he could to advance the empire's aspirations in southern Africa, including promoting White supremacy. The colonization of the region was designed, first and foremost, to extract the region's mineral wealth for the benefit of Rhodes's company. The cultural heritage of the region was not Rhodes's concern unless it suited his larger aims. Being an extremely powerful person, he was able to shape the region's history and archaeology to suit his personal taste. He began with Great Zimbabwe.

About twenty years before Rhodes had arrived in the region, a German geologist had located the massive archaeological site. He was amazed by what he saw but knowing nothing about the history of the region and its people, decided after some reflection that the site must be related to the Phoenicians, the Queen of Sheba, and King Solomon. He believed that black-skinned Africans had nothing to do with its construction, although he admitted that they may have visited the place after its exotic builders had abandoned it. From the very beginning, then, Europeans associated the impressive site with nonlocal people. These observers made the same error as the early scholars who equated the earthen mounds of the eastern United States with the Lost Tribes of Israel, the Phoenicians, and others from outside North America (see chapter 2). In both cases, the interpreters assumed that Indigenous people, were racially inferior to White Europeans and could not build complex structures. Even if non-Europeans had the knowledge, these biased thinkers figured that Native leaders would never have been powerful enough to encourage or coerce large numbers of people to spend time building massive structures. The reasoning behind this belief lay in the racist view that people of color are inherently lazy and uncreative.

Biased observers visiting Great Zimbabwe soon compared the site's Elliptical Building with a seventh-century temple associated with the Queen of Sheba in Yemen. Others observed that the chevron pattern on the walls was like a pattern found on a Roman coin. Thinking that such similarities must reflect cultural association, they made the mistake of equating similar-looking things to one producer rather than imagining that individuals in two cultures can have the same idea without being in contact with one another. Pseudo-archaeologists make the same blunder when they equate the pyramids of Egypt with those in Mesoamerica, similarities between unrelated languages, and ancient artifacts with modern-day objects. Similarity in appearance does not imply a connection in history.

By the time Rhodes appeared in the region, archaeologists had generally decided that the Phoenicians had nothing to do with the site, but many held on to the idea that Great Zimbabwe must be connected to Biblical history. In fact, in 1905, R.N. Hall—who spent two and a half years exploring the site—proposed that the Conical Tower was "the truest evidence of Baal worship." Baal was a pagan god mentioned in the Bible. The Biblical association of the majestic ancient site fit Rhodes's colonialist plans perfectly because it removed the site from local African history and placed it squarely within the Judeo-Christian tradition. The speculative history created a veneer of fantasy that reinforced the Europeans' colonial designs for the African continent.

When professional archaeologists began to excavate Great Zimbabwe in the mid-twentieth century, it was clear to them that the builders and inhabitants of the buildings were a succession of Indigenous peoples. These cultures needed no help from the Phoenicians, the Queen of Sheba, or even wise King Solomon. Excavations revealed a sequence of five periods of occupation extending from about the eleventh to the sixteenth centuries CE, with some deposits being both earlier and later in date. Archaeologists used standard methods of analysis to provide detailed chronologies of the site's pottery, architecture, and soil layers. Their research provided concrete evidence that the history of the peoples who built, inhabited, and finally left the site composed a rich cultural mosaic that was purely African.

The Indigenous peoples living on the Zimbabwe Plateau, the location of Great Zimbabwe, moved and migrated during the sixteenth to the nineteenth centuries. The histories of some of the cultures in the region are poorly documented, but an examination of the artifacts found at Great Zimbabwe testify to the presence of residents at the site in the nineteenth century.

Clan members in the region today still resent the Europeans' desecration of the site that began in the late nineteenth century. They do not distinguish between the treasure hunting escapades of the early European visitors from the more scientific excavations of trained archaeologists. For them, both sets of investigators have disrespected the spirits who inhabit the site. Area residents also criticize the efforts of site managers to protect the World Heritage Site by having constructed a protective fence and by controlling the practice of ceremonies at the site. They also resent the government's management of the site as if it were a business. Tension thus exists between those striving to protect Great Zimbabwe as an archaeological site with worldwide significance and local clan members who continue to lay claim to the site and consider it a sacred landscape. The focus on Great Zimbabwe as an ancient site whose history effectively ends with the site's abandonment has eliminated its post-sixteenth-century history, and silenced the clans' voices.

The interpretation that non-Africans built Great Zimbabwe is an example of biased, racist thinking. It privileges the aspirations and hopes of a foreign power over those of the local people, and thus stands as an example of Trigger's imperialist archaeology. Fueled by speculation and wishful thinking, the prejudiced interpretation silenced what might have been learned about the site's past actuality and created a false chronicle of the region's cultural history. Late nineteenth-and early twentieth-century scholars might have explored the true history of Great Zimbabwe if Rhodes had not had total control over the country that would soon bear his name, Rhodesia. The non-African interpretation suited his colonialist needs, and scholars who sought access to the site and the funds to study it, would have found it difficult (and probably impossible) to challenge the interpretation Rhodes preferred. In fact, R.N. Hall said that the government of Rhodesia had given him the "privilege to explore the Great Zimbabwe" when he really meant that the privilege had been granted by Rhodes himself.

The claim that foreigners created Great Zimbabwe rests on two faulty assumptions:

1. that Africa had no history of its own that did not include Europeans, and
2. that Sub-Saharan Africans could never have built the magnificent site.

Misguided scholars have advanced this kind of biased thinking for many years whenever spectacular archaeological sites have been discovered. The controversy over the construction of America's earthen mounds exactly duplicates the controversy over the origin of Great Zimbabwe. In neither case did a real controversy exist: the nonlocal builders identified by early scholars—whether Israelites, Phoenicians, Egyptians, or Tartars—never had anything to do with the structures in question. As is true of Great Zimbabwe, the only mysteries revolve around how the people built the structures, how they lived there and for how long, and what happened to them after they abandoned the site. These questions require dedicated research and serious archaeological thinking. Speculation and guesswork only cloud the issue and delude the public.

Unsurprisingly, a site like Great Zimbabwe—with its unique architecture and long history—has challenged the interpretive talents of many professional archaeologists. Once they had righted the history of the site once and for all, the people of Zimbabwe adopted it as a national symbol. The Conical Tower appears in the Republic's National Coat of Arms. The use of this ancient archaeological site as a visible symbol of national pride demonstrates how thinking to some purpose in archaeology can impact the contemporary world. Archaeological interpretations, which exist in the present, are not for archaeologists alone.

PSEUDO-ARCHAEOLOGY IN NAZI HANDS

You might be surprised to learn that some of what you've seen in the Indiana Jones movies has a kernel of truth. Stripped of its cinematic effects, heroic deeds, and story arc, the movies offer two insights about archaeological history. The first is that some archaeologists in the past really did act like Indiana Jones, and the second echo of truth is that Nazi archaeologists really did send expeditions of archaeologists in search of the Holy Grail. They also dispatched an expedition to Tibet to discover the birthplace of the Aryans (whose leader Brad Pitt portrayed in *Seven Years in Tibet*).

The history of archaeology has included several remarkable characters, each or all of whom could have served as a model for Indiana Jones. One was Giovanni Battista Belzoni, born in 1778 in Padua, Italy, the son of a barber. His six-feet, six-inch height allowed him to get parts in several London theater productions, and at one time he was known as the "Patagonian Sampson." His archaeological interests developed when he traveled to Egypt in 1815. He rambled through the region for the next several years and became an avid artifact collector who hoped to use the sale of antiquities to acquire financial independence. When he returned to London in 1819, he opened an exhibition of his Egyptian artifacts. Today's archaeologists have an uneasy relationship with Belzoni's exploits. Some view him as a plunderer and dealer of stolen, ancient treasures, but others see him as the founder of Egyptian archaeology. In truth, both perspectives are true.

Another possible model for Indiana Jones is Hiram Bingham. Bingham, born in the United States in 1875, could rely on his social connections rather than on his height, as Belzoni had to do. Bingham at times was a writer, a professor at Yale University, a pilot, and a US senator. As the leader of the Yale Peruvian Expedition of 1911–1915 (cosponsored by the National Geographic Society), he and his team found Machu Picchu, the magnificent Inca settlement high in the Andes. (In truth, Indigenous guides, who had always known about the site, led him to it.) At the time of the expedition, America's elite universities were scrambling for primacy in South American archaeology, so Bingham's "discovery" was a definite plus for Yale's archaeological reputation. Like Indiana Jones, Bingham's exploits found him slashing through dense jungles while trying to decipher faded maps. Bingham and his party removed over four thousand artifacts from Machu Picchu, including mummies. Taking the material was highly controversial because in the late nineteenth century, Peru had enacted a Supreme Decree that forbade defacing and removing objects from its historical properties and archaeological sites. Article 6 of the decree specifically states that any objects found at archaeological sites are national monuments belonging to the Peruvian people. Peru sued Yale over the return of the artifacts and in 2011, the university and Peru signed an agreement stating that the university would return a large collection of artifacts taken from Machu Picchu. In addition, the university agreed to work with the Universidad Nacional de San Antonio Abad del Cusco, in Cusco, to establish a joint center where the artifacts would be conserved, studied, and displayed.

The same year that Bingham was leading the expedition through the underbrush to Machu Picchu, a British aristocrat named Montague Brownslow Parker was entering the Dome of the Rock in Jerusalem. A former captain in the British Army and decorated veteran of the Boer War, Parker had a life-long thirst for adventure. After leaving the army, he had fallen under the influence of Valter H. Juvelius, a Finnish mystic who was in search of the Ark of the Covenant. Using funds obtained from British nobility and American entrepreneurs, Parker led a relic-hunting expedition to the Holy Land. A clairvoyant who knew Juvelius directed Parker to a passage under the Dome of the Rock rumored to contain unimagined riches. A mosque attendant ran screaming into the streets of Jerusalem when he discovered Parker and his English crew hacking away at the holy monument. Parker and his men had to quickly gather their tools and flee without taking any treasure.

The many daring escapades of Parker, Bingham, and Belzoni, though simultaneously remarkable and regrettable, pale in comparison to the archaeology conducted by Nazi archaeologists. In their efforts to exaggerate their findings, they perpetrated the most egregious examples of archaeological fraud ever made. German National Socialists—Nazis—developed a program of archaeological research that consciously set out to promote their brand of counterfeit history with accounts purposefully created to demonstrate Germanic greatness. The era of Nazi archaeology is a dark stain on the history of archaeological research.

Many of the men in Nazi leadership positions, including Hitler himself, strongly believed in the occult and the power contained within ancient artifacts. One of the artifacts that captured Hitler's attention was the Holy Lance (also called the Spear of Destiny), the centurion's spear that pierced Christ's side. Hitler was eager to find the spear because legend said that whoever owned it would have untold power. Thus, the spear would aid him in forcing his evil designs on the world. Happily, at least four relics are claimed to be the Holy Lance. Also, the widespread manufacture of "holy relics" during the Middle Ages means that any alleged "Holy Lance" is likely to be a forgery.

Heinrich Himmler, onetime chicken farmer, was one of Hitler's most trusted and dedicated followers, and like Hitler, he strongly believed in mysticism and the occult. He was so fascinated by the Holy Lance that he had a replica made of it. His interests also included the Holy Grail, Atlantis, the history of Germanic symbols, and Germanic folk tales. An early member of the Nazi party, Hitler awarded Himmler with the leadership of the SS (*Schutzstaffel* or protection squadron). Himmler, who believed he was the reincarnation of Saxon King Heinrich I (who ruled 919–936 CE), was the architect of the Nazi archaeological program. Himmler decreed that the crypt of King Heinrich was a national memorial, and at midnight on every July 2 (the day the king died) he would hold a vigil there, hoping to commune with the king. (Himmler also planned to recreate Mjolnir, Thor's hammer, in the belief that it was a superweapon that would help the Nazis conquer the world.)

The SS was small in number when Himmler gained its leadership, but he soon asked Hitler's permission to increase the size of the unit. Hitler agreed and the SS became a large and powerful organization. The SS would become largely responsible for the genocidal murder of millions of victims.

As part of the growth of the SS, in 1935, Himmler created the *SS-Ahnenerbe* (Ancestral Heritage). One of the organization's main tasks was to study German history, which included archaeology. Hitler had little use for archaeology as a research subject, but understanding its value as propaganda, he permitted Himmler to engage in it. (Hitler, a failed artist, admired Greek and Roman art and architecture, and was embarrassed by the "primitive" culture of the ancient Germans.) Himmler truly believed in the theory of German racial superiority, and the archaeologists of *Ahnenerbe* were expected to provide concrete evidence substantiating his interpretation of German greatness. Much of the research required modifying or even falsifying excavated evidence. In addition to their archaeological work, *Ahnenerbe* groups also engaged in looting antiquities and objects of art.

The idea of using archaeology to investigate and substantiate German greatness did not begin with Himmler or even Hitler. The archaeology of German superiority partly began with the ideas of a German scholar named Gustaf Kossinna.

Born in 1858, Kossinna advocated for the ancient greatness of the German people and used archaeology to identify their historic homeland going back as far as the Neolithic period (around 5500 BCE). He declared the ancient Germans to be the most honorable subject for archaeology and criticized his colleagues studying Egyptian, Greek, and Roman archaeology as unpatriotic. Understanding archaeology's political significance, in 1919, after the end of the First World War, he advised the German negotiators at Versailles not to surrender the Danzig (or Polish) Corridor, a disputed land with Polish and German history. He based his reasoning on the presence of ancient "German" sites in the region.

Kossinna identified cultural and ethnic variations found at archaeological sites with racial differences and argued that the Germans' direct ancestors were a blond Nordic (or Aryan) racial group. This view led him to accept the then-current view that some cultures were naturally passive and that others were naturally aggressive. He believed that these supposed biological differences implied superiority and inferiority, such that an aggressive culture could easily acquire the territory of a passive culture. As a result, he envisioned the ancient Indo-Europeans to have been a powerful, aggressive culture that had migrated throughout Europe, conquering the Indigenous inhabitants and forcing them to build the great civilizations of the Middle East, Italy, and Greece. He claimed that the ancestral Germans who had stayed in their ancient homeland had remained genetically pure. As was shown by his advice at Versailles, Kossinna believed that archaeological research could substantiate a nation's historical right to territorial ownership.

Kossinna died in 1931 but in his final years, he showed an increasing interest in the ideology of the Nazi Party. When the Nazis rose to power in 1933, many of his views were inserted into the school curriculum. In May of that year, Wilhelm Frick, the Reich Minister of the Interior, specifically mentioned Kossinna's views and observed that archaeology was "better fitted than any other discipline to counteract the traditional undervaluation of the cultural level of our Germanic forefathers."

One of the goals of the Nazi regime was to replace Germany's Christian practices with an invented pagan religion based on myth and imagination. Arnold cites a pamphlet circulated by the SS in 1937, which made their position on Christianity clear: "What is Christian is not Germanic; what is Germanic is not Christian! Germanic virtues are manly pride, heroic courage, and loyalty—not meekness, repentance, the misery of sin and an afterlife with prayers and psalms." *Ahnenerbe* archaeologists were charged with discovering runic symbols on ancient pottery and other objects to legitimize the long history of this symbolism and its association with the German people. The swastika and the SS lightning bolts are the most well-known symbols adopted by the Nazis. The swastika has a long history, but the two lightning bolts that became the insignia of the SS were fake runes invented in 1902.

The Nazis' research into symbolism, though totally misguided, represents one of their least objectional projects. The use of runes and other seemingly ancient symbols supported the Nazis' plan to invent a tradition, but such practices were not dangerous in and of themselves, even though they certainly came to represent something sinister. Much more injurious was the Nazis' perversion of archaeological research to support their theory of Germanic racial superiority.

The archaeologists who worked for *Ahnenerbe* often conducted respectable, systematic excavations. The problem was not always with their field methods but with their interpretations. As archaeologists working for a fascist regime, they were expected to provide evidence to support Nazi ideology. Nazi propagandists realized that the discovery of Nazi-themed artifacts would help substantiate both their claims of superiority and their right to annex territory that they deemed belonged to an ancient Germanic empire. Providing backup for interpretations resting on faulty, politically preordained thinking required *Ahnenerbe* archaeologists to mold their interpretations to the ideology rather than letting the evidence guide their interpretations. In other words, the archaeologists had already formulated their interpretations before going into the field to excavate. A Nazi archaeologist might conduct a well-run, systematic excavation but then interpret the findings in concert with the mandated racial theory. This is the worst example of deceitful archaeological thinking.

In keeping with the ideology under which they worked, one Nazi archaeologist, while excavating a settlement inhabited by a culture he termed "the battle-axe people," found weapons he decided were for offensive warfare. Having made this interpretation, he then concluded that the love of weapons was a Germanic trait stretching back in time several thousand years. Not finding shields in association with the axes, he next decided that ancient Germans must have had no interest in protective weapons. This must have meant that their fierce, warlike attitude had been conditioned by their German heritage. When he found chain mail and helmets, however, he concluded that these were emblems of rank rather than pieces of defensive armor! The archaeologist simply adapted his interpretation to suit the regime's politics. His obviously skewed interpretation fit perfectly with Germany's offensive wars against its neighbors. He knew before he had even begun the study that he would mold his conclusions to fit Nazi ideology.

In 1941 Himmler saw pictures of what archaeologists then called "Venus figurines." These statues are ancient carvings in wood and bone depicting women with exaggerated breasts, hips, and buttocks (figure 8.5). Archaeologists are still puzzled by these objects, and do not know whether they were intended to be self-portraits, religious objects, pieces of art, or some combination. They do know that they date to the Upper Paleolithic era (about thirty thousand years ago). Today's archaeologists might be puzzled by the meaning of the figurines, but Himmler most certainly was not. Thinking them to be accurate representations of ancient non-Germanic peoples, he concluded that the statues provided support for his thesis of Germanic superiority. Because archaeologists found these figurines beneath more recent "Germanic" deposits, Himmler decided that the objects had been produced by peoples who had been destroyed thousands of years ago by more powerful, racially superior German invaders. He believed the exaggerated features of the women provided tangible proof of the people's racial inferiority.

Using Nazi pseudo-history for support, Himmler argued it was only right that the twentieth-century Germans should conquer the "lesser peoples" who surrounded Germany. He believed archaeology helped to prove that racially superior peoples have always ruled over the less "racially fortunate."

The Nazis often used archaeology to substantiate their dangerous, race-based thinking. Nazi archaeologists started with the proposition that Germans were racially superior to everyone else, then shaped their interpretations around this view. Their program of research turns archaeological thinking on its head because they should have used the tangible archaeological evidence to shape their interpretations. But this, of course, would have violated their warped racial view of the world. They were ideologically unwilling to let the evidence modify or replace their preordained interpretation. Archaeologists who sought to present ideologically free interpretations were dismissed from their positions and not allowed to practice archaeology until after the end of the war and the defeat of the Nazi regime.

The Nazi's pseudo-history was the official history of the German people from 1933 to 1945. The Germanic theory of racial superiority was a "truth" that dare not be denied during those terrible years. Archaeology, manipulated and cheapened, was merely one tool they used to reinforce their brutality and genocide.

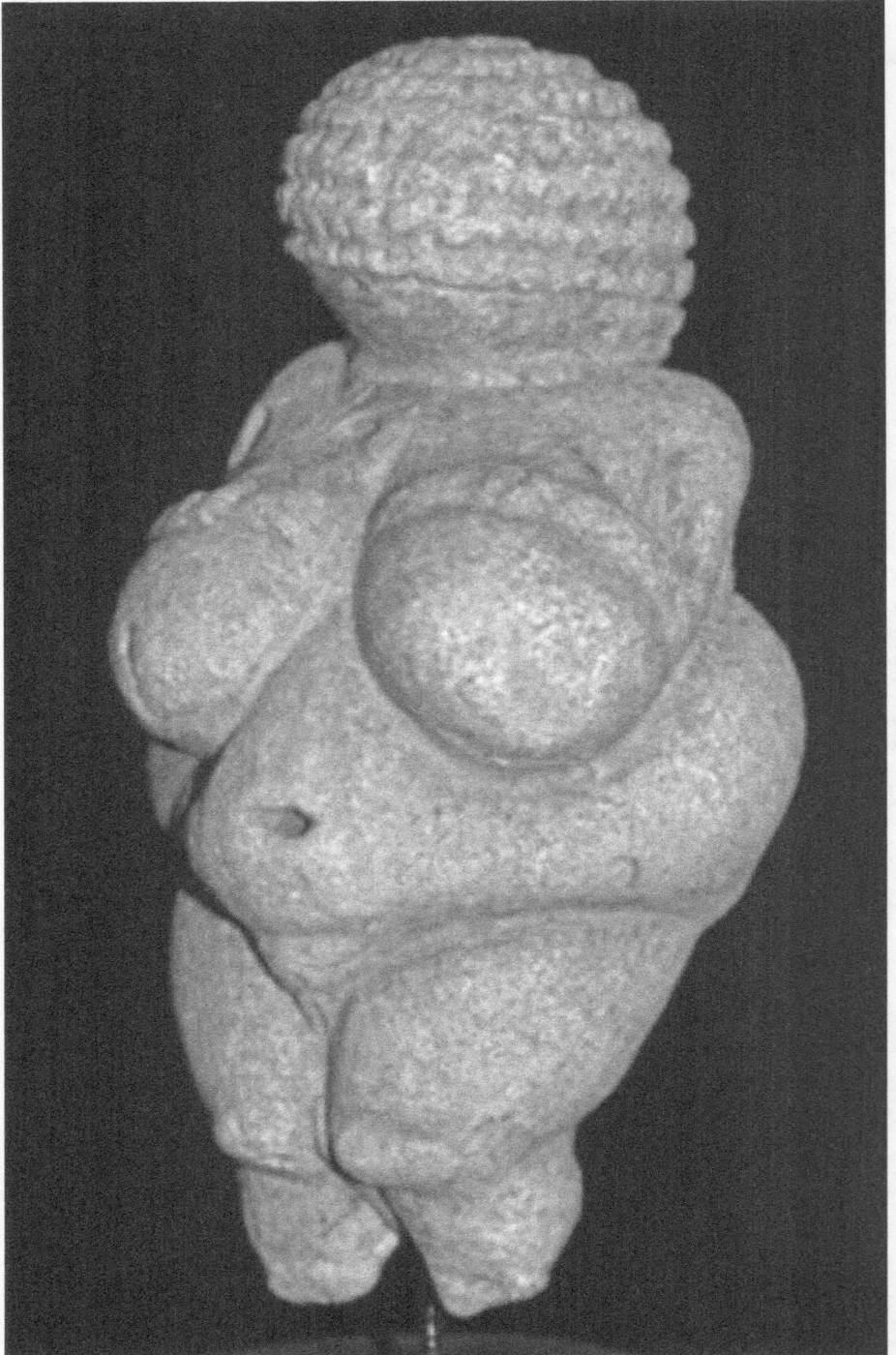

Figure 8.5. The Upper Paleolithic "Venus" of Willendorf in the Natural History Museum, Vienna, Austria

Source: *Photo by Don Hitchcock, donsmaps.com. Used by permission.*

THE DANGERS OF DECEITFUL ARCHAEOLOGICAL THINKING

Archaeological writers have justifiably pointed to Great Zimbabwe and the Nazi's archaeology program as the two most glaring examples of archaeological thinking gone horribly wrong. Archaeological research was used in both cases to falsify the past and to justify discrimination and oppression. In the case of Great Zimbabwe, racist scholars were not able to admit that Indigenous Africans had been responsible for building the impressive walls and buildings. Their acceptance of White supremacy put blinders on their objectivity and the result was the erasure of a significant piece of African history. Only good archaeological thinking was able to right the wrong perpetrated by the biased scholars who looked at Great Zimbabwe and saw the hand of non-Africans. As Joost Fontein writes in his study of the remarkable ruins, by the end of the nineteenth century, accounts of White involvement constituted an important element "feeding a frenzy of European imperial and capitalist discourses and activities in southern Africa." The erasure of African history from the magnificent site by racist writers and visitors, many undoubtedly following the lead of Cecil Rhodes, suited the larger goal of empire and greed.

Nazi archaeology shared many similarities with the early interpretation of Great Zimbabwe because the Nazis, based on their own brand of racism, used archaeological research to erase the history of non-Germans, particularly in Eastern Europe, just those lands they sought to acquire through conquest. The Nazi example is especially horrific because of their party's plan to annihilate an entire people. Archaeology in their hands was a potent political tool they viciously wielded throughout Europe, and one they planned to take to the rest of the world.

One of the key points Jeb Card makes in *Spooky Archaeology* is that much early archaeology had a close relationship to myth and spiritualism, such that some of the earliest research programs were specifically designed to address supernatural questions. The goal of substituting past actuality with false history is obvious at Great Zimbabwe because European visitors to the site, rather than to accept Indigenous involvement, chose to create a mythic past for the site, one that included several peoples from far away. As was true in the early history of American archaeology, all the visitors had to do was to look around them to identify those most responsible for the monuments.

The Nazi case is infinitely troubling because it occurred during an era when archaeology was a well-established discipline. Himmler was a mystic who had no qualms about including the fantastic in his designs for archaeological research. His power and authority meant that he could mandate that his warped view of human history become the official history broadcast to the German people and taught to their children.

Card's point in *Spooky Archaeology* is that professional archaeologists helped overcome their discipline's fascination with the occult, even though the thread of mysticism remains a prominent feature in most pseudo-archaeology. Better-trained archaeologists were able to triumph over the earlier acceptance of a supernatural past by thinking to some purpose, by evaluating the evidence before them and trying to create plausible interpretations from it.

Archaeologists have steadily developed ways to think more profoundly about the past, and the project of refining archaeological thinking continues. One of the most recent and optimistic approaches that have recently come to the forefront of archaeological thinking concerns engaging with and learning from Indigenous peoples and descendant communities. This is the subject of the next chapter.

SOURCES FOR CONTINUED READING

ARCHAEOLOGY

Card, Jeb J. 2018. *Spooky Archaeology: Myth and the Science of the Past*. Albuquerque: University of New Mexico Press.

Fagan, Brian M. 1973. "Belzoni the Plunderer." *Archaeology* 26 (1): 48–51.

Franklin, Maria, Justin P. Dunnavant, Ayana Omilade Flewellen, and Alicia Odewale. 2020. "The Future Is Now: Archaeology and the Eradication of Anti-Blackness." *International Journal of Historical Archaeology* 24:753–66.

Gowlett, J.A.J. 1990. "Indiana Jones: Crusading for Archaeology?" *Antiquity* 64:157.

Heaney, Christopher. 2011. *Cradle of Gold: The Story of Hiram Bingham, a Real-Life Indiana Jones, and the Search for Machu Picchu*. New York: Palgrave Macmillan.

Listing, Rosemary. 2011. "The Treasure Quest: Peru, Machu Picchu, and the Yale Peruvian Expedition of 1911–1916." *Art Antiquity and Law* 16:67–78.

Ryan, Donald P. 1986. "Giovanni Battista Belzoni." *Biblical Archaeologist* 49:133–38.

Salvatore, Ricardo Donato. 2003. "Local versus Imperial Knowledge: Reflections on Hiram Bingham and the Yale Peruvian Expedition." *Nepantla: Views from the South* 4:67–80.

Silberman, Neil Asher. 1982. *Digging for God and Country: Exploration, Archaeology, and the Secret Struggle for the Holy Land, 1799–1917*. New York: Alfred A. Knopf.

Taylor, Kate. 2011. "Yale and Peru Sign an Accord." *New York Times*, February 12, C2.

Trigger, Bruce G. 1984. "Alternative Archaeologies: Nationalist, Colonialist, Imperialist." *Man* 19:355–70.

PSEUDO-ARCHAEOLOGY

Cayce, Hugh L., ed. 1968. *Edgar Cayce on Atlantis.* New York: Warner.

Childress, David Hatcher. 1968. *Lost Cities and Ancient Mysteries of South America*. Stelle: Adventures Unlimited.

Hope, Murry. 1991. *Atlantis: Myth or Reality?* London: Penguin.
Williamson, Phil. 2016. "Take the Time and Effort to Correct Misinformation." *Nature* 540:171, https://doi.org/10.1038/540171; accessed December 2022.

GREAT ZIMBABWE

Chirikure, Shadreck and Innocent Pikirayi. 2008. "Inside and Outside the Dry Stone Walls: Revisiting the Material Culture of Great Zimbabwe." *Antiquity* 82:976–93.
Fontein, Joost. 2006. "Silence, Destruction and Closure at Great Zimbabwe: Local Narratives of Descecration and Alienation." *Journal of Southern African Studies* 32:771–94.
———. 2016. *The Silence of Great Zimbabwe: Contested Landscapes and the Power of Heritage.* Oxford: Routledge.
Garlake, P.S. 1973. *Great Zimbabwe.* London: Thames and Hudson.
Hall, R.N. 1905. "The Great Zimbabwe." *Journal of the Royal African Society* 4:295–300.
Huffman, Thomas N. 2009. "Mapungubwe and Great Zimbabwe: The Origin and Spread of Social Complexity in Southern Africa." *Journal of Anthropological Archaeology* 28:37–54.
Huffman, Thomas N. and J.C. Vogel. 1991. "The Chronology of Great Zimbabwe." *South African Archaeological Bulletin* 46:61–70.
Pikirayi, Innocent. 2013. "Great Zimbabwe in Historical Archaeology: Reconceptualizing Decline, Abandonment, and Reoccupation of an Ancient Polity, A.D. 1450–1900." *Historical Archaeology* 47:26–37.

NAZI ARCHAEOLOGY

Anderson, Ken. 1995. *Hitler and the Occult.* Amherst, NY: Prometheus.
Arnold, Bettina. 2006. "'Arierdämmerung': Race and Archaeology in Nazi Germany." *World Archaeology* 38:8–31.
———. 2006. "Pseudoarchaeology and Nationalism: Essentializing Difference." In *Archaeological Fantasies*, Garrett G. Fagan, ed., pp. 154–79. Oxford: Routledge.
Arnold, Bettina and Henning Hassmann. 1995. "Archaeology in Nazi Germany: The Legacy of the Faustian Bargain." In *Nationalism, Politics, and the Practice of Archaeology*, edited by Philip L. Kohl and Clare Fawcett, pp. 70–81. Cambridge: Cambridge University Press.
Bernbeck, Reinhard. 2018. "An Emerging Archaeology of the Nazi Era." *Annual Reviews of Anthropology* 47:361–76.
Frick, Wilhelm. 1934. "The Teaching of History and Prehistory in Germany." *Nature* 133:298–99.
Klejn, Leo. "Gustaf Kossinna, 1858–1931." In *Encyclopedia of Archaeology: The Great Archaeologists, Volume 1,* Tim Murray, ed., pp. 233–45. Santa Barbara, CA: ABC-CLIO.

McCann, W.J. 1990. "'Volk und Germanentum': The Presentation of the Past in Nazi Germany." In *The Politics of the Past*, edited by Peter Gathercole and David Lowenthal, pp. 74–88. London: Unwin Hyman.

Pollock, Susan and Reinhard Bernbeck. 2016. "The Limits of Experience: Suffering, Nazi Forced Labor Camps, and Archaeology." *Archaeological Papers of the American Anthropological Association* 27:22–39.

Starzmann, Maria Theresia. 2015. "The Materiality of Forced Labor: An Archaeological Exploration of Punishment in Nazi Germany." *International Journal of Historical Archaeology* 19:647–63.

9

Archaeological Thinking in Public

During much of archaeology's history, well-endowed universities, museums, research institutions, and private individuals usually sponsored costly archaeological excavations. In a famous example of personal funding, George Edward Stanhope Molyneux Herbert, the fifth Earl of Carnarvon paid for Howard Carter's world-famous discovery of the tomb of Egyptian King Tutankhamun. Without King Tut, both Carter and Carnarvon would have been minor historical figures because neither man was especially remarkable; it took a long-dead Egyptian pharaoh to make them world famous. In the late nineteenth and early twentieth centuries, most of the elite universities in the United States sponsored archaeological expeditions in Mexico, Central America, Greece, Rome, and the Middle East, all the places that once housed civilizations ruled by ancient elites. The nations in which such excavations occurred often had little say in, or the power to stop or even control, the excavation of archaeological sites or the removal of artifacts by powerful institutions or individuals. As was true of the early diggings at Machu Picchu in Peru (see chapter 8), American and European adventurers could make off with priceless antiquities even if national or local laws had been enacted to ensure that thefts did not occur.

The same class of individuals and institutions who provided funds for archaeological research in the world's "exotic" places also funded research in the United States. The initial excavations at Colonial Williamsburg, Virginia, for example, were largely funded by the Rockefeller family, and Henry Ford sponsored crude excavations at some of the houses he chose to display at Greenfield Village in Dearborn, Michigan. At the time, the role of the United States government in funding archaeological research was extremely limited. Government-sponsored archaeology was conducted by the Bureau of Ethnology (later the Bureau of American Ethnology) beginning in 1879. The Bureau's archaeology was immensely important to the development of American archaeology even though its archaeologists concentrated largely on the American Southwest and the states of the high plains.

In 1906, the US government officially acknowledged its responsibility to the nation's archaeological remains with the passage of the Antiquities Act. The law gave the Department of the Interior, in consultation with the Smithsonian Institution (a governmental institution), the responsibility of managing sites and properties owned by the government. The act applied only to federal land; private property was exempt from the US antiquities law, as it still is today. Further protections for the preservation of archaeological sites followed with the creation of the National Historic Preservation Act of 1966 and with Executive Order 11593 signed in 1971. Section 106 of the Historic Preservation Act changed American archaeology forever because it stipulated that any "federal or federally assisted undertaking in any State" was required to consider the impact of construction on "any district, site, building, structure, or object" that is thought to be eligible to the National Register of Historic Places. The National Register is a state-by-state listing of historic properties and archaeological sites that if damaged or destroyed would adversely affect the nation's understanding and appreciation of its history. Another regulation, 36 CFR Part 60, enacted in 1976, established the nomination process for inclusion in the National Register. In 1979, the passage of the Archaeological Resources Protection Act provided further protections, including law enforcement, for the removal of artifacts from public and Indian land.

The impact of these new laws had an enormous effect on American archaeology because, for one thing, they apply to all construction and land modification projects that use federal money. So, for example, a bank that wanted to construct a new office building in downtown Manhattan, and who used federal monies to help finance it, was required to have archaeologists assess the land prior to construction to determine whether important archaeological remains were hidden below ground. Before the legislation was in place, professional and avocational archaeologists, often assisted by volunteers, might have been allowed to conduct "salvage" or "rescue" excavations at construction sites. In such cases, excavators had to work before the advancing bulldozers. Such excavations were usually conducted as a courtesy and oftentimes the archaeology was rushed and incomplete.

The practical implication of the federal legislation was that the United States would need plenty of archaeologists to conduct excavations prior to the construction or enlargement of office buildings, highways, pipelines, and other efforts involving federal money. It was clear that university and college professors could never fill the need even if their schedules allowed it.

Many archaeologists who supported the federal legislation initially envisioned that research units housed within universities would fill the archaeological need by conducting excavations using students and perhaps a few qualified experts. In this scenario, much of the postexcavation research would be completed by graduate students needing data for their master's theses and doctoral dissertations. This plan worked well in some places, but enterprising professional archaeologists soon realized they could do the archaeological research without university support. The private cultural resource management (CRM) firm was born with this realization. Rather than being employed by universities or museums, consulting archaeologists (called commercial archaeologists in many places) now operated independently, surveying and excavating sites to ensure that federally supported construction projects did not damage or destroy important archaeological sites before they could be examined. By the early decades of the twenty-first century the number of employed archaeologists had risen dramatically because of the needs of CRM. In 2014, Doug Rocks-Macqueen estimated that around 1,630 archaeologists were employed in universities and colleges in the United States, whereas around 7,000 archaeologists were employed by CRM firms. The explosion in archaeological jobs was also felt outside the United States as other countries created or strengthened their antiquities laws. The number of archaeologists in CRM firms in Ireland (where only a handful of academic posts exist) rose precipitously with the economic development boom called the Celtic Tiger (1995–2007), and a report filed in the United Kingdom in 2019 estimated that around 5,300 archaeologists were employed by commercial archaeology firms there. Today, more archaeologists continue to work in CRM companies than in educational institutions. And CRM is not the only place requiring professional archaeologists. The federal legislation has also meant that archaeologists have been employed in state and federal governmental agencies, tribal archaeological offices, planning departments, and other organizations with oversight on federal land, funding, and permitting.

Archaeologists have debated the pros and cons of CRM archaeology since its inception. One positive feature of the legislation is that numerous archaeological sites that may have been otherwise overlooked or ignored have been found, studied, and often saved. The legal requirements have meant that small scatters of ancient chert flakes and small campsites, sometimes viewed as unimportant because of their number, have been examined. The legislation has been especially important for the archaeology of post-Columbian North American history because sites like early twentieth-century farmsteads, nineteenth-century mining camps, and immigrant communities have garnered archaeological attention, often for the first time. Such "unremarkable places" were the living and working spaces of everyday men and women, not the pharaohs and kings that traditionally attracted archaeologists. In the United States, several Native American, African American, and Chinese and Irish immigrant sites have been the subject of study simply because the laws were in place. Another obvious plus is that commercially based archaeology has given individuals the opportunity to use their archaeological education in a work environment. Aspiring archaeologists no longer need a PhD to be a practicing professional.

Some, mostly academic, archaeologists are skeptical of CRM archaeology because of its links to global capitalism and its corporatization of the discipline. These concerns are certainly worth considering. In contrast, other archaeologists argue that irreplaceable pieces of the human story will be lost forever without the hard work and dedication of CRM archaeologists. Such issues have been part of the ongoing dialogue about commercial archaeology and are important for students to appreciate because anyone who continues in archaeology will encounter CRM archaeology at some point in their career.

A key feature of CRM archaeology is that a huge percentage of the funds for conducting archaeological research comes from taxpaying citizens through the federal and sometimes state (provincial in Canada) governments. The transference of archaeological funding from the private institutions and museums to the public sphere has led some archaeologists to use the term "public archaeology" to acknowledge the visible role that the public was now playing in funding archaeological research.

In 1972, Charles R. McGimsey III, the Director of the Arkansas Archaeological Survey and a vocal advocate for the protection of archaeological sites, observed that in the four years between 1960 and 1964, 703,000 acres of land had been stripped in Arkansas without prior archaeological exploration. Extrapolating this figure to the entire United States showed that sites were being destroyed at an alarming rate. Writing in *Public Archaeology*, McGimsey emphasized that "There is no such thing as 'private archaeology'" because the "recovery and study of the past" concerns everyone. He argued that no one has the right to deny the public its right to know the past by damaging or destroying archaeological sites. McGimsey urged that the public must become actively involved in the preservation of the United States' archaeological remains, and he recommended three levels of action. First, citizens must support the archaeological legislation that was then working its way through the government. Second, owners of private property should allow archaeologists to investigate their land before they sell it to developers, and third, the public should educate themselves about the dangers of ill-advised excavation by untrained hobbyists and treasure hunters. McGimsey's primary goal was to stress that the public must become interested in archaeological research and help protect irreplaceable sites.

McGimsey never explained precisely who composed "the public," but the general idea was that it included all nonarchaeologists. With time, however, archaeologists realized that no single "public" exists. Rather, a citizenry as large and diverse as that found in the United States includes several publics, some who love history and wish to protect important sites and properties, but also others who may view archaeology as irrelevant or might even be hostile to it. As Barbara Little noted in 2002, "There is no single public and no single past," meaning that the past, like the present, is immensely complicated. She further optimistically stated that "Members of the public are increasingly aware of the benefits of archaeology, and they are actively involved in guarding those benefits."

Despite the advances made in archaeological funding in the United States, in 2013, two Republican senators argued that the National Science Foundation, the federal agency that awards scientific research funds, must explain to "the public" why they allocate so much money to "questionable" projects when the country faces so many pressing social problems. Five of the nine research programs they highlighted involved archaeology. The senators' opinion might have had a jingoistic element because the projects were located outside the United States, but clearly, not everyone, including some of the nation's lawmakers, was not entirely onboard with McGimsey's plan of action.

The thrust of McGimsey's argument and those of many other archaeologists was that the public should embrace archaeological research because of its inherent importance. From this perspective, the public has an obligation to support the work of archaeologists. But what about archaeologists themselves? What is their responsibility? In the past, it was not uncommon for archaeologists to appear in a town, set up camp, conduct their excavation, and leave town without having much, if any, contact with the town's residents beyond perhaps a landowner and a few shopkeepers. This cavalier attitude toward the living became less sustainable when archaeologists began to think about their responsibilities, especially when they were using taxpayer money. After some reflection, archaeologists had to admit that excavation and interpretation take place in the present and ignoring living people creates what Brian Fagan calls the "arrogant archaeologist." In a similar vein, the great detective writer Agatha Christie had Belgian detective Hercule Poirot, in *Death on the Nile,* describe an archaeologist as "he was all archaeologist, not enough human being."

In the United States, a major impetus for archaeologists to start thinking more critically about their responsibilities came about largely through increased interactions with American Indians. For many years, many archaeologists gave Native Americans little if any thought, believing perhaps that they were too far removed from the past to have any pertinent knowledge about it. This is a continuation of the attitude held by the scholars who debated the origin of the "Moundbuilders" in the nineteenth century (see chapter 2) and still held by many of today's pseudo-archaeologists.

One reason that many archaeologists discounted Native knowledge was that it was handed down orally. Archaeologists often viewed oral information suspiciously because it could not be verified and because it was open to interpretation. By the early 1980s, however, archaeologists were increasingly willing to accept that many Native Americans engaged with their history through oral information and long-held traditions. At the same time, Native American activists were demanding a seat at the archaeological table, and it was becoming clear that archaeologists and members of Native American tribes could work together. In a well-known example, archaeologist Larry Zimmerman had begun collaborating with the Crow Creek Sioux and the Arikaras, as well as members of American Indians Against Desecration (a group seeking the reburial of existing museum collections and a halt to the excavation of Indian gravesites) and the American Indian Movement (a group demanding equal rights for Native

Americans) over the reburial of excavated skeletal remains. At the time, many archaeologists were still "arrogant archaeologists" who saw little use in working with Indigenous individuals and groups, and so were not enthusiastic about including Native Americans in discussions about archaeological remains, even if those remains were the skeletons of their ancestors. Such archaeologists believed they were scientists doing the right thing by collecting, analyzing, and storing human remains, whereas concerned Native Americans viewed archaeologists as defilers and grave robbers who constantly insulted them by tampering with the dead. Archaeologists understand that the past is knowable through the artifacts and other materials left behind at abandoned villages and within graves. Traditional Native Americans know the past spiritually and ritually through their daily existence. Despite the difference in worldviews, American archaeologists found it increasingly difficult to work in isolation from living Native American peoples, especially since so much archaeology was being funded with public, taxpayer money. The only viable option was for archaeologists to collaborate with Native peoples rather than to oppose them.

The dispute between Native Americans and American archaeologists over the deposition of excavated human remains was decided with the passage of the Native American Graves Protection and Repatriation Act of 1990 (NAGPRA). NAGPRA mandates that US museums, universities, and other institutions holding the human remains of Native Americans and their funerary and sacred objects return them to the appropriate Indigenous cultures. The same holds true for skeletal remains and objects found during new archaeological excavations. The passage of the act initially intensified the split within archaeology over the wisdom and desirability of reburial and repatriation, but over time, most archaeologists have accepted that the return of artifacts, sacred objects, and skeletal remains is a human rights issue, one demonstrating that archaeologists can think like sensitive, committed anthropologists rather than as object-obsessed curio collectors. (In another layer of protection, on December 21, 2022, President Biden signed into law the Safeguard Tribal Objects of Patrimony Act [STOP Act] to prohibit the exportation of objects obtained in violation of NAGPRA. As of February 2023, legislation calling for an African American Graves Protection Act is making its way through Congress.)

In the 1990s, two controversial situations involving human skeletal remains changed American archaeology forever and made a dramatic case for collaboration with nonarchaeological communities. The first case, that of Kennewick Man, occurred on the west coast in Washington State, and the second case, that of the African Burial Ground, occurred on the east coast in New York City.

BONES OF CONTENTION

In July 1996, two college students watching a hydroplane race found a human skull that had washed out of the bank of the Columbia River near Kennewick,

Washington. The county coroner collected the skull and several other bones that comprised a nearly complete skeleton. Sensing the bones' antiquity, the coroner took them to archaeologist James Chatters for identification. Chatters was well-versed in the region's archaeology through years of research and when he saw the skull's narrow cheekbones, he assumed that the remains were those of a European settler who arrived in the region either in the eighteenth or nineteenth century. His initial measurements of the bones suggested that the skull was that of a Caucasian male, forty to fifty-five years old when he died. The man had stood about five feet, nine inches tall and was probably right-handed. This all made sense, but one glaring problem cast doubt on Chatters's identification of the "European"—embedded in the skeleton's hip was an arrowhead that archaeologists term a "Cascade point." These chipped stone, lance-shaped points had been made and used by Native American hunters thousands of years before the first European had arrived in the region. Radiocarbon dating of the bones, now called Kennewick Man or the Ancient One, revealed that the skeleton was around nine thousand years old. This date meant that the Kennewick remains were perhaps the oldest near-complete skeleton ever found in North America.

The discovery of the skeleton, and Chatters's attribution that it belonged to a Caucasian, set off a firestorm of media attention. The New Yorker, Discover magazine, U.S. News and World Report, and other prominent media outlets including 60 Minutes played up the idea that Europeans may have discovered America before Native Americans. If true, Kennewick Man would upend everything archaeologists thought they knew about North America's human history. Equally meaningful, Kennewick Man would deny the Native Americans' claims that they were the original settlers of North America. If true, ideologues opposed to Native American rights might claim that Europeans were the first residents of the United States. Conventional history maintains that Europeans, when compared to Native Americans, were relatively recent arrivals in North America. Clearly, the proper identification of Kennewick Man was critically important.

The Army Corps of Engineers, the arm of the federal government with jurisdiction over the riverbed where Kennewick Man was found, seized the skeleton in compliance with NAGPRA. Under the law, governmental agents were required to notify local tribes when suspected human remains were found on federal land. When contacted in August 1996, members of the Nez Perce, Umatilla, Colville, Wanapum, and Yakama tribes claimed Kennewick Man as their ancestor and asked for the return of the bones without further scientific examination. Noting that the skeleton had been found near traditional tribal territory, the Corps of Engineers announced that they would give the remains to the tribes, who would then rebury them with honor. This meant that the bones of a remarkable ancient man would not be available for in-depth scientific study.

Fearing the loss of what they perceived as a highly significant discovery, a group of eight male scholars—professional archaeologists and physical anthropologists (including one from the Smithsonian)—sued the US government claiming that their inability to study the Kennewick Man's remains violated their First Amendment rights. They argued that NAGPRA did not apply because the remains were not those of a Native American. (A pagan group who worshipped Norse gods and goddesses also sued the government arguing that Kennewick Man was one of their Viking ancestors, but this preposterous case went nowhere.) The scientific plaintiffs also claimed that the Corps of Engineers had violated the Civil Rights Act of 1866. This act, an outcome of the Civil War, guaranteed non-Whites the same legal protections as Whites. But if read differently it could be argued that the legislation also gave Whites the same protections as non-Whites. In other words, the scholars claimed that their civil rights were being violated because of their racial identity (they were all non–Native American)

With the courts involved, the Kennewick Man case lumbered on. In 1997, a judge put a hold on the lawsuits and told the Corps of Engineers to rethink its decision about repatriation. Assigning a tribal affiliation to Kennewick Man was the toughest issue because no identifiable artifacts had been found with the bones, except the imbedded arrowhead (which seemed somehow important!). In 2000, the Secretary of the Interior decreed that enough evidence existed to give the tribes the remains, but the presiding judge rejected this decision and said that the scientists' lawsuit could go forward. In August 2002, the judge ruled in favor of the scientists saying that Kennewick Man could be studied. Two months later, the five Native American tribes filed a suit to block the scientific analysis. After a two-year wait, a panel of judges ruled that the tribes had not been able to demonstrate that Kennewick Man was their ancestor, and once again the tribes filed an appeal (which was denied). The archaeologists and physical anthropologists could now begin their study of the bones. Their conclusion was that the skull resembled people from New Zealand or possibly the Ainu of northern Japan, not a European. They conjectured that the Ainu may have reached North America by canoe. In 2015, scientists sequenced Kennewick Man's genome and determined that he was most closely related to today's Native Americans, specifically to the Colville tribe in Washington State (not the Ainu or New Zealanders). After analysis, the tribes received the bones, and the remains were reburied at a secret location. The journey of the Ancient One had finally ended.

Five years before the discovery of Kennewick Man and on the opposite side of the United States, the General Services Administration (GSA) planned to construct a thirty-four-story office building for several federal agencies in lower Manhattan. In keeping with the federal antiquities legislation, archaeologists were hired to investigate the land on which the new building would sit. Their study of an eighteenth-century map revealed that the footprint of the building was in a part of the city that housed tanning yards, a poor house, and a "Negros [sic] Burial Ground." The archaeologists presumed that the cemetery, which was a strip of land enclosing five to six acres, could have once contained around twenty thousand burials of the city's once-enslaved Africans and African Americans. But, according to Ingle, Howson, and Rutsch, because the area had been built over in the nineteenth century with houses having deep basements, the archaeologists concluded that "The construction of deep sub-basements would have obliterated any remains within the lots that fall within the historic bounds of the cemetery." Several of the deep borings they performed at the site supported their assessment that basements had been dug throughout the area. Certainly, they thought, these deep excavations must have uprooted and destroyed the existing burials.

Six weeks before construction at the site was scheduled to begin, the GSA hired archaeologists from a small CRM company to check the lot just in case one or two burials remained. The GSA and everyone else were stunned when the archaeologists discovered dozens of undisturbed graves over the next two months.

After being unearthed, the human remains were removed to Lehman College in the Bronx for study. During the analysis, bioarchaeologists from Howard University in Washington, DC, led by Michael Blakey, questioned the analysts' methods, including that no African Americans were involved in the examination. When they learned about the discovery of the graves, local activists from the city's descendent community held several public meetings to oppose further digging at the property and to demand that all excavated remains be accorded the cultural sensitivity they deserved. The chair of the House of Representatives' Committee on Buildings and Grounds told the GSA that funding for the office building would cease until the controversies swirling around the cemetery were settled. Construction stopped and a larger CRM firm was hired to continue the archaeological excavation. The human remains were transferred to Howard University, an HBCU (Historically Black College or University), where Blakey and his team examined them for the next ten years. In 2004 the remains were respectfully reburied in a ceremony attended by thousands. As Blakey observed, the Howard University effort was profoundly significant because it was "the first major project in which blacks have been able to direct the anthropological study of their early ancestors and to tell the story using bioarchaeological methods." Today, the site of the cemetery, now known as the African Burial Ground, is a National Historic Monument (designated in 2006) (figure 9.1). It is also the resting place of the 419 excavated individuals who were originally interred there.

The controversies over the graves found at the African Burial Ground and Kennewick Man brought home to American archaeologists that archaeology could no longer be viewed as simply about the past. Living peoples—direct descendant communities, affiliated individuals, dedicated scholars, activists, and preservationists—were concerned about the past and committed to having a say in how the human remains of once-living men and women would be handled, analyzed, and interred. Activists' commitment to skeletal remains also includes the repatriation of cultural and sacred objects.

Figure 9.1. African Burial Ground National Historic Monument, New York City
Source: *Public domain image, National Park Service.*

Protests by Native Americans, African Americans, and community activists showed that archaeologists would do well to collaborate with local groups if their discipline was to continue. Thus, by the 2000s, archaeologists were increasingly open to seeing their research projects as collaborative efforts in which nonarchaeologists would play an important role throughout the research process, beginning with the formulation of the research design and continuing to the presentation of the findings. No longer was it going to be possible for archaeologists to ignore those around them. Instead, archaeologists would learn to think differently. Thinking differently changed the power dynamic between archaeologists and communities. Archaeologists could no longer present themselves as oracles of knowledge or as keepers of historical truth. Community members had their own versions of the past, and archaeologists had to take these into account. (This is not to suggest, however, that all interpretations of the past are equally valid. We saw in chapter 1 that some interpretations are speculative and devoid of any evidence whatsoever. All interpretations, regardless of their source, require some form of supporting evidence.)

McGimsey's original concern about how the public could help archaeology had transformed into a concern about how archaeologists could help the public, how they could work with nonarchaeologists to create culturally sensitive and inclusive interpretations of the past. In truth, archaeologists have always collaborated with scholars from different disciplines. Biologists and zoologists have identified ancient plant and animal species, geologists have deciphered ancient landscapes, and historians have provided information on the social contexts of historical epochs. Such scholar-to-scholar collaborations remained firmly fixed within the Ivory Tower. Now archaeologists were being challenged to go outside academia and to consider new collaborations. Many found that applying traditional knowledge and outsider perspectives in equal parts with archaeological evidence created new lines of inquiry.

Two brief case studies will help demonstrate the power of collaboration. In each case, the research benefited from the input of nonarchaeologists.

THE CHEYENNE OUTBREAK OF 1879

In 1867, the US government signed three Medicine Lodge Treaties with American Indian nations, the third of which was with the Cheyenne. Several of the Native leaders who signed the treaty did not understand that one of its conditions was that by signing they had agreed to move from their traditional homeland south to what the United States had designated "Indian Territory" (today's Oklahoma). In early 1872, after learning about the treaty's removal clause, a party of tribal leaders traveled to Washington, DC to inform the government of their intention not to move south. President Grant allowed them to stay where they wished, but with the defeat of General George Custer at the Battle of the Little Bighorn in 1876, the government's position hardened, and the Cheyenne realized that Washington would retaliate and force them into Indian Territory.

Two leaders who had traveled with the party to Washington, Dull Knife and Little Wolf, decided to move with their people into the Big Horn Mountains in Wyoming. When the US Army attacked the band—as retribution for Custer's death and because the band had failed to relocate to the south— many in the band decided to surrender. Under Dull Knife's leadership, they capitulated in April 1877 at Fort Robinson in western Nebraska. After long discussions, the Cheyenne agreed to move to Indian Territory, a journey that took seventy arduous days.

Indian Territory was an unfamiliar place and before long, many Cheyenne were ill or dying. Medical care at the governmental agency where they lived was practically nonexistent and many Cheyenne died during the winter. In 1878, faced with impending sickness, Dull Knife, Little Wolf, and many of their followers fled north to their homeland. The 353 individuals who fled maintained a running battle with the pursuing US cavalry. With their leaders, the followers Dull Knife and Little Wolf decided to split into two groups. Little Wolf's band stopped for the winter in northwestern Nebraska, while Dull Knife and his band decided to go toward Fort Robinson, where they were quickly detained. While at Fort Robinson, Dull Knife's son was found to have left the fort with his wife. Once the pair were captured, they were told that Dull Knife's people would be moved to Indian Territory. Dull Knife flatly refused to go back to the place of such sickness, so in response, the agent in charge decided to cut his rations of food and water. After a few days of privation, Dull Knife's band decided to flee. Sixty-four of the absconding Native Americans were killed by the military, and the rest were captured.

The oral history of the Northern Cheyenne held that the route taken by the escapees was not the one stated in the historical record and supported by White historians. The discrepancy over the route taken by Dull Knife and his followers led representatives of Chief Dull Knife College and the Northern Cheyenne Cultural Committee to collaborate with archaeologists from the University of South Dakota to determined which account was correct. The archaeological research conducted in the late 1980s was supplemented with prayers and storytelling by Cheyenne elders. The archaeologists used a combination of ground surveying, random small excavations, and metal detecting to search for ammunition that had been shot at or by the fleeing Cheyenne. The archaeologists treated all recovered artifacts with the respect expected by the Cheyenne.

The distribution of lead bullets, rifle balls, bullet fragments, and even a small, white, chipped stone arrowhead along the route demonstrated that the Cheyenne's oral tradition was an accurate account of Dull Knife's breakout. The archaeologists found no artifacts within the area claimed by non-Native American historians to be the correct route.

The discovery of the escape route of the Cheyenne in 1879 would have been far less important if it had been conducted without the Cheyenne's traditional history. Archaeologists could have conducted the research independently as a purely research endeavor and reached the same conclusion by examining the location of bullets. In this case, however, they would have had to explain the wide discrepancy between the artifact discoveries and the written documentation. Only by adopting a research design that included the full collaboration of the Northern Cheyenne were archaeologists able to devise the most plausible interpretation of Dull Knife's escape route. Without the help of the Cheyenne, the archaeologists may never have fully appreciated the cultural significance of the breakout's route.

The effort to determine the correct route of the Cheyenne Outbreak of 1879 may appear to be a trivial matter unworthy of archaeological attention. It was merely one small event in the history of US-Native American relations. But if the Cheyenne were to accept the White version of the escape it would mean that Dull Knife made a fatal mistake, one that was totally at odds with how the Cheyenne people understand and venerate him today. The course catalog for Chief Dull Knife College describes Dull Knife as a "respected historical leader of the Northern Cheyenne people," who fought "with great courage and against overwhelming odds" to lead his band back to their homeland and maintain the tribe's sovereignty. They thus see the breakout as an honorable deed that speaks well of Dull Knife's innate wisdom and profound desire to save his people from further humiliation at the hands of the US military. The non-Native American route would have meant that Dull Knife led the band along exposed terrain on a moonlit night. Trees and rocks appear throughout the route accepted by the Cheyenne and verified by the archaeological survey, whereas the historically accepted route is devoid of cover. Exposing himself and others to an attack would have been totally out of character for a respected and thoughtful leader like Dull Knife.

TIMBUCTOO, NEW JERSEY

In 1826, four Black escapees from enslavement in Maryland trekked to south-central New Jersey where they created a settlement they soon called Timbuctoo. The location chosen by the founders had several advantages. First, it was positioned on a part of the Underground Railroad that stretched north from the Slave South all the way across New Jersey and into New York City. This location ensured that other escapees could reach Timbuctoo and find other freedom-seeking women and men. The settlement was also situated on a creek that was large and deep enough to accommodate small boats, meaning that escapees from enslavement could reach Timbuctoo by water in addition to land. The location of the settlement was also close to Mount Holly, a town inhabited by Quakers. The Quakers had a complex association with enslavement, but by the early nineteenth century most of them had concluded that human bondage was incompatible with their Christian beliefs.

The town's advantages meant that the population of Timbuctoo steadily grew. Its residents had indeed found freedom in the North, but they could never ignore or forget the terrible fear that southern slave catchers could arrive at any moment, capture them, and return them to the homes, shops, and plantations of their bondage.

Timbuctoo was plagued with problems throughout the nineteenth century. Racial attitudes and actions by Whites meant that poverty was a constant problem. Educating the young was also challenging. In the late 1890s, the "colored" school in town was in a ramshackle condition and attendance was poor because children had to work to assist their families. The Ku Klux Klan, who was active in the region, provided a visible symbol of the White supremacy that made life at Timbuctoo difficult. The organization had as many as one hundred thousand members statewide.

The population of Timbuctoo slowly dwindled as the nineteenth century continued. Many residents moved away in search of better economic opportunities. Some left to find a more amenable social environment, but others stayed despite everything. Today, several of the residents can trace their ancestry directly to the town's original founders.

Timbuctoo represents just one African American settlement whose residents sought to live on their own terms free of the brutality and humiliation of enslavement. Numerous towns just like Timbuctoo dot the landscape of the northern US states and southern Canada. Each town created by freedom-seeking African Americans is significant because each one tells a unique story of perseverance.

In keeping with the importance of such sites of self-emancipation, in 2009, a group of descendants, community members, and other interested individuals established the Timbuctoo Discovery Project, now called the Timbuctoo Advisory Committee. The committee's chair is a descendant of a settler who arrived in 1829. The committee's task is to advise the local government, the development board, and other municipal agencies on matters concerning the history of the town, including its archaeology. The committee sponsors numerous educational activities including Timbuctoo Day, a day of remembrance that includes inspirational speakers, reenactments, and exhibits.

Archaeological interest in the settlement began in 1999 when an archaeologist with the National Park Service started to gather information about the community. In 2004, the township acquired some of the land on which the town sat and began to discuss archaeological research. In 2009, CRM archaeologists were hired to conduct a survey of the town. They discovered the likely remains of eighteen buildings, five deep shafts (wells, cisterns, or latrines), and three walkways. The Timbuctoo Advisory Committee decided that an archaeological excavation should occur at a place called the Davis property. Historical records indicate that the one-story house that had once stood on the site had been inhabited by one of the town's leaders, but that in 1879, the house and property was sold to William and Rebecca Davis for $2. The members of the Advisory Committee decided to focus on the excavation on this site because it represented a typical homestead at the settlement (figure 9.2). The archaeologists who conducted the excavations decided that all elements of the project from the development of the research design to the dissemination of the results would be a collaborative effort that included members of the community as full partners.

The excavation yielded over fifteen thousand artifacts, with the earliest objects dating to the 1850–1869 period. The most recent artifact dates to the 1950s. Artifacts collected from a midden (a clustered scatter of artifacts strewn across the ground) date from the 1910s to the 1940s. The analysis of this material substantiated that the residents of Timbuctoo lived in a state of poverty.

One of the findings that was particularly telling was the discovery of glassware used for home canning. The rural setting of Timbuctoo made gardens and the preservation of foodstuffs possible. In times of war and economic depression, the US government often promotes canning as a patriotic action, but for members of Black communities like Timbuctoo canning was a way to outwit the racism they might have experienced in White-owned shops. Canning their own homegrown vegetables was a form of survival, but one that included an element of resistance.

Figure 9.2. Excavation of Davis House at Timbuctoo, New Jersey
Source: *Courtesy of Christopher Barton, Francis Marion University.*

*   *   *

Archaeologists have come to understand the importance of thinking in public through a long process. At the beginning, most American archaeologists were of the arrogant variety, believing that only they were able to unravel the mysteries of the past because of their education and privileged social status. This meant that they could blithely ignore everyone around them, even the descendants of the people whose lives they claimed to be interested in understanding. By the mid twentieth century, some practicing archaeologists began to ask for the public's help in saving archaeological sites from destruction. Federal legislation passed in the 1970s required that archaeological investigation should take place at all land-modification projects occurring on federal land or relying on federal sources of funding or permitting. These requirements provided thousands of archaeological jobs. Some archaeologists continued to believe that their research should be isolated from the public, but taxpayer funding made this position difficult to sustain. With time, increasing numbers of archaeologists came to accept that it made little sense to examine the history of a culture and ignore living members of that culture. Part of the realization came from activists and descendants who demanded that their voices be heard and that they be involved in the research from the beginning. Most archaeologists accepted that they must work in collaboration with nonacademic scholars and accept that nonscholars have knowledge and wisdom that must be considered. Twenty-first-century archaeologists know that they must think to some purpose in new ways.

SOURCES FOR CONTINUED READING

ARCHAEOLOGY

Aitchison, Kenneth and Doug Rocks-MacQueen. 2019. *State of the Archaeological Market, 2019*. London: Federation of Archaeological Managers and Employers.

Christie, Agatha. 1937. *Death on the Nile*. New York: Grosset & Dunlap.

Cleary, Kerri and Niamh McCullagh. 2014. DISCO II Employment in Archaeology. *Archaeology Ireland* 28 (4): 10–11.

Fagan, Brian. 1993. "The Arrogant Archaeologist." *Archaeology* 46, 6 (Nov/Dec): 14–16.

Hoving, Thomas. 1978. *Tutankhamun: The Untold Story*. New York: Simon and Schuster.

Judd, Neil M. 1967. *The Bureau of American Ethnology: A Partial History*. Norman: University of Oklahoma Press.

King, Thomas F., Patricia Parker Hickman, and Gary Berg. 1977. *Anthropology in Historic Preservation: Caring for Culture's Clutter*. New York: Academic.

Little, Barbara J. 2002. "Archaeology as a Shared Vision." In *Public Benefits of Archaeology*, Barbara J. Little, ed., pp. 3–19. Gainesville: University Press of Florida.

McGimsey, Charles R., III. 1972. *Public Archaeology*. New York: Seminar.

Orser, Charles E. Jr., 2017. *Historical Archaeology*. Third edition. New York: Routledge.

Rocks-Macqueen, Doug. 2014. "How Many Archaeologists Are in the US? More Than a Couple, Less Than There Should Be." https://dougsarchaeology.wordpress.com/2014/06/18/how-many-archaeologists-are-in-the-us-more-than-a-couple-less-than-there-should-be/; accessed December 2022.

Yetter, George Humphrey. 1988. *Williamsburg Before and After: The Rebirth of Virginia's Colonial Capital*. Williamsburg: Colonial Williamsburg Foundation.

Zimmerman, Larry J. 1989. "Made Radical by my Own: An Archaeologist Learns to Accept Reburial." In *Conflict in the Archaeology of Living Traditions*, R. Layton, ed., pp. 60–67. London: Unwin Hyman.

———. 1992. "Archaeology, Reburial, and the Tactics of a Discipline's Self-Delusion." *American Indian Culture and Research Journal* 6 (2): 37–56.

KENNEWICK MAN

Coleman, Cynthia-Lou and Erin V. Dysart. 2005. "Framing of Kennewick Man Against the Backdrop of a Scientific and Cultural Controversy." *Science Communication* 27:3–26.

Owsley, Douglas W. and Richard L. Jantz, eds. 2014. *Kennewick Man: The Scientific Investigation of an Ancient American Skeleton.* College Station: Texas A&M University Press.

Thomas, David Hurst. 2000. *Skull Wars: Kennewick Man, Archaeology, and the Battle for Native American Identity.* New York: Basic.

Zimmer, Carl. 2015. "New Study Links Kennewick Man to Native Americans." *New York Times* June 9, A14.

AFRICAN BURIAL GROUND

Blakey, Michael L. 1995. "What Makes Burial Ground Project a Milestone." *New York Times,* May 30: A16.

———. 2020. "Archaeology under the Blinding Light of Race." *Current Anthropology* 61:S184–S197.

Ingle, Marjorie, Jean Howson, and Edward S. Rutsch. 1990. *A Stage IA Cultural Resource Survey of the Proposed Foley Square Project in the Borough of Manhattan, New York, New York.* Newton, NJ: Historic Conservation and Interpretation, Inc.

Nelson, Alondra. 2013. "DNA Ethnicity as Black Social Action?" *Cultural Anthropology* 28:527–36.

Paterson, David A. 1993. "It Took a Community to Save Burial Ground." *New York Times,* August 21:18.

Purnell, Brian. 2010. "The African Burial Ground National Monument." *Journal of American History* 97:735–40.

COLLABORATION

Barton, Christopher P. 2022. *The Archaeology of Race and Class at Timbuctoo: A Black Community in New Jersey.* Gainesville: University Press of Florida.

Chief Dull Knife College Catalog, 2022–2023. http://www.cdkc.edu/CATA LOG2022_2023.pdf; accessed December 2022.

Colwell-Chanthaphonh, Chip and T.J. Ferguson. 2008. "Introduction: The Collaborative Continuum." In *Collaboration in Archaeological Practice: Engaging Descendant Communities,* Chip Colwell-Chanthaphonh and T.J. Ferguson, eds., pp. 1–32. Lanham, MD: AltaMira.

McDonald, J. Douglas, Larry J. Zimmerman, A.L. McDonald, William Tall Bull, and Ted Rising Sun. 1991. "The Northern Cheyenne Outbreak of 1879: Using Oral History and Archaeology as Tools of Resistance." In *The Archaeology of Inequality,* Randall H. McGuire and Robert Paynter, eds., pp. 64–78. Oxford: Blackwell.

10

Archaeological Thinking for the Twenty-First Century

We began in chapter 1 with an outrageous interpretation that the Great Pyramid of Giza was originally built and presumably used to generate nuclear power. Individuals who have learned how to think to some purpose understand that the interpretation is nonsense for several reasons, not the least being that absolutely no evidence exists to substantiate the claim. The interpretation simply came out of someone's imagination as pure fiction.

Despite the absurdity of the claim, thousands of people may believe it. Surveyors working for the Pearson Institute at the University of Chicago found in September 2022 that 91 percent of Americans believe that misinformation, "fake news," poses a significant social problem. Fully 70 percent of those surveyed thought that bad or false information contributed to misunderstanding, violence, and even terrorism.

Two months later, data released by Netflix indicated that viewers worldwide watched 24.6 million hours of *Ancient Apocalypse* starring pseudo-archaeologist Graham Hancock. Estimates are that around 3 percent of Americans tuned into the series. On the morning of December 28, 2022, the US Census Bureau reported that the US population was 334,219,740 (and growing by one person every twenty-two seconds). Using these figures, we can estimate that over ten million Americans watched the "fake news" archaeology program. The good news is that the percentage is small when we consider all Americans, but ten million people is still a large population who may believe a fantasy. The bad news is that the individuals obtaining fame and fortune by peddling fake archaeology are vocal, persistent, and, because they are often outlandish, they attract media attention. Simple human curiosity suggests that people are drawn to social media that is outrageous and even bizarre, and such curiosity may extend to the human past as well. In *Spooky Archaeology*, Jeb Card contrasts exciting fictional archaeologists like Lara Croft, or even media-savvy pretend archaeologists like Giorgio Tsoukalos—the well-spoken, high-haired emcee of television's *Ancient*

Aliens—with Professor Dryasdust, the pontificating academic archaeologist who "studies potsherds for reasons that aren't clear or interesting while ignoring valuable treasures of wealth, wisdom, and wonder."

One unavoidable difference between Professor Dryasdust and pseudo-archaeologists—real, fictional, or pretend—is that the latter are usually more entertaining. Lara Croft's fictional exploits and Giorgio Tsoukalos's fabulous stories may attract viewers simply because they're entertaining; they are the very antithesis of sitting in a classroom. After a day of hassles, runarounds, and drudgery, viewers want to be entertained, most people probably don't want to sit through a lecture about the differences between Middle and Late Woodland pottery found in Illinois. Professional archaeologists find the persistence and high media profile of pseudo-archaeologists extremely frustrating, but, then again, most people are not trained archaeologists. The danger that lurks within pseudo-archaeology is that many people undoubtedly fail to understand that ultimately the stories told by pretend archaeologists are simply tales with no evidence behind them. Tales of ancient giants roaming around the United States are great stories, but they are simply that, stories. More distressingly, many fictional accounts are inherently racist because they promote the idea that past human societies could have only created things with the help of ancient aliens. These stories encourage us to think that humans in the past were stupid louts completely unlike us. In this view, ancient Egyptians could never had built a stone pyramid for their dead pharaoh, so they had to have space aliens show them how to build it. (And then the aliens made the pyramid into a nuclear facility.)

Many of the tales spun by pseudo-archaeologists are perfectly harmless, but at their most extreme, fake stories can have consequences as consequential as encouraging racism. In his classic *Frauds, Myths, and Mysteries*, Kenneth Feder acknowledges the tragic character of the fantastical by pointing to the Heaven's Gate cult and its followers' belief in the extraterrestrial connections of its suicide-promoting leader. Pseudo-archaeology, though outrageous, doesn't have the same level of danger if its adherents understand that its stories are entertainment, a kind of Harry Potter for the past filled with mysterious individuals performing incredible acts. The few who unfortunately take pseudo-archaeology seriously are done a tremendous disservice because they are being taught a false human history, one that however entertaining, bears no relation to the epic story of the human adventure.

The crux of the matter, and the central theme of this book, is that the practice of real archaeology involves gathering, studying, and interpreting tangible evidence. Rather than to create fanciful stories about the past, archaeologists learn to think with the evidence they have at hand, while accepting that more evidence is bound to be collected by someone in the future. The reality of scientific investigation is that new evidence may refine or even negate the older evidence. Professional archaeologists accept, embrace, and encourage this possibility. Archaeologists' use of fragmentary, confusing, and partial evidence to devise interpretations is part of the process of detection (see chapter 1), and this is why archaeologists are so often compared to detectives. In fact, comparing archaeologists to detectives has been a consistent theme in Western popular culture, which partly explains the appeal of characters like Indiana Jones and others.

Agatha Christie is famous for having commented on the similarity between archaeologists and detectives. Her interest in archaeology was honest because she was no armchair theorist viewing archaeology from the safety of her parlor. She was married to an archaeologist, and she attended many excavations under harsh conditions, often serving as an on-site photographer. She detailed her archaeological experiences in *Come, Tell Me How You Live* (1946) and in *An Autobiography* (1977). She inserted archaeologists into her novels as characters and used archaeological sites as crime scenes. In *Murder in Mesopotamia*, one of her archaeology-themed mysteries, she has Hercule Poirot being told, "You would have made a good archaeologist, M. Poirot. You have the gift of re-creating the past." For Christie, detectives and archaeologists have a close relationship because both investigate fascinating puzzles requiring resolution.

Christie's desire to link archaeologists and detectives soon gained widespread acceptance, even among archaeologists. In 1949, the doyen of southwestern US archaeology, A.V. Kidder, noted that "in popular belief" two kinds of archaeologists exist. The "hairy-chested archaeologist" is a "strong-jawed young man in a tropical helmet, pistol on hip, hacking his way through the jungle in search of lost cities and buried treasures." He wears high boots to protect himself from deadly snakes, and often has his shirt "enough unbuttoned to reveal the manliness of his bosom" (Indiana Jones). In contrast, the "hairy-chinned archaeologist" is more refined, older, and absent-minded. His only weapon is a magnifying glass. This archaeologist is thoughtful, careful, and not at all adventurous (Professor Dryasdust). Kidder observed that both kinds of archaeologists exist in the real world. The treasure hunter attracts attention because of his daring-do, while the staid academic quietly goes about the business of the past unbothered by the present. (Note that women archaeologists are absent from the profiles, even though women did conduct archaeological research at the time.)

In 1973, William Y. Adams, an acclaimed archaeologist of the Nile Valley and a dedicated Sherlock Holmes enthusiast, stated that the similarity between detectives and archaeologists occurs because both reconstruct "large events from small clues." Adams further used detective fiction to highlight the differences between observation and deduction and argued that "a brilliant series of observations may be betrayed and invalidated by an inept series of deductions." For him, the problem was that archaeologists, like fictional detectives, might choose ingenuity over common sense, such that "probability values are wildly inflated; the possible becomes the probable, and the probable becomes the certain." In other words, if archaeologists, like detectives, stray too far from logic—thinking to some purpose—they may come to believe too strongly in their abilities and miss important links between lines of evidence.

In his study of archaeology's image in today's popular culture, Cornelius Holtorf explores the archaeologist-as-detective theme in depth. He notes that the connection between the two is perhaps unsurprising because many archaeologists today work closely with police detectives in forensic cases involving the excavation and removal of skeletal remains. It is no longer unusual to see police at crime scenes using archaeological techniques of recovery or consulting with archaeologists and bioarchaeologists. (In fact, forensic archaeology is now an important archaeological specialization.)

Holtorf also notes that the connection between detectives and archaeologists is so close that several academic archaeologists have written their own detective novels. Unsurprisingly, many of their main characters are archaeologists. In *The Cambridge Murders* (first published in 1945), archaeologist Glyn Daniel's character Sir Richard Cherrington, clearly one of Kidder's hairy-chinned archaeologists, is a slightly absent-minded archaeologist who describes himself as "rather a connoisseur of tweeds." (Daniel, being Welsh, used the pen name Dilwyn Rees in the first edition. He probably used the name for numerous reasons, but one may have been to avoid his stuffy colleagues' disapproval. In any case, his real name now appears on later editions.)

Holtorf observes that today's popular culture characterizes archaeologists much the same as in Kidder's time, but with more variations as the number of media options have grown. Today, some archaeologists are depicted as adventurous (Lara Croft, Indiana Jones), some are boring (Dr. Dryasdust, Cherrington), some are corrupt (Alex West in *Lara Croft: Tomb Raider*), and some are evil (Dr. Elsa Schneider in *Indiana Jones and the Last Crusade*). In short, it seems that while the archaeologist-as-detective has been a constant theme in works of fiction, the one overriding characteristic they all share despite their individual motives is the ability to think. Their intentions might not meet the standards of twenty-first-century archaeology, but all archaeological characters who appear in detective fiction, if they are presented as legitimate scholars, must be shown to have based their interpretations on the evidence they have at hand. They cannot simply make it up as they go, as do pseudo-archaeologists. It would be a strange story indeed if a detective solved a murder by creating evidence from nothing. It would be like playing a game of Clue without any rules. (I think Col. Mustard used a lead pipe to kill Mr. Boddy in the dining room. Why? Because I say so, I don't need evidence.)

The human story is as vast as it is infinitely fascinating. Humans have accomplished so much in the three million or so years that we've been on Earth. The discovery of fire, the creation of stone tools, learning how to make usable pots from the soil, and the vast array of objects designed, invented, and produced since the earliest days demonstrates the enormous creativity and capability of humans to create useful, and oftentimes even highly dangerous, material things.

Faced with the huge numbers of incredible stories of humanity's achievements and failures, no need exists to create fictional tales about space aliens, giants, and other strange creatures who lived on earth in some distant past. Human history is complicated enough without adding fantastic stories having no tangible evidence. Archaeologists devote their lives to unraveling the mysteries of a human past that is complicated and often difficult to understand. Only by learning how to think clearly will new strands of the human story be unraveled.

SOURCES FOR CONTINUED READING

Adams, William Y. 1973. "The Archaeologist as Detective." In *Variation in Anthropology: Essays in Honor of John C. McGregor*, Donald W. Lathrap and William Y. Adams, eds., pp. 17–29. Urbana: Illinois Archaeological Survey.

Card, Jeb J. 2018. *Spooky Archaeology: Myth and the Science of the Past.* Albuquerque: University of New Mexico Press.

Christie, Agatha. 1935. *Murder in Mesopotamia: A Poirot Mystery.* New York: P.F. Collier and Son.

———. 1977. *An Autobiography.* New York: Dodd, Mead.

Colavito, Jason. 2022. "Netflix Releases Data About Who Is Watching 'Ancient Apocalypse.'" https://www.jasoncolavito.com/blog/netflix-releases-data-about-who-is-watching-ancient-apocalypse; accessed December 2022.

Daniel, Glyn [Dilwyn Rees]. 1945. *The Cambridge Murders.* London: Gollancz.

Feder, Kenneth L. 2006. *Frauds, Myths, and Mysteries: Science and Pseudoscience in Archaeology.* Fifth edition. Boston: McGraw Hill.

Holtorf, Cornelius. 2007. *Archaeology Is a Brand! The Meaning of Archaeology in Contemporary Popular Culture.* Walnut Creek, CA: Left Coast Press.

Kidder, A.V. 1949. "Introduction." In *Prehistoric Southwesterners from Basketmaker to Pueblo*, by Charles Avery Amsden, pp. xi–xiv. Los Angeles: Southwest Museum.

Mallowan, Agatha Christie. 1946. *Come, Tell Me How You Live.* New York: William Morrow.

Tolkacz, David. 2022. "Most Americans Concerned with Fake News, but 'Fake News' May Be Old News." *Skeptical Inquirer* 47 (1): 7.

Index

Page references for figures are italicized.

About the Author

Charles E. Orser, Jr., is an anthropological historical archaeologist who investigates the modern world as it was created after about 1492. He received his PhD in 1980 and has conducted excavations in the United States (Midwest and South), Europe (Ireland and England), and South America (Brazil). He has lectured throughout the United States and in Ireland, England, Sweden, Portugal, Brazil, Colombia, Italy, Canada, Iceland, New Zealand, and Australia. A retired distinguished professor at Illinois State University, he is now affiliated with the School of Human Evolution and Social Change at Arizona State University. He is the author of one hundred professional articles and several books, including *Historical Archaeology* (now in its third edition); *A Historical Archaeology of the Modern World*; *The Archaeology of Race and Racialization in Historic America*; *Race and Practice in Archaeological Interpretation*; *Unearthing Hidden Ireland: Historical Archaeology at Ballykilcline, County Roscommon*; *A Primer on Modern-World Archaeology*; *Archaeological Thinking*; and *An Archaeology of the English Atlantic World, 1600–1700*. He is the founder and editor of the *International Journal of Historical Archaeology*. In 2019, he received the Society for Historical Archaeology's highest award, the J.C. Harrington Medal, for lifetime achievement in the discipline.

www.ingramcontent.com/pod-product-compliance
Lightning Source LLC
Chambersburg PA
CBHW030651270326
41929CB00007B/306